Illinois Department of Commerc

ɟh

orge H. Ryan
Governor

February, 2001

As director of the Illinois Department of Commerce and Community Affairs, I am proud to present the Illinois Trade Office's, 'Trade Secrets' guide to assist Illinois companies in their international trade efforts.

Illinois has historically recognized the importance of international trade. Since the birth of the Illinois Trade Office in 1965, DCCA has played an influential role in educating and assisting small and medium-sized companies in preparing and executing international commerce.

Today, Illinois is the 6th highest exporting state in the nation, and over 600,000 jobs here are linked to exports. Our Illinois Trade Office has increased and enhanced our efforts to bring more Illinois firms to trade and catalog shows, promote Illinois as an international tourism destination, and attract foreign direct investment.

The Illinois Trade Office continuously conducts various seminars and individual counseling sessions as well as provides a multitude of research materials to educate and assist Illinois firms to enhance their presence overseas. I encourage you to take advantage of this guide and all of the services that the Illinois Trade Office has to offer.

Best regards,

Pam McDonough

Pam McDonough
Director

Internet Address http://www.commerce.state.il.us

620 East Adams Street
Springfield, Illinois 62701
217/782-7500
Fax: 217/785-6454 ▪TDD: 800/785-6055

James R. Thompson Center
100 West Randolph Street, Suite 3-400
Chicago, Illinois 60601
312/814-7179
Fax: 312/814-6732 ▪TDD: 800/419-0667

325 West Adams Street, 3rd Floor
Springfield, Illinois 62704-1892
217/785-2800
Fax: 217/785-2618 ▪TDD: 217/785-0211

2309 West Main, Suite 118
Marion, Illinois 62959
618/997-4394
Fax: 618/997-1825 ▪ TDD Relay: 800/526-0844

Published by the Michigan Small Business Development Center
Wayne State University
2727 Second Avenue
Detroit, MI 48201
(313) 964-1798 (P)
(313) 964-3648 (F)
stateoffice@misbdc.wayne.edu

Printed in the U.S.A.
Reprinted in 2001

Graphic Designer: Constance Fekete
Printer: ImageMasters, Wixom, MI
Second Edition

ISBN 1-88641-03-x

Library of Congress Cataloging-in-Publication Data
McCue, Sarah S., date.
Trade Secrets : the export answer book /
p. cm.
Includes bibliographical references and index
1. Export marketing—Handbooks, manuals, etc.

The Michigan Small Business Development Center is partially funded under Cooperative Agreement No. 3-7770-0023-11 by the U.S. Small Business Administration. Any opinions, findings, and conclusions or recommendations expressed in this publication are those of the author(s) and do not necessarily reflect the views of the U.S. Small Business Administration. The Michigan Small Business Development Center is an outreach program of Wayne State University in partnership with the U.S. Small Business Administration and local Center sponsors.

DEDICATION

A publication of this breadth and depth is impossible to produce without the research, experience, and contributions of many international trade experts. Trade Secrets: The Export Answer Book is an attempt to include the opinions and expertise of as many international trade specialists as possible. It to them that this second edition is dedicated.

To Julie Clowes of the U.S. Small Business Administration, Detroit District Office. Without her extensive contributions to the first and second editions, this publication would not have been published.

To Connie Fekete and Roy Meissner of the Michigan Small Business Development Center for their exceptional graphic design skills and patience in light of continuous edits.

To Jeanne Gerritsen of the Michigan Small Business Development Center for her intellect, exceptional editing skills, and infectious enthusiasm.

To my boss Ronald R. Hall for his have-at-it attitude, entrepreneurial spirit, and constant support.

To Zakeya Hatch for her outstanding organizational skills, follow through, and administrative support.

To Chris James of the U.S. Department of Commerce's Trade Information Center for his extensive edits to keep the information contained herein accurate, comprehensive, and current.

To my friend and colleague, Dr. Jacqueline Stavros of Madonna University for her editing talent and support during hectic times.

To Graduate Research Assistants from the Wayne State University School of Business Administration and School of Library Science who checked, re-checked, and checked again the information contained in these pages: Giri Badanahatti, Ambush Goeloe, Michelle Harvey, Andrew Leamy, Irene Mokra, Jawahar Muthukrishnan, and Jayshree Singh.

And a special note of thanks to R. Badrinath, Senior Trade Adviser on Institutional Capacity Development for SMEs, International Trade Centre UNCTAD/WTO in Geneva, Switzerland. It is due to his leadership, vision, and belief in the need to expand trade opportunities with firms in transition economies that Trade Secrets: The Export Answer Book will be adapted in twenty developing countries.

Sarah McCue, Ph.D.
Michigan Small Business Development Center
Wayne State University

TABLE OF CONTENTS

Transportation

Documentation

Packaging and Labeling

Trade Agreements

Importing

Appendix

Special Insert for International Business Educators, Consultants, and Researchers

INTRODUCTION

Because of the title, many people ask me, "So, what's the secret to exporting?" Truth be told, really there is no secret. Becoming a successful exporter is simply a matter of finding a market niche, identifying where foreign buyers or representatives need your product, and learning what public and private sources exist to help you succeed in the global marketplace. *Trade Secrets: The Export Answer Book* provides a comprehensive overview of the export transaction in a logical, step-by-step approach using a question and answer format. A very important element of the book is that each question is accompanied by related resources so that the firm, economic development professional, or international trade specialist may delve deeper into a particular topic.

Trade Secrets was written to assist business counselors and business managers who are not familiar with trading in this ever-changing, evolving global economy, in understanding the terms, processes, and possibilities of exporting. It is a deceptively simple, yet comprehensive tool covering all elements of the export process, from conducting market research to identifying foreign customers to packaging the product for shipment. The underlying goal in producing this book was to provide the most accurate, up-to-date exporting guide which has both breadth and depth of focus on common exporting issues.

This second edition contains updated answers to the most commonly asked international trade questions, a contact guide to international business service providers, an international business plan template, the most comprehensive list of international publications available, and a special section for the international trade professional seeking to develop model export development programs and services.

Currently less than 12% of American small- and mid-sized businesses compete in the global arena. This lackluster performance in exporting is attributed to many factors, including the perceptions that the U.S. market is large enough, that it is simply too difficult to find foreign buyers, it is hard to get paid, and that the paperwork is not worth the hassle. In response to such perceptions, *Trade Secrets* was written in clear, non-legalistic language to provide you with the "secret" or little known resources and information that seasoned exporters and trade consultants use on a daily basis to successfully complete an export transaction. *Trade Secrets* is a reference guide that provides no-nonsense advice in an easy-to-use format. The *secret* aspect of this book is that we let you know what the "export experts" are using as resources and we tell you how they would generally answer a question on exporting.

We at the Michigan Small Business Development Center feel our obligation is to disseminate practical, actionable information to small businesses owners who play a pivotal role in the new world economy and to the trade professionals who must be armed with the resources necessary to assist them. Small business consultants and firms must work together to identify trade opportunities with firms not only in developed countries such as Great Britain, Canada, Germany, and Japan but also with firms in transitional economies and emerging democracies such as African countries, Brazil, China, Indonesia, Mexico, India, Russia, and other former Soviet republics. An unprecedented democratization of our world has occurred, the continuation of which is dependent on economic growth and stability in all countries. Just five years ago, who would have imagined that the economic crisis in Asia would have created not a ripple but a resounding tidal wave of financial instability that has effected firms in developed and developing countries throughout the world? As a result, firms in the United States must be proactive and ready to respond to the challenge of competing in a global economy and to opportunities inherent in markets that just a few years ago were closed to U.S. exporters.

Simply put, the massive restructuring of our social, political, and economic world has created a worldwide market of savvy and knowledgeable consumers ready to buy your product or service. We hope that this publication helps you respond to such unprecedented opportunities.

May you achieve remarkable success!

Ronald R. Hall, State Director
Michigan Small Business Development Center
Wayne State University

Why Should I Export?

Exporting offers numerous advantages for the firm but, unfortunately, many firms have not taken advantage of the incredible opportunities that exist in the worldwide marketplace. The massive restructuring of political boundaries, the collapse of Communism, the opening of new consumer markets, historic trade agreements, and the new World Trade Organization have created unprecedented opportunities for businesses to export. Ours is a global economy, influenced by the worldwide access of manufacturing technology which has created competitive manufacturers able to produce cheaper, faster, and better. Formerly underdeveloped countries have become serious rivals to established economies due to worldwide links to communication systems and the explosion of television, print, and electronic access to information. There has never been a more opportune time for U.S. firms to capitalize on these market shifts. Therefore, it is critical to a country's and firm's growth and competitive advantage to export for the following reasons:

Increase Sales and Profits. If the firm is performing well domestically, it is likely that expansion into foreign markets will improve profitability. Yet the U.S. Department of Commerce found in 1997 that only 3 of 25 businesses export, although they are all capable of it.

Gain Global Market Share. Over 95% percent of the world's economic activity is outside the United States.

Reduce Dependence on Existing Domestic Markets. By expanding into foreign markets, the firm will increase its marketing base and reduce internal country competition.

Stabilize Market Fluctuations. By expanding into global markets, firms are no longer held captive to economic changes, consumer demands, and seasonal fluctuations within the domestic economy.

Sell Excess Production Capacity. By exporting, production capacity and length of production runs may increase, thereby decreasing average per unit costs and increasing economies of scale.

Enhance Competitiveness. Exporting is proven to enhance competitive advantage. While the firm will benefit from exposure to new technologies, methods, and processes, the country will benefit from an improved balance of trade.

Create Domestic Jobs. It is estimated that in 1997, U.S. exports of goods and services supported a total of 1.3 million jobs.

Help Reduce the Trade Deficit. Exports represent eight percent of the U.S. Gross Domestic Product (GDP) out of $7,500 billion of annually traded goods and services.

Find Excellent No Cost/Low Cost Experts in Export. For many firms, the decision not to export is based on the fear of the unknown which are often known as the myths, myopia, and misperceptions of exporting. Trade promotion organizations throughout United States have been established to assist companies that are strong domestically but have not contemplated export markets. These organizations help businesses with every step of the export process.

RESOURCES

Basic Guide to Exporting, A ($16.50) S/N 003-009-00604-0 ISBN 0-16-0003296 NTIS, Springfield, VA 22161 (703) 487-4650 (p).

Basic Guide to Exporting, A ($16.50) World Trade Press, 1505 Fifth Avenue, San Rafael, CA 94901 (800) 833-8586 (p); (415) 453-7980 (f).

Building an Import/Export Business ($15) ISBN 0-471-53627-X John Wiley & Sons, Inc., 605 Third Avenue, New York, NY 10158 (800) 225-5945 (p)

Services: The Export of the 21st Century ($19.95) World Trade Press, 1505 Fifth Avenue, San Rafael, CA 94901 (800) 833-8586 (p); (415) 453-7980 (f)

What Are the Most Common Mistakes Made by New Exporters?

According to the U.S. Small Business Administration, the following are the 12 most common mistakes small firms make as they begin to export or expand into foreign markets:

- Failure to obtain qualified export counseling and to develop a master international strategy and marketing plan before starting an export business.
- Insufficient commitment by top management to overcome the initial difficulties and financial requirement of exporting.
- Insufficient care in selecting overseas sales representatives or distributors.
- Seeking orders from around the world rather than concentrating on one or two geographical areas and establishing a basis for profitable operations and orderly growth.
- Neglect of the export business when the domestic market booms.
- Failure to treat international distributors and customers on an equal basis with domestic counterparts.
- Assuming a given market technique and product will automatically be successful in all countries.
- Unwillingness to modify products to meet regulations or cultural preferences of other countries.
- Failure to print service, sales, and warranty messages in foreign languages.
- Failure to consider use of an Export Management Company when the firm cannot afford its own export department or has tried one unsuccessfully.
- Failure to consider licensing or joint venture agreements when import restrictions, insufficient resources, or a limited product line cause companies to dismiss international marketing as unfeasible.
- Failure to provide readily available servicing for the product.

RESOURCES

Breaking Into The Trade Game (free) U.S. Small Business Administration, Office of International Trade, 409 Third Street, S.W. Washington, DC 20416 (202) 205-6720 (p)

Export ABCs, ($25), The Journal of Commerce, 445 Marshall Street, Phillipsburg, NJ, 08865-9984, (800) 221-3777 (p)

Illinois Trade Office, Illinois Department of Commerce and Community Affairs, 100 W. Randolph, Suite 3-400, Chicago, IL 60601 (312) 814-7164 (p), www.commerce.state.il.us (w)

Key Words In International Trade, ($59.95) ICC Publishing, 156 Fifth Avenue, Suite 305, New York, NY 10010 (212) 206-1150 (p), iccpub@interport.net (e)

What Are the Advantages and Risks of Exporting for My Firm?

Direct advantages to the exporting firm include an opportunity to

- expand market share
- increase production if underutilized in the domestic market
- decrease dependence on domestic sales or compensate for a stagnate domestic market
- diffuse domestic competition by expanding into less competitive foreign markets
- follow domestic leaders into foreign markets to reduce foreign market research costs

It is important to note that many of the risks to exporting are similar to those faced in the domestic market. Potential risks of expanding into new markets include the facts that:

- sales may not meet projections
- competition may be greater than anticipated
- customers may be slow in payment, or not pay at all

There are some risks that are unique to exporting including the facts that:

- repatriation of profits from the target country may be constrained or forbidden
- fluctuations in exchange rates may decrease or eliminate profits
- in cases of non-payment or other contractual problems, there may be questions of jurisdiction (*i.e.*, U.S. courts may not be able to enforce contracts between parties in different countries)
- instability in the target country can lead to losses from war or civil strife or nationalization by the foreign government
- the product may not be accepted in foreign markets

RESOURCES

Background Notes ($68) S/N 044-000-91214-7 U.S. Superintendent of Documents, P.O. Box 371954, Pittsburgh, PA 15250-7954 (202) 512-1800 (p); (202) 512-2250 (f); gpoaccess@gpo.gov (e)

The Exporter ($180 for 12 issues), Trade Data Reports, Inc., 90 John Street, New York, NY, 10038 (212) 587-1340 (p); exporter@exporter.com (e); http://exporter.com (w)

Going International ($28.00) ISBN 0-394-54450-1 Random House, 201 East 50th Street, New York, NY 10022 (800) 733-3000 (p)

What Is Involved in a Typical Export Process?

The export process involves three critical functions: feasibility analysis, foreign market entry planning, and implementation. These functions involve 20 steps:

Feasibility Analysis

1. Analyze domestic performance
2. Assess firm's capacities
3. Consider demographic, social, political, and economic factors of target market
4. Confer with international trade experts (marketing, finance, legal, and logistics)
5. Select target markets

Foreign Market Entry Planning

6. Conduct industry sector market research
7. Evaluate market research
8. Plan market entry strategy
9. Comply with target country licensing, standards, and certification requirements
10. File for necessary patent, trademark, and copyright protection
11. Identify taxes, tariffs, duties, quotas or other non-tariff trade barriers
12. Establish pricing schedule

Implementation

13. Determine methods of distribution
14. Establish marketing methods
15. Choose representative or sales methods
16. Negotiate financial instruments
17. Obtain insurance
18. Complete necessary paperwork
19. Package and label
20. Ship product

RESOURCES

Export/Import Basics: The Legal, Financial, and Transport Aspects of International Trade, $39.95, ICC Publishing, 156 Fifth Avenue, Suite 305, New York, NY 10010 (212) 206-1150 (p), iccpub@interport.net (e)

International Business Quick Reference Guide ($35) International Division Publications, U.S. Chamber of Commerce, 1615 H Street, NW, Washington, DC 20062-2000 (202) 463-5460 (p); (202) 463-3114 (f)

Export Process Assistant: http://venture.cob.ohio-state.edu:1111/tutorial/openingscr.html

ExporTutor: http://web.miep.org/tutor/index.html

Illinois Trade Office, Illinois Department of Commerce and Community Affairs, 100 W. Randolph, Suite 3-400, Chicago, IL 60601 (312) 814-7164 (p), www.commerce.state.il.us (w)

What Questions Should I Answer Before Making the Decision to Export?

Before exporting or expanding into foreign markets, it is important to first assess the firm's management capabilities. Decide whether the dedicated personnel, resources, and management support are strong enough to complete numerous export transactions. Then it is necessary to conduct appropriate research. To select a market based on research and rationale, look into foreign market trends; country demographics; political, economic and social environments; possible language barriers; and the local business environment. This information is necessary to help select a target market or markets that will be profitable. After researching, develop an export business plan. A plan will allow management to anticipate the future and better understand the company so that informed decisions may be reached. Included in this plan will be a rationale for selecting a particular foreign market which answers the following questions:

Analysis of Domestic Performance

Why is the business successful in the domestic market?
What is the current domestic market share of the product?

Firm's Commitment and Desire to Export

What are the firm's objectives in exporting?
At what level in the firm's hierarchy are exporting decisions made?
Who on your staff will be involved with the export process?
What international experience does management (or any of its employees) have?
What level of involvement in the export process is the firm willing to have?
How much risk is the firm willing to take on?

Competitive Analysis

What makes the firm's products or services competitive in a foreign market?
What makes the products or services unique?
What are the firm's overall competitive advantages (e.g., technology, patents, skills)?

Finding Out About Targeted Foreign Markets

What market segments are being targeted?
How is the firm's competition performing in international markets?
Will the product or service be restricted due to tariffs, quotas, or other non-tariff barriers?
Will patent/trademark protection abroad be essential for your product?
What product labeling requirements must be met?
What sort of target market environmental regulations need to be adhered to?

Marketing the Product

How will the product or service be advertised?
What companies, agents, or distributors have purchased similar products?
Will an agent or distributor be appointed to handle the export market?
What territory should the agent or distributor cover?
Is there a trade show or trade mission that will best highlight your product or service?
Will the product/service be sold under the same name in the foreign target market?

Pricing and Commercial Terms

How will a price be calculated?
What are your service terms?
What are your payment terms? Credit terms?
What are your warranty and guarantee terms?
What are your discount terms?

RESOURCE

Questions & Answers For Export/Import ($44.50) International Trade Institute, 5055 North Main St., Dayton, Ohio 45415 (800) 543-2453 (p); (937) 276-5920 (f)

Who Can Help Me Answer My Exporting Questions?

A local Small Business Development Center, U.S. Department of Commerce local district office or Country Desk Officer in Washington, D.C., or a Small Business Administration branch office is a good place to start. These trained professionals will answer many of your general questions, gather some information, help with directed research, or provide referrals to either a private sector international business professional or a public sector agency. Most government-sponsored export assistance programs are offered at no charge to the public.

The Trade Information Center (TIC) is an invaluable, free resource. Trade specialists in the TIC advise exporters on how to locate and use government programs available from 19 trade-related agencies, direct callers to sources of general market information, and provide basic export counseling. Information provided to exporters range from basic, how-to information to sophisticated reports and statistics. The TIC offers information on export counseling, seminars and conferences, overseas buyers and representatives, export financing, technical assistance, and tariff rates for export destination countries. To speak with a trade specialist, call (800) USA TRADE, fax at (202) 482-4473, or visit its web site at http://www.ita.doc.gov/tic. The center is open 8:30-5:30 EST, Monday through Friday. There is an after hours message service.

International Economic Policy Country Desk Officers are the U.S. Department of Commerce's source for information on trade to specific countries. They monitor the pulse of potential markets to highlight new opportunities for trade and investment. Desk officers collect information on their assigned country's regulations, tariffs, business practices, economic and political developments, trade data, market size and growth, economy, trade policies, and political situation. Call the Trade Information Center at (800) USA TRADE to obtain this information.

The Export Hotline and Trade Bank is a free international information service available to any company with a fax machine. Export and import information, collected from more than 150 sources, is instantly available on more than 50 industries and 78 countries from a collection of more than 5,000 reports. The information includes industry sector analysis, country commercial overviews, trade environment, investment regulations, trade shows, key contacts, samples of export and import documents, business travel and protocols, and government assistance programs. To utilize the system, call (800) 872-9767.

Working in partnership with the Small Business Exporters Association ((703) 761-4140), and the South Carolina Small Business Development Center, the Export Opportunity Hotline helps small- and medium-sized businesses assess their export readiness, develop their export potential, and successfully introduce their products into international markets. The Export Opportunity Hotline offers a knowledgeable trade consultant, an assessment of a firm's export readiness, basic market research and information on the best prospective market for a product, and materials on the international trade process. These services are generally free. Call (800) 243-7232; e-mail at exporthot@darla.badm.sc.edu; or visit its web site at http://exporthot.badm.sc.edu.

The Census Bureau compiles and maintains up-to-date global demographic and social information for all countries in its International Data Base (IDB) which is accessible to U.S. companies seeking to identify potential markets overseas. Call the U.S. Census Bureau Foreign Trade Division at (301) 763-4100 or (301) 763-4811 or fax at (301) 763-7610. It also maintains a web site at http://www.census.gov.

The Foreign Agricultural Service produces Country Reports on various commodities in more than 40 overseas markets. These reports highlight market trends and information on U.S. market positions and competition. Contact the Foreign Agricultural Service at U.S. Department of Agriculture Information Division, Reports Office, 14th and Independence Avenues, S.W., Room 6072-S, Washington, DC 20250-1000 or call (202) 720-0924 or fax at (202) 720-3229.

RESOURCES

Directory of U.S. Government Resources (free) Trade Information Center, U.S. Department of Commerce, HCHB 7424, 14th and Constitution, NW Washington, DC 20230 (800) 872-8723

Exporting From Start to Finance ($42.95) ISBN 0-0706-9300-5 McGraw Hill, 13311 Monterey Avenue, Blue Ridge Summit, PA 17214-9988 (800) 262-4729 (p)

Export Today ($49/year) ISSN 0882-4711 Trade Communications, 733 15th St, N.W., Suite 1100, Washington, DC 20005 (202) 737-1060 (p)

Key Officers of Foreign Service Posts: Guide for Business Representatives. ($5.00) State Department, Document S/N 744-006-00000-7, U.S. Superintendent of Documents, P.O. Box 371954, Pittsburgh, PA 15250-7954 (202) 512-1800 (p); (202) 512-2250 (f); gpoaccess@gpo.gov

What Are the Best Web Sites That Will Help Me Export?

The following web sites have been qualified as valuable and worthwhile to exporters:

ATA Carnet Forms	http://www/uscib.org
Bureau of Export Administration	http://www.bxa.doc.gov
Commerce Business Daily	http:cbdnet.access.gpo.gov
Commercial News USA	http://www/cnewsusa.com
Creditreform Credit Service Providers	http://www.creditreform.de/creditreform/
Culturgrams	http://www.byu.edu/culturgram
Dun & Bradstreet	http://www.dbisna.com/
Embassies	http://www.embassy.org
Environmental Labeling	http://unixg.ubc.ca:780/~ecolabel/cel.html
Export-Import Bank	http://www.exim.gov
Export Legal Assistance Network	http://www.miep.org
Export Today	http://enews.com:80/magazine/export/
Financial Times Online	http://www.ft.com
Global Network of Chambers of Commerce	http://www1.usa1.com/ibnet/chamshp.html
Global Trade Point Network	http://www.unic.org/unctad
International Business Resources - Michigan State University	http://www.ciber.bus.mus.edu/busres.htm
International Trade Centre UNCTAD/WTO	http://www.unicc.org/itc/welcome.html
International Trade Law	http://itl.irv.uit.no/trade_law
Internet Tradelines	http://www.intrade.com
Journal of Commerce	http://www.joc.com
Library of Congress	http://www.loc.gov
National Association of Export Companies	http://www.imex.com/nexco
National Export Offer Service	http://www.tradecompass.com/neos
National Trade Data Bank	http://www.stat-usa.gov
Prohibited Foreign Traders	http://www.fedworld.gov
Schedule B Numbers	http://www.census.gov/foreign-trade/www/scheduleb97.html
Small Business Development Centers	http://www.sba.gov
Small Business Exporter's Association	http://web.miep.org/sbfa/
Trade Compass	http://www.tradecompass.com
Trade Information Center	http://www.ita.doc.gov/tic
Trade Leads	http://www.imex.com/trade/opport.html.
Trade Negotiation Information	http://www.ustr.gov/reports/tpa/1996/contents.html
Trade Point USA	http://ww.tpusa.com
Trade Shows	http://www.expoguide.com/shows/location.htm
U.N. Commission on Trade & Development	http://www.unctad-trains.org
Unibex Foreign Partner Search	http://www.unibex.com
UNZ and Company	http://www.unzexport.com
U.S. Agency for International Development	http://www.info.usaid.gov
U.S. Chamber of Commerce	http://www.uschamber.org
U.S. Council for International Business	http://www.uscib.org
U.S. Census Bureau	http://www.census.gov/foreign-trade/www
U.S. Customs Service	http://www.treas.gov/treasury/bureaus/customs/
U.S. Department of Agriculture	http://www.usda.gov
U.S. Department of Commerce	http://www.doc.gov
U.S. Department of State	http://www.state.gov
U.S. National Trade Estimates	http://www.ustr.gov/reports/nte/1996/contents.html
U.S. Small Business Administration/Trade Net	http://www.sba.gov or http://www.gits.gov/
World Bank	http://www.worldbank.org
World Fact Book	http://www.odci.gov/cia/publications/95fact/

What Are the Essential Elements of an International Business Plan?

Before making a commitment to enter into international business agreements, the development of an international business plan is a key step for assessing your company's readiness to export. An export plan is useful in three ways. One, it articulates the rationale behind selecting a particular foreign market based on fairly extensive research that you have conducted. Two, it explains to potential financiers and customers why you want to penetrate or export to a particular market. Three, and most importantly, it helps you understand the costs and profits involved in exporting by developing financial projections, short- and long-term budgets, and cash flow projections. Simply put, the plan will help you decide if you should export, if there is a market for your product, how much it will cost to export a product, and how much profit you can expect. If you follow this outline, you'll be able to clearly articulate the goals for marketing and financing your export expansion plan. Each of these sections should be concise and to the point, from one to three paragraphs. The core elements of any business plan include:

ELEMENT	EXPLANATION
Executive Summary	State what makes your company successful domestically and then list your competitive advantages over domestic and foreign competition.
Present Situation	Identify the company's products with export potential.
Objectives	Define long-term goals and how exporting will help to attain them.
Management	Conduct a company analysis and ensure that the decision to export is supported by all levels of management. Develop an action plan to decide who will execute what functions and make export decisions.
Description	Explain why the product/service is unique in an international market.
Market Analysis	Decide how to market the product/service.
Target Customers	Describe the demographic and socioeconomic profile of your customer.
Existing Competition	Conduct a global industry analysis. The company should determine its competitiveness within the global industry.
Focus Group Research	Gather a small group of potential customers to give you constructive feedback and criticism.
Calculated Risk	Forecast the industry growth or decline over the next three to five years.
Marketing Strategy	Explain how you will attract and keep customers.
Pricing/Profitability	Define your international pricing and promotion strategy.
Selling Tactics	Identify various methods of reaching potential customers, including perhaps direct mail, trade shows, cold calling, and advertising.

RESOURCES

BizPlan*Builder*, ($129), JIAN, Inc., 1975 West El Camino Real, Suite 301, Mountain View, CA 94040-2218 (p); (415) 254-5640 (f)

IDIC Newsletter (free) U.S. Chamber of Commerce, 1615 H Street, N.W., Washington, D.C. 20062 (202) 463-5460 (p); (202) 463-3114 (f); http://www.uschamber.org

International Commodity Trade Series - Wine, Gold, Silver, Grain, Cotton, Cocoa, Lead, Nickel, Rice, Steel, Sugar, Tin, Wool, Zinc ($95.00 each, 3 for $249) World Trade Press, 1505 Fifth Avenue, San Rafael, CA 94901 (800) 833-8586 (p); (415) 453-7980 (f)

Methods of Distribution Determine where and how to sell overseas.

Advertising Consider foreign labeling and packaging requirements, literature translations, and customer relations.

Public Relations Develop a regular and consistent product/service update program, an internal newsletter, technical magazine articles, press releases, etc.

Business Relationship Articulate a plan for developing international business relationships which includes cultural training for sales and management. Determine the type of relationship (e.g., agent/distributor, rep, supplier, direct export, etc.) you wish to establish.

Manufacturing Plan Indicate the initial volume of sales and production, expansion requirements, sources of materials, location of manufacturer, etc.

Financial History Include a five-year Profit and Loss Statement.

Financial Projections Be realistic and conservative.

12-Month Budget Determine your anticipated costs for the first year of exporting.

Cash-Flow Projection Outline cash receipts vs. cash disbursements.

Balance Sheet Illustrate your liquidity and cash position.

Break-Even Analysis Calculate the number of units you must sell to reach your break-even point.

Source of Financing Explain how you will obtain the money to start or expand your export operation.

Use of Proceeds Explain how profits and loan amounts will be allocated.

Conclusions Approach in beginning to export, total capital required, profit expected, schedule, comments.

Appendices Resumes, key accounts, potential customers, market survey data, drawings, agreements, financial projections, etc.

RESOURCES

International Trade Reporter's "Current Reports" ($1104/year) BNA Editorial Offices, 9435 Key West Avenue, Rockville, MD, 20850 (800) 372-1033 (p); (800) 253-0332 (f)

World Trade Almanac: Economic, Marketing, Trade, Culture, Legal & Travel Surveys for the World's Top 100 Countries ($87.00) World Trade Press, 1505 Fifth Avenue, San Rafael, CA 94901 (800) 833-8586 (p); (415) 453-7980 (f)

What Are Some of the Tips, Tricks, and Avoidable Traps When Developing an International Business Plan?

After you've gathered your resources, conducted research, and become familiar with those in the field who can assist you, it is time to begin writing the international business plan. Following are some tips and tricks, and some avoidable traps that have become problematic for firms writing their international business plans.

Seek No-Cost/Low-Cost Advice. Companies that are new to exporting or those companies expanding into an unfamiliar foreign market often do not obtain qualified export counseling before developing the international business plan. Public and private sector professionals are available throughout the United States to help you clearly define goals, objectives, and a foreign marketing and finance strategy. These assistance organizations include Census Bureau's Foreign Trade Division, country desk officers, freight forwarders, industry desk officers, Small Business Development Centers, U.S. and District Export Assistance Centers, U.S. Small Business Administration, and World Trade Centers Association. All of these organizations are listed in the appendix.

Obtain Management Commitment. Before researching and writing the plan, the person charged with developing a foreign market entry strategy must obtain commitment from top management so that potential financiers and foreign partners understand that the key players in the firm are willing to overcome the initial difficulties and financial requirements of exporting. The president and all departments including accounting, finance, logistics, marketing, research, and training must understand and embrace the firm's export expansion plans. Detailed experiential resumes of all senior staff should be included in the international business plan.

Conduct Thorough Market Research. The best market research tool available at no cost or limited cost is the National Trade Data Bank (NTDB). Free access to NTDB is available at all federal deposit public libraries. You may also order it in CD-ROM or Internet formats. No matter how technical or obscure, what you need to know will likely be found in the NTDB. Updated monthly, the NTDB contains more than 160,000 documents of current information on topics such as trade leads; available resources; import and export opportunities by industry, country, and product; foreign companies or importers looking for specific products; how-to market guides; demographic, political, and socio-economic conditions in countries throughout the world; and much more. Call (202) 482-1986.

Analyze Market Research. Many international business plans are weak on market research. Market research is simply confirming your gut instinct that somehow a product will be accepted in a particular market. You learn this by conducting focus groups on the usefulness, design, size, color, and all other characteristics of your product; by sending product samples; and by coming to understand the unique preferences of your potential foreign customers. The *Market Factor Assessment*, found on page 21, should be included in an international business plan. It is a 36-question diagnostic tool which considers demographic, political, economic, social, consumer, and competitive factors and allows you to rate each country based on a market condition scale.

Determine Export and Import Flow (Industry Analysis). Many companies find it difficult to learn where a particular product is being exported to or imported from. If you are going to be successful in a particular market, it is absolutely critical to determine whether your product can be competitive. The best way to find this out is through the Census Bureau's Foreign Trade Division which tracks the number of shipments leaving and coming into the United States by a 10-digit code. For $160 a year (or $25 for a one-time only report), you can subscribe to the Selected Commodity Service 1 To 10 List. This lets you track the product's export or import transactions, value, quantity, and country of destination *on both the import and export side of the equation.* This allows you to develop a unit price on a product to competitively sell anywhere in the world. You can then determine the average price of the product category. For example, you can find out the unit price of widgets imported from Japan by dividing the total quantity by the total value. Call (301) 457-2311.

RESOURCES

Exporter's Encyclopedia ($545/year) ISBN 0732-0159-3896 Dun and Bradstreet, 3 Sylvan Way, Parisppan, NJ 07504 (800) 234-3867 (p); (201) 605-6911 (f)

International Business ($48/year) ISSN 1060-4073 American International Publishing Corporation, 500 Mamaroneck Avenue, Suite 314, Harrison, NY 10528 (800) 274-8187 (p) or (914) 381-7700 (p) for subscriptions only

International Information Report ($160/year) Washington Researchers, Ltd., P.O. Box 19005, 20th Street Station, Washington, DC 20036-9005 (202) 333-3499 (p); (202) 625-0656 (f)

Journal of Commerce ($205/year) The Journal of Commerce, 445 Marshall Street, Phillipsburg, NJ 08865-9984 (800) 221-3777 (p); haddock@interport.net (e); http://www.joc.com (w)

Determine the "Just Right" Export Price. Pricing a product is the most important factor that will affect your financial projections in the export business plan. Many first time or infrequent exporters do not consider the various non-domestic costs that can contribute to the per unit price. Among the special elements to consider when exporting are the percentage mark up, sales commissions, freight forwarder processing and documentation fees, financing costs, letter of credit processing fee, export packing charges, labeling and marking, inland freight charges, unloading at the terminal, insurance, translation of product materials, etc. Make sure that each of these costs is clearly articulated in your financial projections and 12-month budget. On page 69 you will find an Export Pricing Worksheet.

Articulate the Firm's Capacity. It's important to stress that pricing is not the only factor which contributes to a buyer's decision to purchase a product or service. In order of importance, following are other factors which are important to your foreign buyers and which constitute the total "price package:" management capability; production capacity and processes; quality control system; technical cooperation, if any, with foreign firms; structure for handling orders; export experience, including types of companies dealt with; and financial standing and links with banks. All should be included in the international business plan, along with credit terms, payment schedules, currencies of payment, insurance, commission rates, warehousing costs, after-sales servicing responsibilities, and costs of replacing damaged goods.

Address the Buyer's Decision Points. It is important to address the primary decision points buyers consider so that readers of your business plan realize that you understand what is important to foreign buyers. In priority order, from most to least important, the primary buying decision points are quality, delivery schedule, price, warranties, liability for claims/damages, patents and infringement protection, technical assistance, confidentiality, changes in drawings/specifications, packaging, terms of payment, mode of transportation, and ability to provide a progress report on orders.

Marketing. Many first-time exporters are reactive rather than proactive exporters, in that the only reason they are exporting is because someone from another country contacts them. Many firms don't export because they don't know of the low-cost or no-cost marketing opportunities available to them. The best marketing opportunities are found using *Commercial News U.S.A.*; (212) 490-3999; National Export Offer Service (301) 596-5187; *Export Yellow Pages* (202) 482-5131; International Buyer Program (202) 482-0146; Agent/Distributor Service (202) 482-4204; Catalog Exhibitions and Shows (202) 482-3973; and trade associations.

Internet. Small firms must begin to use the Internet to advertise as well as to conduct research. A significant component of your business plan should be an explanation of how you intend to use the Internet to expand internationally. Some of the best ways to promote on the Internet include designing a web site and registering with all search engines; sending out postcards to those on your mailing list that you now have a web site; requesting e-mail addresses from current customers and obtaining e-mail addresses of firms in other countries so that you can communicate at virtually no cost; establishing reciprocal links to firms and organizations that will visit kindred web sites, etc.

Checking a Buyer's Credit. Before you agree to any deal, it is essential that a potential buyer, distributor, or partner's credit be checked. The best sources are America's Business Information Association (770) 667-1818; Dun and Bradstreet Information Services (800) 932-0025; Graydon International (212) 633-1434; J. I. International (800) 589-1698; LIDA Credit Agency, Inc. (800) 423-0026; Owens On-line, Inc. (800) 745-4656; Standard and Poor's Rating Service (212) 208-1527; and Veritas (800) 929-8374.

Methods of Distribution. Many firms consider direct exporting as the only means of conducting international business. Direct exporting does allow for greatest control of marketing, financing, and growth of the export market. However, other methods of distribution include appointing a commissioned sales agent; letting an export management company handle the sale of your product; appointing a sales representative; negotiating a distributor agreement; or forging a licensing, joint ventures, or off-shore production venture.

RESOURCE

Washington Researcher's International Information Report ($160) ISSN 0748-206X Washington Researchers, 2612 P Street, N.W. Washington, DC (202) 333-3533 (p)

Who Can Assist Me with Research and Market Planning?

Many public and private organizations offer excellent market and research assistance. Some of the best international trade professionals to consult are:

Freight Forwarders. These individuals can provide specific country information on requirements regarding documentation, shipping, insurance, and packaging.

International Departments of Banks. International departments deal with foreign banks, letters of credit, and all other facets of international financing. These banks can also provide information on the credibility of the foreign banking institutions.

Export Management Companies. EMCs, as they are commonly called, can provide vital information on the status of the overseas market of a product, methods of transport, and marketing information of a particular region.

Small Business Development Centers. SBDCs, located at community colleges and universities or chambers of commerce, employ counselors who are trained specialists to answer the various questions of business owners.

U.S. Department of Commerce, its Commercial Service and the U.S. Small Business Administration. Through local branch offices of these government agencies, a company will find experts who can offer advice on how to go about breaking into the global marketplace, plus a variety of free publications on different international markets. The Small Business Administration also has loan programs to help businesses expand. Both agencies employ international trade specialists in the district offices who are available for counsel to the public.

Country Desk Officers. These individuals reside in Washington, DC, but maintain an expertise in their respective assigned countries by communicating with U.S. diplomats overseas and the foreign embassies in the U.S. With their knowledge base of a particular country, they are qualified to provide current, market-specific information that may not yet be in print. To speak with a country desk officer, call (800) USA TRADE.

Industry Desk Officers. Similar in expertise and knowledge to the country desk officers, these individuals are involved with a specific industry and will provide foreign marketing information regarding a particular industry. To be referred to a specific industry desk officer, call (202) 482-2000.

State International Offices. Most states offer some form of market planning assistance. The Illinois Trade Office (ITO) of the Illinois Department of Commerce and Community Affairs provides international marketing assistance to Illinois companies seeking distribution channels for their products in foreign markets. The ITO maintains a network of International Trade Centers and NAFTA Opportunity Centers located throughout the state, and has State of Illinois Foreign Offices located throughout the world. For further information, please call (312) 814-7164 or visit www.commerce.state.il.us.

Export Hotline and Trade Bank. You can call this free service provided by the Small Business Exporters Association to receive market and country specific reports via facsimile or the Internet. This fully automated service allows callers to receive their reports instantly. To receive, register your fax number, call (800) USA-XPORT.

Private Firms/Consultants. Check your local yellow pages for any consultants, such as the World Trade Centers, in your area. Also look for any ethnic-based social groups or professional organizations related to the area on which you desire information. These people will tell you firsthand about their homeland and attempt to link you to business owners who may buy your product.

RESOURCES

Country Commercial Guides U.S. Department of State. Available on the National Trade Data Bank, at the State Department web site at www.state.gov, or by visiting a local federal depository library

Country Reports ($350 each) The Economist Intelligence Unit, 111 West 57th Street, New York, NY 10019 (212) 554-0600 (p); (212) 586-1181 (f)

Journal of International Marketing ($75/year) Michigan State University, Center for International Business Education & Research, MSU University Press, 14055 Harrison Road, Suite 25, East Lansing, MI 48823-5202 (517) 353-4336 (p)

What Is the National Trade Data Bank (NTDB)?

Produced by the U.S. Department of Commerce, the National Trade Data Bank (NTDB) is a comprehensive database which selects the best and most up-to-date international trade and economic information available and provides it in a convenient format. Updated monthly, the NTDB is an invaluable resource for exporters as they make crucial decisions about today's complex and competitive international market.

It is a one-stop location for trade information from more than 20 federal sources. While the following topics only scratch the surface of the more than 160,000 documents (over one gigabyte) available, here is a selected listing of the types of information you can find on the NTDB: basic export information; calendars of trade fairs and exhibitions; capital markets and export financing; country commercial guides; country reports on economic and social politics and trade practices; energy production, supply and inventories; exchange rates; export licensing information; guides to doing business in foreign countries; international trade regulations; international trade agreements; maritime and shipping information; market research reports; overseas contacts; price indexes; trade opportunities; worldwide import and export statistics by country and commodity; the World Fact Book; World Minerals Production; and worldwide agricultural commodity production and trade.

No matter how technical or obscure, the relevant information will probably be found on the National Trade Data Bank. The trick is to find it. A free, easy-to-understand "Magic Bullet Guide To The NTDB" is available on the NTDB itself. Call 1-800-STAT-USA for a free five-page guide by mail or fax.

The cost of a single monthly issue (two discs) is $59 and an annual subscription of 12 monthly issues is $575. You can use the NTDB CD-ROM on any IBM compatible PC with at least 640K of memory. You may also use a Macintosh that is equipped with software capable of running DOS programs.

If you're not inclined to purchase this resource for your business, all federal depository libraries are required to have this information. There is most likely a federal depository at your public library or university or community college library. Librarians should be skilled and available to teach you how to use this resource. Also, many Small Business Development Centers, International Trade Administration district offices, state departments of commerce, and international business centers have the NTDB.

RESOURCES

FINDEX: The Directory of Market Research Reports, Studies, and Surveys ($390) ISBN 0-942189-08-6 Cambridge Information Group, 7200 Wisconsin Avenue, Bethesda, MD 20814 (800) 843-7751 (p) or (301) 961-6750 (p)

Worldcasts 60,000 abstracted product forecasts for 150 countries ($975 per volume or $1,450 for 8 volumes) Predicasts, 11001 Cedar Avenue, Cleveland, OH 44106 (800) 321-6388 (p) or (216) 795-3000 (p)

World Trade ($24/year) World Trade, P.O. Box 3000, Department WT, Denville, NJ 07834-9815

National Trade Data Bank Manual ($22.50) Bermam Press, 4611-F Assembly Drive, Lanham, MD 20706 (800) 865-3457 (p); (800) 865-3450 (f); order@bernan.com (e); http://www.bernan.com (w)

How Can I Obtain a Phone Book From Overseas?

Foreign phone books are an excellent way to find current addresses of businesses that may want to purchase your product. High-priced international marketing firms utilize this technique as an integral part of finding buyers. Despite what you might think, acquiring a telephone book for a foreign city is quite simple. Aside from actually visiting the foreign country and obtaining a telephone book there, a U.S. export manager can call Ameritech and speak with the Directory Services Division. Simply request a telephone book from a certain city and Ameritech will send the book to you. If the Ameritech center you call has the book on hand, you should receive the phone book within three to five days. If the phone book must be ordered, you can expect to receive the book in approximately three weeks. Fees for the phone book may range from $20 to $275 for large cities that have several volumes.

For more information on acquiring a foreign telephone book, you may also wish to call the operator of your long distance company. Foreign embassies and consulates within the United States will also have phone directories from their home country. Large public libraries usually have phone directories for major foreign cities. And lastly, there are a few private agencies that sell foreign phone books, such as M. Arman Publishing. Call (904) 673-5576 for more information.

What Are the Rules of International Business Etiquette?

Each country has a culture that is unique to itself. Indeed, it probably has sub-cultures as well. It is critical for anyone who wishes to be successful in selling to people of another country to learn about, understand, and appreciate that culture. Culture influences consumer preferences, buying patterns, negotiations, arrangements, and a host of other daily business practices. Your investment in learning about the cultural environment now should save you great grief from gnawing problems and festering feelings later.

Be aware that what is considered polite or standard business practice in the U.S. may be considered rude or outside the norm elsewhere in the world. Your international business counterparts will realize that you are a foreigner, and make some allowance for your behavior and speech and lack of knowledge. As well, you will be forgiven for any inadvertent cultural *faux pas*. However, the more you know before you go, the greater your opportunity for success. Your counterparts will appreciate what you learned before entering the country.

You might sense differences in conceptions of time and priorities, family dynamics as they relate to business, styles of leadership and decision-making, the process of negotiating relative to reliance on laws and rules, business courtesies, and values and ethics. If you witness something that you find to be morally objectionable, culturally insensitive, socially outrageous, "backwards," or simply incomprehensible, it would be a good idea for you to try to understand why the people of the people of that culture act as they do. Particularly where values are concerned, you should be open-minded, non-judgmental, and flexible. That is not to say that you must ignore your moral standards, but that you should be cautious and question before you judge.

Business Manners

You will find people in many other cultures are more formal in their business relationships than in the United States. It is important to use full names and titles in introductions. Never call an individual by his or her first name, unless you are invited to do so, and only upon appropriate occasions. You will notice that most cultures are

RESOURCE

Overseas Phonebooks (prices vary) M. Arman Publishing, Inc., P.O. Box 785, Ormond Beach, FL 32175 (904) 673-5576 (p); (904) 673-6560 (f) Available 24 hours ($15-$250 per phone book)

much more "stiff" in their initial meetings with you, as Americans tend to be more effusive and outgoing in initial meetings. Because of the heightened formality, err on the side of caution and use "Herr" or "Herr Doktor" or "Senor" rather than the first name or a derivative (e.g., Joseph or Joe). Because you will make introductions more frequently, you should try to know ahead of time the correct names and their pronunciation. Practice saying the names out loud until they come easily to your tongue.

You might also be shaking hands more often than you would in the U.S. — or not shaking them at all. There are many different types of hand shakes and what in the U.S. would be called "limp" is the style preferred by most Arabians. French prefer a quick handshake and Chinese generally pump the hand. Bowing—from the nod of a head to a deep bow—is customary in many countries. In Japan, the level of the bow is an indication of the relative level of prestige of both parties. In many countries of South America, it is customary for men to keep on holding hands or embracing even while walking the street.

Socializing

If you are invited to a social affair, accept the invitation, because it is a sign of respect. It may also be a prerequisite for doing business, because in many cultures, people will not do business with those whom they do not know. Moreover, declining a social invitation may be taken to be a rudeness. On the other hand, if you ask someone to dinner, and are refused, be sure to ask again and again, because your intended guests may not accept until you have offered it for the third time. Do not press to discuss business, however, during this social time. Simply enjoy the hospitality extended to you — and learn about the people, their belief, opinions and their ways. In the U.S., "time is money." In other countries, time is for relationships.

Becoming inebriated in any society undermines business. In some cultures, it is considered a severe loss of face. Even for mild drinking, the alcoholic beverage of choice various from country to country. There are also nuances in the ways of consuming a drink, ranging from taking sips to drinking it all in one swallow, as well as how many drinks are too much and not enough. If you don't drink, you may want to fake it with tonic water or ginger ale, or simple say without fuss that you do not drink.

Gifts

The custom of giving gifts is not limited to the U.S., although the U.S. government has regulations and businesses frequently have policies limiting what you can give (and receive). Check out the local practice, not only of giving gifts, but of what kind and to whom they should or should not be directed. If you are invited to someone's home in Japan, and wish to give flowers, they should be neither an uneven number (because it is not easily divided) nor white (because it is a symbol of death). A gift of a knife there means you wish to sever the relationship.

Business Cards

It is standard international business practice to make your business card bilingual, with English on one side and the host country language in the other. If you are going to several countries, have a bilingual card for each. Be careful if you are going to several countries that used to share a common business language (e.g., Russian in the former Soviet Union republics). Although Russian may still be spoken in business, having your card in the official national tongue will speak well of you.

Take plenty of cards. You will be using them more frequently and more widely than in the U.S.

In come countries, the business cards are treated quite reverently, as they are a declaration of status. The card may be carefully handed to you, with both hands, with the writing facing you, and perhaps also presented with a nod or a bow. Do not bend, write on, nor put away the business card while in the company of the presenter of the card. Instead, place it carefully on the table directly in front of you where you sit so that it faces it towards you at all times during the discussion.

RESOURCES

Do's and Taboos Around the World ($14.95) and **Do's and Taboos of International Trade** 3rd ed. ($14.95) ISBN 0-471-59528-4 John Wiley & Sons, 605 Third Avenue, New York, NY 10518-0012 (800) 225-5945 (p)

A Short Course In International Business Culture ($19.95) World Trade Press, 1505 Fifth Avenue, San Rafael, CA 94901 (800) 833-8586 (p); (415) 453-7980 (f)

Trading With . . . ($25) from The Journal of Commerce ($365 annual subscription price) The Journal of Commerce, 445 Marshall Street, Phillipsburg, NJ 08865-9984 (800) 221-3777 (p); haddock@interport.net (e); http://www.joc.com (w)

What Are Some Cultural Norms of Our Biggest Trading Partners?

Here are some guidelines to use with people who are our country's most active and important trading partners.

Canadians probably are more familiar with U.S. customs than the reverse. However, because there are many similarities, the differences are often overlooked by people of the U.S. — or overemphasized and/or made light of, particularly when it comes to using, pronouncing, and spelling words. For example, discussing the use of "eh?" at the end of a sentence, "a-boot" or "a-bowt" for "about," or "color" or "colour" is often patronizing and counterproductive.

Formal but warm, Japanese like to preserve harmony. Raising your voice or losing your temper will cause you to lose "face," a very important concept in Japanese living, along with showing respect. They are generally group-oriented, rather than individualistic, and strive for consensus before a decision is made. Silence during a business meeting does not mean displeasure, but a processing of information. Rushing to fill a silence may jeopardize the value of the outcome of the negotiations. Moreover, a nod or a "yes" does not mean approval or a go-ahead, but merely "I see" or "I understand."

With Mexicans, be warm and approachable. The man-to-man *abrazo* is typical, as well as standing closer than the U.S. norm in conversations. In negotiating, leave a margin for bargaining. Shake hands at the beginning and conclusion of a meeting. Use professional titles when addressing or naming an individual. Mexicans value courtesies and place an emphasis on tactfulness.

Formality and politeness are inherent to Chinese business discussions. A bow or nod in greeting or farewell may be sufficient; in general, the Chinese are not a touching society. Remember the sequence of names: the first name is the family name; in dealing with Westerners, they will often adopt a Western first name. The reversion of Hong Kong to China in 1997, and Taiwan, are sensitive subjects for conversations.

In Brazil, friendliness and formality go hand-in-hand. While titles are important, first names are often used. Conversations are animated with large gestures, but be careful: the hand sign in the U.S. for "ok" is an extremely rude gesture. Expect the "friends first," before doing business. However, business entertainment is usually done in a restaurant, not in the home, with family and soccer typical topics of conversation.

A well-educated, hospitable people, Russians love the cultural arts and their contributions of music, literature, fine arts and crafts to the world. They also love to debate issues, ideas, and history, and theirs is a terrible history of survival over the centuries. The U.S. has offered millions of dollars to train and support the Russians as they move toward a free market economy; however, if they perceive a benevolent or condescending attitude towards them during this transition, or a regard that their country is an empire for a capitalist to conquer, they will resent it. Be committed to developing personal relationships over the long haul, for they are the basis for business.

The answers to this and the foregoing question was written by Jeanne Gerritsen, author of *Gaining the Export Edge: International Business for Small Business*, published by the Michigan Small Business Development Center.

RESOURCES

CulturGrams ($80/nonprofit; $120 without a tax-exempt id number). Kennedy Publications, Brigham Young University Publications, P.O. Box 24538, Provo, UT 84602 (800) 528-6279 (p); (801) 378-5882 (f) http://www.byu.edu/culturgram

The Global Road Warrior ($24.95) World Trade Press, 1505 Fifth Avenue, San Rafael, CA 94901 (800) 833-8586 (p); (415) 453-7980 (f)

Managing Cultural Differences ($39.95) Pub. No. 5078; ISBN 0-88415-078-X Gulf Publishing Company P.O. Box 2608 Houston, TX 77252-2608 (713) 520-4444 (p) or (800) 231-6275 (p)

World Population ($4.50) S/N 003-024-06706-4 U.S. Superintendent of Documents, P.O. Box 371954, Pittsburgh, PA 15250-7954 (202) 512-1800 (p); (202) 512-2250 (f); gpoaccess@gpo.gov (e)

Will Being a Female Business Owner Affect My Business Success Abroad?

The United States is one of the most progressive countries in the world with respect to how women are treated in business environments and in the work-force. It also is currently considered the most advanced country in the world for women in business management positions. However, many foreign businesses have lowered barriers to women and allowed them to assume management positions. Biases, prejudices, and tradition still deny women true equality in the international business world. Don't take abuse, but don't expect respect either.

For example, in Arab countries, hosts commonly use "separate but equal" dining facilities. Even if a woman heads the delegation, the fact that she is female may prompt the host to place her in the women's dining room. It is important to also note that the treatment of women who are residents of a particular country does not necessarily indicate how businesswomen from the United States will be treated. However, how women are regarded is a testament to the unique culture, history, and social structure of a particular country. If you feel women are not treated as you would treat them in the United States, do not start a debate on this issue unless your local host asks for your opinion.

When businesswomen travel abroad, they must be prepared to handle sexual overtures by remaining in control while showing no anger or other emotion. If a woman becomes flustered by the situation, she should excuse herself, leave the room, regain composure, and resume negotiations.

Regardless of which country a woman conducts business, it is important to dress conservatively, avoid being flirtatious, be careful about dining alone (some may see it as an open invitation to join you), avoid giving business gifts unless they are for the family, offer but do not insist on picking up the check during business lunches/dinners, and if you are or were married, use the title "Mrs."

RESOURCES

International Businesswoman, A Guide to Success in the Global Marketplace ($19.95) ISBN 0-275-9200-1(pb) Greenwood Praeger, 88 Post Road West, P.O. Box 5007, Westport, CT 06881 (203) 226-3571 (p)

Women's Guide to Overseas Living ($15.95) Intercultural Press, Inc.; P.O. Box 700, Yarmouth, ME 04096; (207) 846-5168 (p); intercultural@internetmci.com (e)

Do I Need to Know a Foreign Language?

Although it is extremely beneficial to know the host country's language, speaking their language is not usually mandatory since English is the current language of international business. However, this is not to say that there may not be communication problems in international transactions. Americanized-English is full of idiomatic expressions and slang which make it extremely difficult for non-native English speakers to comprehend fully the true meaning of what is said. When speaking, watch eye contact for signs of confusion and misunderstanding, summarize your point often, speak slowly, avoid acronyms and slang, enunciate your words, be careful of your body language, do not pretend to be fluent in a foreign language if you are not, and listen well. When engaging in foreign correspondence, remember to use short, simple sentences, avoid idiomatic expressions and slang, be polite, objectively reread your correspondence to see if there may be any misunderstandings, and make sure handwritten numbers are precisely formed.

If you need to learn a foreign language, contact the Defense Language Institute at (408) 242-5748. The non-resident division sells foreign language courses. The Language Training Center has a large holding of all types of foreign books. These books are available through the national interlibrary loan program.

To obtain foreign language books prepared by the State Department's Foreign Services Institute, call the National Technical Information Service at (800) 553-6842.

Some large bookstores are also expanding their foreign language sections. Some dictionaries, phrase books, and learning tapes focus upon business and travel needs.

RESOURCES

PC-Translator ($985) Linguistic Products, Inc., P.O. Box 8263, The Woodlands, TX 77387 (713) 298-2565 (p); (713) 298-1911 (f)

Translation Services Directory ($75) American Translators Association, 1800 Diagonal Road, Suite 220, Alexandria, VA 22314 (703) 683-6100 (p), 73546.2032@compuserve.com (e)

Your Trip Abroad and **Tips For Travelers** ($1.00 each) Booklets for Travelers U.S. Superintendent of Documents, P.O. Box 371954, Pittsburgh, PA 15250-7954 (202) 512-1800 (p); (202) 512-2250 (f); gpoaccess@gpo.gov (e)

Do I Need a Visa to Travel?

The best person to answer this question is the U.S.-based foreign embassy/consulate for that particular country. Generally, most countries do require a visa and the length of time required to obtain the visa, the actual duration of the visa, and their fees are different for each country.

Plan ahead! Most visas, obtained from the foreign consulate within the United States, are available anywhere from 24 hours to eight to 10 weeks. Work permits for a foreign country can take months. To apply for a work permit, you generally need a corporate sponsor located in the country to which you are traveling. You may also need to prove you are HIV negative.

If you know you will be traveling abroad, apply for a passport now, as the processing can take several months. Once you receive your passport you can apply for the visa at major local post offices or U.S. courts. Or you can obtain an application form from http://travel.state.gov/passport_services.html. For current travel advisories and warnings, be sure to contact the U.S. Department of State's travel advisory section at (202) 647-5225.

Also, if you plan to travel with product samples, inquire about an ATA Carnet, to make travel simple and avoid excess customs fees. More information about an ATA Carnet can be found on page 98.

RESOURCES

Health Information for International Travelers ($7.00) U.S. Superintendent of Documents, P.O. Box 371954, Pittsburgh, PA 15250-7954 (202) 512-1800 (p); (202) 512-2250 (f); gpoaccess@gpo.gov (e)

Personal Safety Guide for International Travelers ($25.00 - quantity discounts available) Lee Security Consultants, 2044 Reynolds Street, Falls Church, VA 22043; (703) 237-3151; (703) 237-0804 (f)

Where Can I Sell My Product?

Market research allows firms to determine which foreign markets have the best potential for a particular product. The goals for market research are to determine the largest and fastest growing markets for the product, identify market trends, identify market conditions and practices, and determine competitive firms and products. New-to-export firms should seek a few target markets based on the demographic and physical environment, the political environment, economic factors, social and cultural environment, market accessibility, and product potential. Conducting a thorough market factor assessment will help the firm predict the demand for its products or services and how well it will perform in each target market. In order to identify the top two or three foreign markets, it is important to conduct the following market factor assessment of several countries that appear to offer export opportunities:

1. What is the overall population of each country, considering growth and density trends?
2. Is the population of your target age groups adequate? (e.g., 1 - 10, 11 - 24, 25 - 40, 40 - 60, etc.)
3. Where is the population located? (e.g. urban, suburban, and rural areas.)
4. Study climatic and weather variations, if fluctuations may affect the product or service offered.
5. Calculate the shipping distances from the point of export for the various target countries.
6. Consider the age and quality of transportation and telecommunications infrastructure.
7. Are there adequate shipping, packaging, unloading, and other local distribution networks?
8. Is the system of government conducive to conducting business?
9. To what degree is the government involved in private business transactions?
10. What is the government's attitude toward the importation of foreign products?
11. Is the political system stable or do governing coalitions often change radically?
12. Does the government seek to dismantle quotas, tariffs, and other trade barriers?
13. What is the country's commitment to fostering higher levels of imports and exports?
14. What are the predicted economic growth levels for each country?
15. Identify the GNP of each target market and the balance of payment for each country.
16. What is the percent of imports and exports in the overall economy?
17. What is the country's import to export ratio?
18. Find the rate of inflation for each country and identify currency or exchange regulations.
19. What is the per capita income of the target country? Are income levels increasing?
20. What is the percentage of discretionary income that can be spent on consumer goods?
21. What is the literacy rate? What is the average educational level achieved?
22. What percentage of the population is identified as middle class?
23. To what degree is the target market similar to the home market?
24. Will the product or service need to be translated?
25. Summarize the legal aspects of distributor agreements for each country.
26. What are documentary requirements and other technical or environmental import regulations?
27. Is the market closed to foreigners, despite the appearance of a free and open market?
28. Identify intellectual property protection laws which would affect the product or service.
29. If a commercial dispute arises, does the judicial system offer a fair and unbiased review?
30. Are the tax laws fair to foreign investors? What is the rate of tax on repatriated profits?
31. Is there an identified *need* for the product in the target market?
32. What percentage of the product or service is produced in the target market? Imported?
33. Is the product or service understood and accepted by the target market?
34. What is the general level of acceptance toward imported products?
35. How many foreign competitors are in the market now? From what regions?

The Market Factor Assessment

The Market Factor Assessment provides a complete breakdown of the factors identified above. Rate each prospective country based on a market condition scale of 1 (poor) - 5 (excellent). Tally the results of your research to identify your target markets.

	Country	Country	Country	Country
Demographic/ Physical Environment				
1. Population size, growth, density				
2. Age distribution				
3. Urban and rural distribution				
4. Climate and weather variations				
5. Shipping distance				
6. Physical distribution and communication network				
7. Regional and local transportation facilities				
Political Environment				
8. System of government				
9. Government involvement in business				
10. Attitudes toward foreign business trade				
11. Political stability and continuity				
12. Fair/free trade mindset				
13. National trade development priorities				
Economic Environment				
14. Overall level of development				
15. Economic growth: GNP, industrial sector				
16. Import and export percentage of total economy				
17. Balance of payments				
18. Currency: inflation rate, availability, controls, stability				
19. Per capita income and distribution				
20. Disposable income and expenditure patterns				
Social/Cultural Environment				
21. Literacy rate, educational level				
22. Existence of middle class				
23. Similarities and differences in relation to home market				
24. Language barriers				
Market Access				
25. Adequate distribution network				
26. Documentation and import regulation				
27. Local standards, practices, and other non-tariff barriers				
28. Patent, trademark, copyright protection				
29. Adequate dispute resolution mechanisms				
30. Tax laws, rates				
Product Potential				
31. Customer needs and desires				
32. Local production, imports, consumption				
33. Exposure to and acceptance of product				
34. Attitudes toward products of foreign origin				
35. Competition				

RESOURCES

Consumer International ($900) EP262 1995, Find/SVP, 625 Avenue of the Americas, New York, NY 10011-2002 (800) 346-3737 (p); (212) 807-2676 (f)

Export Marketing and Sales ($69.50) International Trade Institute, 5055 North Main St., Dayton, Ohio 45415 (800) 543-2453; (937) 276-5920 (f)

Foreign Labor Trends ($36/60 issues) U.S. Superintendent of Documents, P.O. Box 371954, Pittsburgh, PA 15250-7954 (202) 512-1800 (p); (202) 512-2250 (f); gpoaccess@gpo.gov (e)

Market Share Reports ($11) National Technical Information Service, US Department of Commerce, 5285 Port Royal Road, Springfield, VA 22161 (703) 487-4600 (p)

What Are the Best Sources With Which to Conduct International Market Research?

Market research allows entrepreneurs to determine which foreign markets have the best potential, identify market trends and practices, and determine competitive firms and products. Yet research has found that small businesses are reluctant to export because of an inability to locate information on foreign markets and to locate foreign buyers. The small international trader should consider the following no-cost and low-cost sources for foreign market research and locating foreign buyers:

Country Desk Officers are employees of the U.S. State Department or Commerce Department who are experts in a particular country. They will personally answer questions regarding any facet of marketing in their region.

Flash Fax is an instant information source available through the U.S. Department of Commerce Trade Information Center. By calling (800) USA-TRADE, you can obtain information which will automatically be faxed to you. Flash Fax is available for Central and Eastern Europe (2); Russia and NIS (3); Latin America, Caribbean, and NAFTA (4); Japan (5); Asia including Australia, Pacific Islands, India, and Pakistan (6); Africa and Near East (7); Northern Ireland and border countries (8); and Uruguay Round/GATT which is now WTO (9).

Trade Development Industry Officers work with manufacturing and service industry associations to identify trade opportunities by product or service, industry sector, or market, and develop export marketing plans and programs. They also provide trade information and analysis, and statistical data.

The *National Trade Data Bank* (NTDB) contains Census data on U.S. exports and imports by commodity and country, hundreds of current market research reports, *the Country Directories of International Contacts* (CDIC) – formerly known as the Foreign Traders Index – which contains names and addresses of foreign firms abroad interested in importing U.S. products, and thousands of pages of documents specifically related to international business research and marketing.

U.S. Department of Commerce *Country Market Profiles and Industry Analyses* are country-specific descriptions evaluating 40 overseas markets which provide a market overview, market trends, and information on the U.S. market position, the competition, and labeling and licensing requirement.

Contact other excellent market research sources such as the *Center for International Research* at the *U.S. Census Bureau* at (301) 763-4100 for up-to-date global demographic and social information through its International Data Base. Also, contact the U.S. Postal Service at (202) 268-2263 for a free copy of the *International Direct Marketing Guide* which describes all the facts about foreign direct marketing techniques. The Michigan Small Business Development Center ((313) 964-1798) also offers a comprehensive listing of market research sources in its *Low Cost/No Cost International Business Resources.*

Other sources include *Background Notes,* a U.S. Department of State ((202) 512-1530) publication which offers in-depth profiles on hundreds of countries. Produced by Brigham Young University, *CulturGrams* are another source of country-specific profiles which highlight cultures throughout the world ((801) 378-6528). Another source of import and export statistics is *Market Share Reports* which gives import statistics and U.S. export share of the import total of 80+ countries ((703) 487-4600). *FINDEX: The Directory of Market Research Reports, Studies, and Surveys* contains descriptions of consumer and industrial studies and surveys, audits, market reports, and research services ((301) 961-6750).

RESOURCES

BNA Export Reference Manual ($675) Bureau of National Affairs, Inc., Distribution Center, 9435 Keywest Avenue, Rockville, MD 20850 (800) 372-1033 (p) or (301) 961-6750 (p); www.newstand.lotus.com

Encyclopedia of Associations ($460) Gale Research, Inc., 835 Penobscot Building, Detroit, MI 48226-4094 (313) 961-2242 (p)

How to Find Information About Foreign Firms ($145) ISBN: 1-56365-044-4 Washington Researchers Publishing, Box 19005, 20th Street Station, NW, Washington, DC 20036-9005 (202) 333-3499 (p); (202) 625-0656 (f)

Inside Washington: Government Resources for International Business ($49.95) ISBN 0-96-285 1353; Delphos Publishing, 1101 30th Street, N.W., Suite 200, Washington, DC 20007 (202) 337-6300; ssgatchev@delphos.bocc.com

What Are the Best Sources With Which to Find Foreign Buyers?

After you've conducted your market research, you will need to find foreign buyers and make contacts. The *Agency for International Development* (AID) at (703) 875-1551 provides lists of importers in select AID recipient countries who are interested in importing specific U.S. products. Additionally, the annual *Export Yellow Pages* buyer's guide and sourcebook of U.S. suppliers is used worldwide by agents, distributors, and importers who are looking to buy American products and services. Call (800) 288-2582.

If you want access to thousands of potential buyers from throughout the world, you really cannot pass on the opportunity to advertise in *Commercial News USA*. It is published ten times yearly to promote U.S. products and services in 141 countries worldwide. Used by thousands of small businesses in the U.S., advertising in *Commercial News USA* is an excellent way to let foreign businesses know that your product is available. Advertisement rates start around $325 ((212) 490-3999). *Washington Researchers* at (202) 333-3533 also produces a number of excellent, low-cost publications which list foreign buyers in various markets.

One low-cost technique is to locate foreign buyers in *foreign phone books*. Despite what you might think, acquiring a telephone book for a foreign city is quite simple. Call Ameritech Directory Services Division at (800) 346-4377 or M. Arman Publishers at (904) 673-5576. Fees for a particular foreign phone book range from $20 to $275 for large cities that have several volumes. Also, check with large *public libraries and consulates* within the U.S. for foreign phone directories. Other readily accessible resources to help small businesses find foreign buyers include advertising in trade journals which focus on a particular product.

Check with your *national association* for your particular product. The association will likely produce a trade journal which advertises members' products to readers throughout the world. Also, actively exhibiting at *trade shows*, and passively participating in *catalog and video exhibitions* are excellent ways to generate foreign buyer contacts. Use exhibitions administered by the U.S. Department of Commerce ((202) 482-3973) or various private sector organizations as low-cost mechanisms to advertise a product abroad. You can gain access to the Canadian market for just $100 - $200 — without leaving your business — as representatives from various state and federal agencies display your company brochures at locations throughout Canada, collect all interested inquiries, and pass them on to you ((416) 369-9630). Also useful are *Worldwide Trade Show Directory* from Gale Research and web sites such as *Expo Guide*.

Also, it is important to *review existing company files* to determine if the company received requests from foreign entities in the past and chose not to respond to the requests. This is a highly overlooked but excellent place to begin a search.

Don't underestimate the power of any *trade lead* — hot or cold! Search for foreign companies that have looked or are currently looking to buy your product. Although a new export manager tends to discount "stale" leads as not worth the time, he should remember that if a buyer was considering the purchase of a product, most likely that product will be bought again. "Hot" leads may be so hot that the foreign buyer is inundated with quotes. Trade leads are available from the U.S. Department of Commerce's Trade Opportunities Program, World Trade Centers, or on the National Trade Data Bank. Consult a local office of the U.S. Department of Commerce for details.

The Illinois Trade Office of the Illinois Department of Commerce and Community Affairs provides trade leads to interested Illinois companies. For further information, please call (312) 814-7164.

RESOURCES

AID Importer List and Guide to Doing Business with AID Agency for International Development, Office of Small and Disadvantaged Business Utilization, 1100 Wilson Blvd., Suite 1220A, Roslyn, VA 22209; (703) 875-1551 (p); (703) 875-1862 (f)

American Export Register Thomas Publishing Company International Division (212) 629-1131 (p); (212) 629-1140 (f)

World Trade and Customs Directory ($399) International Division Publications, U.S. Chamber of Commerce, 1615 H Street, NW, Washington, DC 20062-2000 (202) 463-5460 (p); (202) 463-3114 (f)

Worldwide Trading Partner Locating System ($495) Applied Technologies International Corp., 2255 Morello Avenue, Pleasant Hill, CA 94523-1850 (510) 680-0200 (p); (800) 406-1581 (f)

The International Trade Resource and Data Exchange was established in cooperation with the United Nations Conference on Trade and Development. Launched in 1992 as part of the United Nations' Trade Efficiency Initiative, I-TRADE integrates vital public- and private-sector trade resources into a comprehensive, user-friendly clearinghouse of trade-related information, leads, and sources. Drawing from and working with the most respected suppliers of trade information in the world, I-TRADE provides small- and medium-sized entrepreneurs (SMEs) with access to current trade leads at a reasonable cost. Find information on I-TRADE via internet at http://www/tpusa.com/.

Although it may take nine to twelve months to set up, the U.S. Department of Commerce's *Matchmaker* program involves an overseas trip to meet with foreign buyers. The department offers sessions on how to maximize your participation in a trade mission ((202) 482-0692).

Multi-lateral development banks often seek small businesses to provide goods and services to the developing countries receiving their financial assistance. Major banks include the World Bank ((202) 477-1234), International Monetary Fund ((202) 623-7430), and Inter-American Development Bank ((202) 623-1000), all located in Washington, DC.

The *Customized Sales Survey* is a tailored research service which provides information on marketing and foreign representation for the product. Surveys determine such factors as the marketability of products, names of local competitors, trade barriers, comparative pricing levels, and names of local firms wanting to represent your type of product. The cost for this service ranges from $600-$3,500 per country. Contact a local U.S. Department of Commerce District Office, or call (800) USA-TRADE.

The *Economic Bulletin Board* (EBB) is an online and fax service that posts the daily trade opportunities (TOPS) that arrive from the U.S. embassies. The TOPS are solicited from foreign governments and private companies looking for bids from U.S. companies on needed products and services. To obtain more information, call (800) STAT-USA.

The *U.S. Census Bureau Foreign Trade Division* offers exceptional data services which are easy to acquire, accurate, timely, and dependable. The services are truly the most inexpensive and valuable resources for trade data currently available and are not to be missed.

RESOURCES

Commercial News USA (free) Associated Business Publications International, 317 Madison Avenue, New York, NY 10017 (212) 490-3999 (p) or (212) 482-4918 (p); (212) 822-2028 (f)

What's Working for American Companies in International Sales and Marketing ($391/23 issues per year) Progressive Business Publications, P.O. Box 3019, 370 Technology Drive, Malvern, PA 19355-0719 (800) 220-5000 (p); (610) 647-8089 (f)

What Are the Services Provided by the Census Bureau?

The Foreign Trade Division of the Census Bureau works with the data the U.S. Customs Service collects on every commodity that enters or exits the United States. You can use these data to find opportunities to expand the market for a product, break into new markets, determine what products are selling at what prices in what markets, and identify competition from imports. Few exporters know of the Census Bureau's outstanding services which include the following:

The Selected Commodity Subscription Service. From a list of 16,000 import codes or 9,000 export codes, from acorns to zinc oxide, select up to 10 commodities and track their trading pattern each month. Find data for your product(s) (like golf clubs) rather than broad categories (like sporting goods). You'll receive quantity and value data by country and customs district for each month and year-to-date. For example, you can discover how many snowshoes the United State imports from other countries which indicates where the foreign competition is located. Also, see how many fishing rods are made in the United States and where they are being exported. This information helps you find new markets. The cost is $180 per year (or $160 per year when received electronically) for each set of 10 commodities.

A wealth of international trade data can also be found on the Census Bureau's Foreign Trade Division web site. It offers merchandise trade statistics for the United States, including trade balances with international trading partners; historical trade data, country by 1-digit SITC commodity trade data, Schedule B Keyword Search (you don't have to browse the entire book!), Shipper's Export Declaration form and instructions for filling it out, a guide to foreign trade statistics, and links to other trade pages on related subjects. The web site address is http://www.census.gov/foreign-trade/www.

The Foreign Trade Division provides the official monthly import and export CD-ROMs to customers as soon as the FT 900 U.S. International Trade in Goods and Services report is released. These are the data that reporters use in TV/radio news and newspapers to describe the strength of the U.S. economy. Small exporters can use the data to determine where to establish new markets; find countries in which your product can compete; find the domestic and foreign exports free along side (FAS) value and quantity; and find the air and vessel value and shipping weights. Importers can use the data to track trade flows with any of 240 trading partners; determine competitiveness of the U.S. with foreign competitors; and determine Customs value and quantity, consumption value and quantity, and the cost, insurance, and freight (CIF) value and calculated duty.

Exporters can also get the detailed official merchandise trade statistics, on the day of release, from the Census Bureau's Internet Subscription services called CenStats. Subscribers will receive import and export data at greater commodity detail (3-digit SITC level instead of just the 1-digit level on the public Internet site), commodity data by country or country by commodity, enhanced search capabilities, and access to county demographic profiles, small-area economic activity by ZIP code, and census tract.

For further information, contact the Foreign Trade Division of the Census Bureau at (301) 457-2227 or view its web site at http://www.census.gov/foreign-trade/www.

RESOURCES

Customs Duties & Taxes Worldwide ($500) World tariff, Suite 448, 220 Montgomery Street, San Francisco, CA 94104-9490 (800) 556-9334 (p); (419) 391-7537 (f)

Market Research International ($790) S/N: EP245 sub. 1994, Find/SVP, 625 Avenue of the Americas, New York, NY 10011-2002 (800) 346-3787 (p); (212) 807-2676 (f)

What Are the Top U.S. Industry Targets?

The U.S. International Trade Administration highlights outstanding markets for American industries, ranked by potential gain in export sales over a two-year period. Among 29 key countries with strong sales potential for U.S. goods and services, there are 361 individual market sectors judged as "top Targets" for increasing U.S. exports through 1997. Top markets were initially identified by U.S. Commerce Department commercial attaché staffs overseas and then analyzed by the Office of Export Promotion according to a common set of market factors which gauge potential demand and overall economic growth of the countries. Market factors include measures of the size and projected growth of a total market, imports, and U.S. exports, as well as judgments on local and third-county competition. For further information, contact Dr. Alan O. Maurer at (202) 482-3486.

Aircraft and Parts - (202) 482-1229
Korea, United Kingdom, Taiwan, Italy, Germany, Singapore, Netherlands, South Africa, Russia

Apparel - (202) 482-5078
Japan, United Kingdom, Mexico, Netherlands, Switzerland, Belgium, Saudi Arabia, Kuwait

Automotive Parts and Accessories - (202) 482-0554
Japan, Australia, Germany, Mexico, Netherlands, France, Brazil, Thailand, Belgium

Computers and Software - (202) 482-0572
Germany, Japan, France, United Kingdom, Australia, Korea, China, Malaysia, Netherlands

Construction and Mining Machinery - (202) 482-0558
Thailand, Indonesia, Chile, China, Australia, Mexico, Hong Kong, Philippines

Drugs and Pharmaceuticals - (202) 482-0128
United Kingdom, Germany, Switzerland, Korea, Hong Kong, China, Sweden, Malaysia

Electronics - (202) 482-5466
Germany, Japan, France, Taiwan, China, Hong Kong, Singapore, Malaysia, Italy, Israel

Environmental Technologies - (202) 482-5225
France, China, Mexico, Indonesia, Spain, United Kingdom, Chile, Korea, Taiwan, Italy

Food Processing and Packaging - (202) 482-3494
China, Australia, Mexico, India, Egypt, Russia, Turkey, Saudi Arabia

Instrumentation - (202) 482-5014
Japan, Malaysia, Australia, Taiwan, Singapore, Germany, Thailand, Italy, Netherlands, Mexico

Medical Instruments and Equipment - (202) 482-5014
Japan, United Kingdom, Korea, France, Taiwan, Spain, Brazil, Australia, Netherlands

Metalworking Equipment - (202) 482-0315
China, Thailand, Mexico, Brazil, South Africa, Israel

Plastic Materials and Resins - (202) 482-0128
Taiwan, Hong Kong, China, India, Belgium, Egypt

Sporting Goods and Recreation Equipment - (202) 482-0337
United Kingdom, Chile, Malaysia, Singapore, Switzerland, Portland, South Africa, Egypt

RESOURCE

International Mail Manual ($17) U.S. Superintendent of Documents, P.O. Box 371954, Pittsburgh, PA 15250-7954
(202) 512-1800 (p); (202) 512-2250 (f); gpoaccess@gpo.gov (e)

What Are the Services Provided by the U.S. Department Of State?

According to the U.S. Department of State, the success of American business in international markets is of vital national interest. Eleven million American jobs now depend on exports — jobs that pay 13 to 17% more than non-trade related jobs. America's economic well-being, global leadership, and national security are all reinforced when American companies successfully compete in the global economy. Supporting American firms in the global economy is a principal objective and core mission of State Department officers around the world.

The Office of the Coordinator for Business Affairs is a good point of contact for firms seeking State Department support and assistance. CBA works directly with American companies to help them tap the worldwide resources of the State Department when they need advocacy or help in solving problems. As a business ombudsman and adviser to the Secretary of State and senior officials, the Coordinator ensures that U.S. business concerns are at the forefront of the foreign policy process.

The State Department produces Country Commercial Guides, Background Notes, and Dispatch Magazine. They are available through the State Department home page at http:www.state.gov under Business Services, along with economic policy updates, county analyses, congressional reports, briefings, and speeches. To order print versions, contact the Government Printing Office at (202) 512-1800.

Key Contacts at the State Department

Coordinator for Business Affairs (202) 647-1625
Defense and Sensitive Dual-Use Articles to Sell Overseas (202) 647-4231
Diplomatic Security (202) 663-0533
Economic and Business Affairs (202) 647-7950
International Organizations/Procurement Opportunities (202) 647-1155
Oceans and International Environment and Scientific Affairs (202) 647-1069
Public Affairs, State Department (202) 645-6575
Small and Disadvantaged Business Utilization (703) 875-6822

Key Regional Contacts at the State Department

African Affairs Information Center (202) 647-3502
East Asian and Pacific Affairs Information Center (202) 647-6594
European and Canadian Affairs Information Center (202) 647-2469
Mexico, Caribbean, Central and South America Information Center (202) 647-6754
New Independent States of the Former USSR Information Center (202) 647-7647
North Africa and the Middle East Information Center (202) 647-1552
Indian Sub-continent Information Center (202) 736-4331

RESOURCE

Export Sales & Marketing Manual ($295) Export-Link; 9302 Lee Highway, Suite 800, Fairfax, VA 22031 (800) 876-0624 (p); (703) 293-7829 (f); http://www.export-link.com

How Can I Obtain Lists of Potential Foreign Buyers?

The *Trade Opportunities Program* provides private and public trade leads that arrive daily from U.S. embassies abroad. These leads are printed in the *Journal of Commerce* (800) 223-0243, extension 7185, and other private sector newspapers. They are also available through the U.S. Department of Commerce's Economic Bulletin Board. Information on this bulletin board is accessible by Internet, modem, and fax machine. Call the Trade Information Center at (800) USA-TRADE for cost and ordering information.

Formerly known as the Foreign Traders Index, the *Country Directories of International Contacts* lists, by country, foreign directories of importers (showing name, address, telephone number, contact, etc.), government agencies, trade associations, and other organizations, country by country, where the U.S. Commercial Service maintains a presence. This list can be found on disk two of the National Trade Data Bank or, for more information, call (800) USA-TRADE.

The *Agent Distributor Service* (ADS) is a government program that helps locate interested and qualified overseas agents and distributors. A file, containing up to six representatives with interest in your company, containing names, addresses, and brief comments about themselves is available for approximately $250 per country or Canadian province. Allow 30-60 days for processing. To utilize this service, contact a local U.S. Department of Commerce office (202) 482-2505.

The Illinois Trade Office of the Illinois Department of Commerce and Community Affairs can provide Illinois companies lists of contacts or agent/distributor searches for $100-$250. Contact the Chicago Headquarters at (312) 814-7164.

Also, in *Appendix E* of the *U.S. Department of State's Country Commercial Guides* there is a list of names and addresses of government agencies and trade associations in the respective countries that you may wish to contact for names and addresses of firms in that country. Names of individual firms are not included in this list.

Finally, the *Export Yellow Pages, Commercial News USA*, and the *National Export Offer Service* are probably the three best sources to utilize to actively search for foreign customers. Descriptions of these services follow.

RESOURCES

Commerce Business Daily ($324) U.S. Superintendent of Documents, P.O. Box 371954, Pittsburgh, PA 15250-7954 (202) 512-1800 (p); (202) 512-2250 (f); gpoaccess@gpo.gov (e); free online at http:cbdnet.access.gpo.gov

Companies International CD-ROM ($2,495) Gale Research Inc., PO Box 33477, Detroit, MI 48232-5477 (800) 877-4253 (p); (313) 961-6083 (f)

How Can the *Export Yellow Pages, Commercial News USA,* National Export Offer Service, and Trade Compass Help Me Find Foreign Buyers?

Annually produced in cooperation with the U.S. Department of Commerce, *The Export Yellow Pages* is a sourcebook of U.S. suppliers used worldwide by agents, distributors, and importers who are looking to buy American products and services. This buyer's guide is designed to promote exports and help U.S. companies remain competitive in the global marketplace by listing information on more than 15,000 U.S. companies involved in or seeking international business. The U.S. Department of Commerce spearheads the distribution of 50,000 copies through U.S. embassies and consulates worldwide. It is one of the least expensive and most lucrative ways to tap into a worldwide distribution network, by allowing businesses to advertise for a fee starting at $295 or list contact information at no charge. To learn about export promotion opportunities (including how to get your company listed free of charge in the *Export Yellow Pages*) and how to obtain a free copy of the latest directory, call (202) 482-5131. Request that an "Export Yellow Pages Directory Registration Form" be sent to you or ask them to send you a copy of the *Export Yellow Pages.*

U.S. firms looking for buyers, dealers, distributors, or joint venture partners advertise in the U.S. Department of Commerce's *Commercial News USA.* It is distributed by U.S. embassies and consulates in more than 150 countries to screened buyers of U.S. products and services. It circulates to more than 140,000 business readers and two million electronic bulletin board users. Published ten times yearly, each issue of *Commercial News USA* offers 1/9 page listings in *USA Marketplace,* a one-stop bulletin board appearing in print and on-line versions, for announcing the latest news about U.S. export products and services. From potato chips to computer chips, each listing contains an 80-100 word product/service description, photo (optional) and company contact information. For added impact, firms can be positioned in special industry sections matching products and services. Call (212) 490-3999, visit on-line at http://www/cnewsusa.com, or contact a local U.S. Export Assistance Center for more information. Rates start at $395.

The *National Export Offer Service* (NEOS) gives exporters worldwide market exposure at little cost or risk. In one comprehensive directory, NEOS profiles thousands of U.S. export products and services. It displays detailed descriptions and images, allowing importers from throughout the world to find products of interest, review and compare product features, link directly to an exporter's web page, and contact the exporter by e-mail, phone or fax. View the NEOS web site at http://www.tradecompass.com/neos. Search by keyword, industry code, product name, brand name, supplier's name or location to find specific export products and companies. Companies that want to advertise their products or services and become part of the NEOS database pay an annual fee that depends on a variety of available features and begin at $125. Information on advertising rates is available online at www.tradecompass.com/neos; or by calling (202) 783-4455 (p); (800) 598-3220 (p); (202)-783-4465 (f) or by e-mail at wayne@tradecompass.com.

Trade Compass offers the most comprehensive Internet-based resource for critical market intelligence information and logistics for companies engaged in international business. Found on the Internet at http://www.tradecompass.com, the service provides real-time international business news, trade leads, country and company market intelligence reports, and a book store. *Trade Compass* also has a logistics management system including electronic export documentation filing, shipping schedules, cargo book, air and ocean cargo tracking, and the only Internet Electronic Data Interchange (EDI) connections with the U.S. Customs Service. For more information, contact Trade Compass at (202) 783-4455 or e-mail at sales@tradecompass.com.

RESOURCES

Export Yellow Pages (free from the SBA, USEACs, and U.S. West) ISBN 0-9628513-2-9; Venture Publishing or Delphos Publishing, 1101 30th Street, N.W., Suite 200, Washington, DC 20007; (202) 337-6300 (p) or (800) 288-2582 (p)

International Business Export Catalogue American International Publishing Corporation, 10711 Burnet Road, Suite 305, Austin, TX 78758 (512) 873-7761 (p)

What Internet Sources List Foreign Buyers and Contacts?

The following sources provide credible trade leads, buyer/seller matching, lists of buyers, and advertising opportunities:

Web Sites

http://www.buyused.com

http://www.std.com/intltrade

http://www.cityscape.co.uk

http://www.connexx.org/connexx

http://www.ios.com/~intlnet

http://www.stat-usa.gov

http://www.ibex-gba.com

http://www1.usa1.com/~ibnet.com

http://www.std.com/intltrade

http://www.ijs.com/naafetee/

http://www.tradematch.com/

http://www.tradecompass.com

http://www.gopher://una.hh.liv.umich

http://www.i-trade.com

http://www.tradenet.org/

http://www.trading.wmw.com/

http://www.tpusa.com/

http://www.tradeport.org

http://www.exporthotline.com

http://unibex.com

http://www.expoguide.com

http://www.joc.com

http://www.ita.doc.gov/exportmatch

http://www.iserve.wtca.org

http://www.fx4business.com/et

http://www.jetro.go.jp/japan/index.html

http://www.usitc.gov/tr/tr/htm

E-mail

Catalist inga@pnwer.org

Global Market Resources gmri@worldnet.alt.net

International Trade Data Network ptivey@itdn.net

Tradebank sales@exporthotline.com

How Can I Use the Internet to Promote My Product?

According to the July-August, 1997 edition of the *Clearinghouse on State International Policies,* Web-based transactions amounted to $318 million in 1995. By the year 2000, the International Data Corporation estimates there will be 34 million Web users, 45 percent of whom will use the Web to purchase $95 billion goods and services. Frederick W. Smith, Chairman and CEO of Federal Express, asserted that the Internet is revolutionizing trade on a scale like that caused by the laying of undersea cables and introduction of high speed airplanes. "What the Internet allows you to do is sit anyplace . . . and become a global competitor with no investment, no infrastructure, no representative, nothing except your ability to put your products and offering on the Internet."

Yet it is just recently that small firms are discovering how effective a tool the Internet can be in their global marketing strategy. The Internet is a relatively inexpensive tool for firms who wish to market their products and services throughout the world. While the upfront costs to develop a web site may be relatively high, the expected return on investment from this marketing medium should greatly surpass the initial expense. Following are elements of a good web site that will help to better market your product internationally:

- Keep it "fast" by using a minimal number of graphics and photos
- Know what your potential buyer wants and needs to know before deciding to buy
- Navigate from the top
- Encourage feedback
- Establish discussion groups to discuss industry trends, answer questions, etc.
- Post employment opportunities
- State your business philosophy
- Post business partnering opportunities
- Provide a guest book to create a mailing list of individuals who desire more information
- Allow a mode of registry for those who wish to continue to receive information
- Make the logical, key words of your business your button links
- Have a "comments from satisfied customers" section
- Have a "most commonly asked questions" section
- Promise to answer e-mail within three days or less
- Include any quality or registration marks your firm has received
- Provide links to kindred organizations and firms so that your viewer can find more information regarding your industry
- Provide information that is educational about your product or service
- Include copyright, trade mark and patent marks
- Make it easy to make the purchase

RESOURCES

Exporters Directory: www.exporter.i411.com

Cyber advertising: info@inexchange.net

What Are the Ways to Enter a Foreign Market?

Before considering the different ways to enter a market, first determine how much financial risk the firm can assume and how much control over the product is necessary in the foreign market. The answers to these questions will help you decide which type of representation to use. There are essentially four ways to enter the global market: direct or indirect exporting, joint venture, licensing your product, and off-shore production. When choosing an entry method, consider the similarity of the foreign market to the home market, level of service required, tariffs and shipping, lead time requirements, brand awareness, and competitive advantage.

Indirect Exporting Methods With indirect exporting, the company is not directly involved in the export process, rather, the company uses the services of an intermediary middleman. This method provides a good way for a small business to break into the international market place without the complexities and risks of direct exporting. Disadvantages with indirect exporting are the possible loss of control over the product to an aggressive representative and risk of non-compliance with your requests.

Commissioned Agent (a.k.a. Purchasing Agent) A commissioned agent is usually an expert in a particular product who earns income through a commission from the net export price. Agents find foreign firms that want to buy the products and place orders on behalf of the buyers. They do not become involved with packaging and shipping of the products, nor do they take title of the products they represent.

Export Management Company (EMC) or Export Trading Company (ETC) An EMC or ETC has well-established networks of foreign distributors which provide immediate foreign market access. Products are purchased at a discount, and transportation and marketing costs are incurred by the EMC or ETC. Loss of control over foreign sales could affect customer service and overall image. Therefore, it is important to negotiate with an EMC to maintain a certain degree of control over the product. ETCs, like the EMCs, sell products in foreign markets; however, ETCs usually represent a number of identical or similar products from a single industry. ETCs assume the risks associated with exporting by taking title to goods and handling subsequent export operations for the firm. Both ETCs and EMCs typically export large volumes of products from many sources at lower per-unit costs. They use established networks of overseas offices, transportation, insurance, and warehouses. ETCs can offer a range of goods and services to potential buyers, secure more favorable prices, or develop additional sales channels typically denied individual exporters.

While there are many different forms of ETCs, the primary advantage of exporting through a well-developed ETC is that for you the selling process is simply a domestic transaction. ETCs are also capable of monitoring markets more efficiently and are better equipped to recognize potential opportunities.

Some of the functions an ETC performs include warehousing and storage of goods; loading and unloading of cargo at shipside or in transit area; coordinated handling services for air freight at airports; freight forwarding including customs clearance of freight, freight consolidation, and shipping documents preparation; transport clearinghouse, brokerage, and freight rate information; packing, crating and otherwise preparing goods for shipping; domestic and international telecommunications; purchasing and selling foreign currency exchange and transmitting funds abroad for international trade transactions; furnishing short- or long-term financing to business enterprises; placement of marine, casualty, and war risk insurance contracts with carriers for international trade transactions; preparing and placing advertising for international trade; market analysis and

RESOURCE

International Direct Marketing Guide (free) U.S. Postal Service, International Products Management, Room 1140, 475 L'Enfant Plaza, SW, Washington, DC 20260-6520 (202) 268-6095 (p) or ask your local U.S. Postal Business Office

research for international trade transactions; and legal services for international trade-related matters.

Direct Exporting Methods The major advantage to direct exporting is that the firm is afforded more control over the exporting process; profit potential is greater because the company does the work, thereby foregoing the payment of a profit share to a middleman; and the exporter will also develop a closer relationship with the foreign buyer. As a result, the direct exporter will also gain greater insight and knowledge of the foreign market. Disadvantages of direct exporting include exposure to greater risk and a chance that excess time and resources will be devoted to creating a successful overseas market.

Sales Representative An individual who represents the company in the foreign market is a sales representative. Representatives use the company's literature and samples, usually work on a commission basis, and assume no risk or responsibility. Signed prior to hiring the representative, a contract should outline the territory, terms of sale, method of compensation, reasons for termination of services, etc. A representative may not necessarily work on an exclusive basis.

Distributors A distributor purchases merchandise from an exporter, usually at discount, and resells it in the foreign market for a profit. The distributor maintains an inventory of the supplier's products, and usually provides support and service. The distributor does not usually sell to an end user. Payment terms and other agreements between the distributor and the company are established via contract.

Direct Sales to End Users Via exporting, a firm directly sells to an end user in a foreign country. Buyers are identified through trade shows, international publications, word of mouth, or government contact programs. The firm is responsible for shipping, payment collection, product servicing, and all other facets of the export process.

Licensing A firm may contractually assign the rights to certain technical know-how, design, and intellectual property to a foreign company in return for royalties or some kind of reimbursement payment. Licensing offers rapid entry into a foreign market, there is no capital investment, and the return is usually realized more quickly. However, licensing also involves some loss of control over production and marketing and the potential theft of technological know-how by the licensee. Licensors should take care to protect intellectual property through proper legal contracts.

Joint Ventures A joint venture is a partnership in which the in-country firm and the foreign firm negotiate interest, performance, responsibility, investment, and profit. Joint ventures can spread costs, mitigate risks, offer in-country knowledge and details, and ease market entry. Laws regulating joint ventures often require that a majority percentage of stock belong to an in-country national.

Off-Shore Production A firm may need to establish a manufacturing plant in the targeted foreign market to reduce transportation costs, avoid prohibitive tariffs, lower labor costs, lower input costs, or gain government incentives. This option typically requires a large capital outlay and therefore is most suitable for advanced exporters.

RESOURCE

A Short Course in International Marketing (19.95) World Trade Press, 1505 Fifth Avenue, San Rafael, CA 94901 (800) 833-8586 (p); (415) 453-7980 (f)

What Is the Difference Between an Export Management Company and an Export Trading Company?

An Export Management Company (EMC) is a private firm that serves as the export department for manufacturers, either by taking title or by soliciting and transacting export business on behalf of its clients in return for commission, salary, or retainer. An EMC usually specializes by product or by foreign market and usually has well-established networks of foreign distributors to allow immediate access to the foreign market. If using an EMC, keep in mind that you may lose control over foreign sales and the image of the product. If this is a major concern, make sure to have a secure contract which outlines the responsibilities and liberties between the EMC and your firm.

The terms EMC and ETC (Export Trading Company) are sometimes used interchangeably, since the two entities perform essentially the same function. The ETC is also a private firm that serves as the exporting department for a U.S. manufacturer. However, ETCs often take title to goods and receive compensation in the form of a purchase discount from the manufacturer. ETCs tend to specialize by industry and they pay all the exporting expenses.

The concept of an ETC was created with the Export Trading Company Act of 1982 which was designed to stimulate U.S. exports by reducing uncertainty about applying U.S. antitrust law to export operations. This law also called for the financing options of export transactions to be more accessible.

Contact the Office of ETC Affairs at the U.S. Department of Commerce, Room 1800, Washington, DC (202) 482-5131 or etc@doc.gov for any specific questions you may have on export trading companies.

RESOURCES

Export Trading Company Guidebook ($11.00) S/N 003-009-00523-0, ISBN 0-16-000-336-9 U.S. Superintendent of Documents, P.O. Box 371954, Pittsburgh, PA 15250-7954 (202) 512-1800 (p); (202) 512-2250 (f); gpoaccess@gpo.gov (e)

Registry of Export Intermediaries ($59.95) National Association of Export Companies (NEXCO) (212)725-3311 (p); (212)725-3312 (f)

Trading Company Sourcebook International Business Affairs Corporation, 4938 Hampden Lane, Suite 346, Bethesda, MD 20814 (301) 907-8647 (p)

Are Brand Names Important to Promote My Product in Foreign Markets?

Positive product name recognition is always beneficial. If the product has a simple, well-known name in the United States, you would want to maintain that name recognition overseas. Conversely, if the name brand is difficult to pronounce, is a "play-on-words" in the English language, or does not translate in the foreign tongue (or translates as something negative), you may wish to change the product name. The classic example of improperly naming a product is when Chevrolet witnessed dismal sales of its *Nova* car in Mexico. *Nova* translates to "no go" in Spanish. Even the best marketing managers would have a difficult time selling a car with this name.

In addition to brand names, the design of your product package is equally important. Gerber had a tough time selling its baby food in countries with low literacy rates where visual images are often utilized to compensate for poor reading levels. Mothers were horrified by Gerber products because the picture of the baby on the label caused them to believe that babies were inside the jar!

Although selling in a foreign country, most of your marketing strategy will remain the same; it just needs to be tailored to appeal to new customers. If you research the unique culture, history, language, traditions, customs, social structure, and environment of the country in which you are trying to sell a particular brand, you will probably avoid a marketing fiasco.

Should I Modify My Product?

Although the answer to this question will depend on your product and the destination, typical modifications of exported products include:

- Changing the product to metric standards
- Altering the number of units contained in a package
- Changing the size of a product
- Translating packaging and product language
- Changing color schemes
- Changing advertising campaigns to reflect the country's culture
- Gaining certification to ISO 9000 or other in-country standards
- Changing electrical voltage

RESOURCE

Profitable Exporting: A Complete Guide To Marketing Your Products Abroad ($90) ISBN 0-471-61334-7 John Wiley & Sons, Inc., 1 Wiley Drive, Sommerset, NJ 08875 (800) 225-5945 (p); http://www/wiley.com (w)

What Functions Does a Distributor Perform?

A distributor represents one or more manufacturers or service organizations as an independent sales function. The distributor serves related but non-competitive lines in a well-defined and exclusive territory, and is compensated primarily on a commission basis for goods shipped or billed from the factory of the company represented. The distributor also supplies other valuable services such as credit reports, marketing information, sales analysis, and in some cases, design engineering. Typically, a distributor receives credit for all sales within the territory. As part of the sales operation, the distributor maintains a sales office, compensates sales personnel, and assumes responsibility for all sales expenses. The distributor has little, if any, control over pricing and terms and does not take title to goods.

Benefits and necessity of contracting with an in-country distributor:

- A distributor can easily identify and communicate with the foreign market
- A distributor is more familiar with local business practices
- A distributor is more familiar with a specific industry in a foreign market
- A distributor acts as the manufacturer's "eyes and ears," letting it know of acceptance or resistance to a product and any need to make adjustments to the product
- A distributor can aid in obtaining necessary import licenses or other regulatory approvals, clearing goods through local customs, and arranging for delivery
- A distributor can install products and provide service repairs for guarantees/warranties
- The laws of some foreign countries prohibit a foreign company from selling its products locally unless it has established a local representative who will ensure the continued availability of parts, provide necessary servicing, and be "present" in order to stand behind the products

Advantages of selling through a distributor:

- Sales of one product can "trigger" sales of other products
- Provides more complete coverage in specific geographic areas and markets
- Provides objective evaluation of new products
- Sales costs are known: distributor is paid only for orders received and shipped
- Distributor has local acceptance (*i.e.*, a permanent resident in the selling territory)
- Provides quick response to customer problems due to proximity
- Provides quick entry into the market
- Reduces cost for sales and product training

Disadvantages of selling through a distributor:

- Lack of control of sales personnel
- Lack of in-depth product knowledge
- Less detailed sales reporting
- Distributor may not be as familiar with technical concerns in certain situations
- Because the distributor relies solely on commission, without the "perks" of other sales professionals, motivating the distributor may prove difficult
- Lack of knowledge of customer base
- No control over marketing (how product may be perceived by a foreign audience)
- If distributor loses his reputation so may your product by association
- Possible loss of identity

RESOURCE

Standard Handbook of Industrial Distributors ($95) Bergano Books Co., P.O. Box 190, Fairfield, CT 06430 (203) 254-2054 (p)

How Do I Find Information About Foreign Agents or Distributors?

The costs associated with selecting a representative are no more — and probably less — costly than having to replace a representative who is unqualified or incapable of handling the job. There are a number of ways to locate qualified, interested agents or distributors including:

Word of Mouth. Ask customers if they can recommend a suitable agent. (If the same company appears time and again, the manufacturer may consider them a good candidate for the job.) Other manufacturers may provide names of effective agents in a territory, though they may be reluctant to suggest their better agencies for the simple reason of competition.

Trade Shows. At trade shows (foreign and domestic), agents circulate among exhibits and talk with others about their interest in representing product lines. These conversations often produce a source of candidates. Be warned, however, that many other manufacturers may have had similar conversations.

Commercial Lists. Trade associations as well as commercial organizations publish directories of manufacturers' representatives. Listings are available from a few sources, including:

National Directory of Manufacturers' Representatives (from McGraw-Hill Book Co.), 1221 Avenue of the Americas, New York, NY 10020, 212-512-4100.

Agency Sales magazine, Manufacturers' Agents National Association, 23016 Mill Creek Road, P.O. Box 3467, Laguna Hills, CA 92654, 714-859-4040.

Industry trade organizations also publish lists with a brief description of their registered agencies. An example would be the Electronic Representative Association, 233 E. Erie St., Chicago, IL 60611.

Advertising Media. Classified ads can be used to locate industry-specific representatives. Newspapers or industry trade publications contain classified sections that list manufacturers' representatives. Foreign telephone directories, such as the telephone Yellow Pages, can be used. Follow-up is often necessary to determine if the agent fits the manufacturer's needs.

Phone Books and the *Export Yellow Pages* are excellent ways to locate distributors in a specific geographical area. Please see page 23 to find out how to obtain foreign phone books.

Search Organizations. These organizations are responsible for locating agents for client companies. The search organizations usually meet with the manufacturing client to discuss requirements and pass along the information to agencies that may be appropriate for the client. Search organizations charge for their services, but the time saved and the benefit of having an agent or distributor screened and questioned for the client typically makes the process cost effective.

RESOURCE

Export Sales Agents ($49.95) ICC Publishing, 156 Fifth Avenue, Suite 305, New York, NY 10010 (212) 206-1150 (p), iccpub@interport.net (e)

How Else Can I Find an Agent or Distributor?

To locate a reputable agent or distributor, also consult your local U.S. Department of Commerce office, chamber of commerce, trade associations, international departments of banks, or an international trade specialist. U.S. Department of Commerce services include:

Agent Distributor Service (ADS) A federal program that locates and qualifies overseas agents and distributors. A file containing up to six representatives with interest in your company is available for approximately $250 per country or Canadian province. Allow 30-60 days for processing. To utilize this service, contact a local U.S. Department of Commerce office or call (202) 482-2505.

Customized Sales Survey (CSS) Formerly known as the Comparison Shopping Service, a custom-tailored service providing firms with targeted information on marketing and foreign representation for specific products in specific countries. Interviews or surveys are conducted to determine the sales potential and possible distribution channels of a product. Fees for CSS surveys vary. Contact the nearest U.S. Department of Commerce District Office or (202) 482-2000.

Matchmaker Trade Delegations Planning and recruitment of firms by the U.S. Department of Commerce, to introduce new-to-market businesses to prospective agents and distributors overseas. Trade specialists evaluate the potential of a firm's product, find and screen contacts, handle product transportation logistics, and host a trip filled with meetings of prospective clients. Contact the Export Promotion Services, Office of Marketing Programs, U.S. Department of Commerce, Washington, DC 20230; (202) 482-4231 (p); (202) 482-0178 (f).

Gold Key Service A custom-tailored service for U.S. firms planning to visit a foreign country. It combines market research, assistance in developing sound market strategies, orientation briefings, introductions to potential partners, interpreters for meetings and effective follow-up planning. The fee varies. Contact a local Department of Commerce office or call (800) USA-TRADE.

State Trade Office The Illinois Trade Office of the Illinois Department of Commerce and Community Affairs offers Agent/Distributor searches through their network of foreign offices. Contact the Chicago Headquarters at (312) 814-7164.

RESOURCES

Industrial Reps of Overseas Countries and Overseas Buying Reps ($25) International Wealth Success, Inc., 24 Canterbury Road, Rockville Centre, NY 11570 (800) 323-0548 (p)

Pre-Screening Prospective Agents: Some Guidelines ($3.25) Research Bulletin #534, Manufacturers' Agents National Association, P.O. Box 3467, Laguna Hills, CA 92654 (714) 859-4040 (p)

How Can I Best Select an Agent or Distributor?

Review the content of a potential agent or distributor's letter, letterhead and typing, and general show of interest and enthusiasm. If initial contact is made by telephone, listen to the content of the call, acceptability of voice, show of interest, and eagerness to sell. In order to conduct the interview effectively, it is important that you have both background information and data on the sales territory, and have previously developed market potential for your product line in the geographical or industrial area of interest. During the interview, consider discussing the following points:

Normally, the distributor is paid on commission.

Tell the candidate up front what the company policy is regarding territory which can be divided in a variety of ways, such as by counties, metropolitan boundaries, postal codes, or other methods.

Some distributors sell to customers in a specific industry, such as automotive or electronic, while others organize themselves according to specific product type such as metal fabrication or plastic parts. Most distributors sell by territory; however, some specialize by market application or customer type within a territory. Knowing exactly what companies the distributor currently represents is one of the most important pieces of information the prospective exporter must know. If there is a possible conflict between product types, or if there is a principal within the distributor's portfolio which the new manufacturer feels is not compatible or supportive of his products, the relationship should not be fostered. Product line compatibility is a must for successful marketing through distributors and for avoiding cannibalization.

Knowledge of the distributor's sales volume is necessary to determine if the distributor is looking for additional business or is comfortable with current profitability. Manufacturers should compare products sold, usual commission rates, total sales dollars, number of personnel, and other factors to determine whether selling time is available for another product line.

An examination of the distributor's customer list may prove helpful, and as a principal, you have a right to ask for a list of the major customers in the agent's territory. You need to be assured the distributor is calling on major customers in that specific market, though the information disclosed must be kept confidential.

Technical backgrounds, education and personal experiences are all necessary to know in order to determine how well-versed the distributor is on the practical aspects of the products represented.

It is a good idea to know the banking institution of the distributor, and though confidential figures will not be disclosed, a conversation with bank officials will determine the general nature of the agent's financial situation.

In sum, when evaluating prospective distributors or agents, check out their reputations with suppliers, bankers, and customers. Make sure you understand their overall experience and knowledge of your market. What territory do they currently cover? Do they have experience with product lines like yours? If yes, ask for the names and addresses of U.S. firms they currently represent. What about the technical capability and capacity to service your product? In addition to documented financial strength and a history of sales volume and growth, you should be given a list of the lines that have been handled in the present and past, both complementary and competitive. Also, make sure your potential distributor or agent understands English and has a knowledge of U.S. business methods. And, be sure to ask about the promotion and marketing techniques used.

RESOURCES

How to Find Manufacturing Agents and Agency Salesmen ($3.50) Manufacturers' Agents National Association, P.O. Box 3467, Laguna Hills, CA 92654 (714) 859-4040 (p)

How to Get More of Your Agent's Time ($3.25) Manufacturers' Agents National Association, P.O. Box 3467, Laguna Hills, CA 92654 (714) 859-4040 (p)

What Are the Standard Contractual Clauses, Penalties, and Protections That Should Be Considered When Drafting an Agent or Distributor Contract?

Standard contractual clauses of representative contracts include the length of the appointment, sales and promotion, minimum quantities, payment and terms, legal compliance, intellectual property protection, non-competition, confidentiality, assignment, termination notice, governing law, and prior agreements. Following are hints on how to structure a protective contract.

- Make the contract of a fixed duration (perhaps a six-month or two-year period).
- Include a cancellation clause (reasons could include lack of orders within a specified period of time; failure of agent to pay; if agent become financially insolvent, etc.).
- Changes to the agreement cannot occur without the written authorization of both the exporter and the agent.
- Define the specific sales territory (e.g., city, state, region, country, multi-country) and the products covered within each territory. Do not use nebulous definitions such as "Europe."
- Ensure that the agent agrees not to promote, market, or sell products that are directly competitive with the exporter's products. The agent should be authorized to sell merchandise that is complementary to the exporter's products.
- You, the seller, must agree not to authorize another agent to establish a sales base in your agent's territory.
- Quote all prices in U.S. dollars.
- The delivery should be the date upon which the order is available for pickup at the seller's facility. If a sale is lost because of late delivery, seller must compensate the agent on a reasonable basis for such late delivery. Include clause of nonliability for late delivery beyond manufacturer's reason able control.
- Include the payment method for all products. An irrevocable letter of credit is still the best assurance of payment other than payment in advance.
- The agent should agree to order a set amount of annual purchases. The seller must reserve the right to establish a minimum charge for orders. Unsold items should be returned only at the written authorization of the seller which determines the repurchase price after deducting costs for return transportation, damage, and deterioration from the original purchase price.
- All disputes arising from the contract should be settled under the Rules of Conciliation and Arbitration of the International Chamber of Commerce. Make sure the award will be binding in the distributor's country.
- Products must be free from defect for (x) days from the date of use or purchase by the buyer.
- The seller must reserve the right to make design changes, improve design, or change specifications. Also, the manufacturer must reserve the right to change prices, terms, and conditions at any time.
- The seller shall not be liable if failure to enforce the contract are the result of *force majeure* circumstances such as floods, earthquakes, transportation strikes, labor disputes, or any other conditions beyond the control of the seller.
- Clarify tax liabilities, payment and discount terms, etc.
- Governments are very protective of their agents, representatives, and distributors. Many courts will insist that compensation be paid to the representative for loss of income and cost of establishing the territory in the event of "unjust" termination, even at the end of a contract period.
- The cost of a legal agreement drafted before there is a problem between the distributor and the manufacturer can save you thousands of dollars in the long run.
- It is critically important that you seek the advice of an experienced international trade attorney before making any agreements.

RESOURCES

Guide to Drafting Distributorship Agreements ($29.95) ICC Publishing, 156 Fifth Avenue, Suite 305, New York, NY 10010 (212) 206-1150 (p); iccpub@interport.net (e)

International Exporting Agreemenis ($108) Pub. No. 424; Matthew Bender & Company, International Division, 11 Penn Plaza, New York, NY 10001 (800) 223-1940 (p) or (212) 967-7707 (p); damian@a.burns@bender.com (e); http://www.bender.com (w)

Agent or Distributor Contract

We ________________ (company name), herein referred to as ________________ headquartered in ________________ (city, state, country) offer the opportunity to act for our company as our exclusive sales representative, subject to the terms and conditions in the sales territory named below. The territory to be covered is as follows:

- Exempted from your sales territory and your commissions are the following accounts:
- It is understood that the addition or deletion of accounts is open for review at all times. The right to reject any and all orders is reserved without qualification.
- The following rates of commission apply: The foregoing percentages will be applicable to all sales credited to you, except sale of merchandise as may be offered by us at less than regular price, in which case you will be advised of the rate of commission prior to offering merchandise at such price.
- Commissions will not be computed or paid on discount allowances that may be included in the selling prices of the merchandise.
- Commissions, as stated, will be paid to you only when the buying, warehousing and disbursing offices are located within the stated territory. Commissions will be computed and paid only on orders accepted and shipped. All commissions will be paid to you on the 15th of the month following date of shipment.
- Under the following conditions your commissions will be debited: (a) With any commissions paid to you on orders shipped and subsequently returned. (b) With any commissions paid when the account becomes insolvent or bankrupt before they have remitted to us in full for any unpaid balance.
- It is requested that you accord full cooperation to all direct representatives of the company in your territory and that you will follow our instructions in this connection.
- All travel and incidental expenses will be borne by you. You will not assume responsibility for any expenditures for this company. You will not make statements to customers regarding terms, deliveries, and conditions not specifically authorized by us in writing. You will at all times quote prices from price lists furnished to you by us and take orders only at the prices which we shall specify for individual accounts or trade classifications.
- The relationship hereby established between parties does not constitute that of employer and employee but that of independent contractors.
- You are not authorized to, and agree not to enter into any contract or agreement in the name of or on behalf of this company.
- There are no understandings or agreements relative to this contract that are not fully expressed herein and no changes shall be made in this contract unless reduced to a new written contract signed by both parties.
- This agreement between the parties hereto shall continue in force until terminated by either party upon thirty (30) days notice by registered mail to the last known address, and within said thirty (30) days all samples, catalogues, price lists, and other materials belonging to us are to be returned.

ACCEPTED:

Signature: ________________

Typed Name: ________________

Company Name: ________________

Address: ________________

City, State, Zip, Country: ________________

Date: ________________

How Do I Select the Proper Trade Fair?

A trade fair can help locate foreign buyers and provide a first-hand account of how the product will fare in the international target market. You will be able to assess the competition and meet potential distributors/agents for the product first-hand. To receive the most benefit from a trade show, first determine the company's trade show objective. Most managers would say it is to generate sales, but there are other valuable reasons to participate. The export manager can establish contacts and meet with inquirers, distribute company literature, announce the product, generate publicity and excitement for the product, and meet with distributors and set up future arrangements. Increasing market share is yet another reason to participate. Also, do not forget that a trade show provides the opportunity to conduct detailed research of a local market and check out the competition first-hand. Dun and Bradstreet offers an annual conference, Exhibiting At Trade Shows: Techniques for Success From Start to Finish. Call (212) 692-6600 for more information.

With the proliferation of shows offered throughout the world, it is important to be selective when considering when and where to exhibit. This is especially true for those companies with small budgets. If you take time to research trade show opportunities and plan ahead, you will be successful in reaping the benefits offered by smaller functions. Following are some tips on what to consider when deciding which show to participate:

- Don't be lured into a show just because it is big and promises to provide hundreds or even thousands of potential customers. Firms that have niche products or services are usually better served attending smaller, regional, more focused shows.
- If you can find a show that is tied to an educational program, you may experience even greater results. In times of downsizing and reduced budgets, companies are more likely to send people to a show that is allied with an educational opportunity as opposed to an exhibit-only function.
- Smaller shows offer other advantages. They may be less expensive to participate in and attend. Booth costs will usually be less than the $13.80/sq. ft., U.S. average. Smaller shows require fewer expenditures for show marketing because the audience is usually smaller. This is a much more comfortable venue for your staff and will enable them to spend more time getting to know prospects.
- Shows also often provide an opportunity for exhibitors to sponsor, or share in sponsoring, receptions or hospitality suites. A recent survey by *Sales and Marketing Management Magazine* reports that hospitality suites do open the door to sales. Of those executives asked how they felt attending a hospitality suite would influence purchases from the sponsoring company, 32% said they would probably increase their level of business.
- Smaller shows provide a good opportunity to let clients mingle with top management. Most clients want to know who makes the decisions in the firm
- If you choose to host a suite, remember: don't skimp. Companies whose suites lack food and drink are perceived as cheap. No one wants to work with a company that cuts corners.
- There are a number of resources, guides, and directories which contain information on industry- or country-specific trade shows. Listings provide the names of the shows; their dates and locations; contact information for the show's exhibition management; profiles of products and exhibitors; registration fees and admission charges to exhibits, seminars, and social events; founding data and frequency of event; number of attendees; and hotel rooms and meeting rooms needed.

RESOURCE

TradeshoWeek Data Book ($355) Reed Reference Publishing.; 121 Chanton Road, New Providence, NJ (800) 521-8110 (p); info@reedref.com (e)

Where Are Trade Shows Being Offered?

Thousands of trade shows are offered throughout the world. While many reputable overseas shows are sponsored in part by the U.S. Department of Commerce, there are numerous private sector organizations that also sponsor quality shows. Certain industry associations also have an international draw to their shows and conferences.

U.S. Department of Commerce Trade Fairs and Exhibitions About 80 international worldwide events are selected annually by the Commerce Department or by the private sector under Commerce's Certification Program. Companies recruited by Commerce to exhibit receive pre- and post-event logistical and transportation support, plus the design and management of the USA Pavilion. Commerce also provides extensive overseas market promotional campaigns to attract appropriate business audiences. Call the Trade Information Center at (800) 872-8723 for the telephone number of the office responsible for that industry.

U.S. Department of Commerce Catalog and Video Exhibitions These events provide a low-cost, low-risk vehicle to generate leads, whether the company is looking for sales or overseas representation. Using the resources of U.S. embassies worldwide, product catalogs or videos are shown by Commerce commercial officers to potential agents, distributors, or buyers in selected world markets. Contact the Export Promotion Services at (202) 482-3973.

U.S. Department of Commerce International Buyer Program The IBP supports major domestic trade shows featuring products and services of U.S. industries with high export potential. Qualified foreign buyers worldwide are recruited to attend the shows. The shows are extensively publicized through embassies, government agencies, travel agents, regional commercial newsletters, catalogues and magazines, and foreign trade associations. An international business center is sponsored at each foreign buyer show, providing interpreters, multilingual brochures, counseling and private meeting rooms. Contact the Export Promotion Services at (202) 482-0146.

According to Gale Research, publishers of a comprehensive guide to 6,839 trade shows worldwide, trade show activity throughout the world continues to grow. Trade shows are considered one of the best ways to meet with current customers, reach previously unidentified prospects, and offer goods and services to the international market. Over the course of the next decade, the trade show industry is expected to grow by a third. Five hundred new shows are expected to be launched by the end of 1999.

For those firms with Internet access, the Expo Guide Index will help you locate trade shows throughout the world. http://www.expoguide.com/shows/location.htm.

Information on Gale Research's *Trade Shows Worldwide* may be obtained by contacting Gale Research, Inc., 835 Penobscot Building, Detroit, Michigan USA 48226-4094 or call toll free at (800) 347-GALE or fax at (313) 961-6815.

Reed Exhibition Companies also produces a yearly *Tradeshow Week Databook* and a free newsletter "Going International? Trade Show Tips for Exhibitors and Exporters." Reed sponsors 335 events in 25 countries servicing 53 industries. For a free list of Reed events call (203) 840-5436. To order their Databook or for other information contact Reed Exhibition Companies, Export Division, 383 Main Ave. Norwalk, CT 06857 (203) 840-5570 (p), (203) 840-9570 (f), http://www.reedexpo.com (w).

RESOURCE

Trade Shows Worldwide ($255) ISBN: 0-8103-8079-X; ISSN: 1046-4395; Gale Research, Inc., 835 Penobscot Building, Detroit, MI 48226-4094 (800) 347-GALE (p); (313) 961-6815 (f); galeord@gale.com (e)

What Types of Buyers Will Attend a Trade Show?

Before deciding to exhibit at any show, determine how many people attending the show are potential end users of your product or service. First, determine the Audience Interest Factor (AIF) index which predicts the percentage of visitors who stop at two out of ten exhibits. The greater the AIF index, the easier to attract booth visitors. Most show producers or trade associations will be able to provide the AIF for their particular show. Once the AIF is determined, the potential audience can be calculated by multiplying the expected attendance at the show by the AIF. The resulting figure will give you the number of high-interest attendees.

Next the step is to determine the Product Interest Factor (PIF) which is the number of people interested in seeing any one product. The product interest factor may be obtained from trade show management or the sponsoring organization. On average, the PIF is 16%. By multiplying the AIF by the PIF, you will determine your potential audience.

For example:
20,000 Attendance x 47% AIF = 9,400 High-Interest Attendees x 16% PIF =1,504 Potential Audience

To determine if your product fits this show, classify exhibitors and buyers as vertical or horizontal. A vertical show is one in which the exhibitors and attendees represent a single-niche market or job classification, for example, the Canadian Tire Dealer Retreaders Association. The exhibitors as well as the attendees are interested in tire retreading exclusively, which is a narrow or vertical group. A horizontal show is one in which the exhibitors and attendees might represent a vast range of automotive products from tires to bumpers to radios and other auto related items. Vertical seller/vertical buyer shows have the highest AIF (57%) and Horizontal seller/vertical buyer shows have the lowest AIF(35%).

A trade show booth is an expression of the firm and, as such, the design should quickly convey the image of the firm. Studies show that firms exhibiting at trade shows have approximately seven seconds to capture the interest of those passing by. Unless the product itself is eye-catching or large, convey the image and message of the product with large, bold, colorful graphics. Do not put chairs in the booth. Chairs make for inattentive employees and prospects. Your objective should not be to provide an oasis for show patrons who are tired and need a quick rest. Hold more intimate, time consuming conferences in another location. Allow enough room in the booth so people can come into your booth and look at your products. If possible, allow people to handle products. If a demonstration is needed, make sure the booth is large enough to allow a sufficient amount of space so people have a clear view. If buyers should not handle the product, leave the product at home and use videos to demonstrate the product. Buyers are wary of products that say "do not touch." Use professional, well-designed literature. Engineering drawings and artist renderings are not by themselves good literature. Many good displays are built around "literature stations" which are often used as the focal point for a booth, allowing people to browse and more deeply delve into a product.

RESOURCE

Trade Show and Convention Guide ($115) BPI Communications, Amusement Business, Box 24970, Nashville, TN 37202 (615) 321-4250 (p); (615) 327-1575 (f)

How Do I Prepare for a Trade Show?

Letting potential buyers know that the firm will be participating in a particular trade show will boost trade show visits and sales. Investment in pre-show promotional activities will reap rewards for the firm in terms of a more successful show experience and an improved bottom line. A recent survey indicated that a major percentage of show participants report they are involved in pre-show promotional activity, but only 20% indicated a strong commitment to creative pre-show marketing. However, that 20% reported a higher than average Audience Interest Factor and higher than average levels of person-to-person contact.

It has been clearly established that a personal invitation from an exhibitor is the most important reason someone will visit an exhibit. Personal invitations are not to be confused with a postcard merely indicating the booth location. Invitations should be handwritten if possible and contain a compelling reason to visit the exhibit. Many show attendees visit only those exhibits to which they have received a personal invitation. Some firms follow-up invitations with a phone call to make sure the invitation was received and to reinforce the need to "stop and talk with us."

Some companies send a "teaser" item that requires a booth visit to receive the rest of the item or an item of greater value. All items need to be imprinted with company name, logo, phone number, address, and booth number. Besides creating interest before and during the show, these items will return home with the attendees and continue to be a constant reminder of the firm's product.

A 1997 survey by *Exhibitor Magazine* found that more than 70% of buyers use trade shows as the major source of information when making a buying decision. The survey also found that the average cost of a trade show lead is $180. Many companies fail to recognize the link between the design of trade show exhibits and the overall objective of the show itself. A firm's booth speaks volumes about the capabilities, efficiency, and commitment of the firm. Think of the booth as an introduction. Does it make a good first impression? Even firms with limited space can compete in the trade show arena by using good design techniques and a well-trained staff.

RESOURCE

How to Get the Most Out of Trade Shows ($29.95) ISBN: 0-8442-3193-2 NTC Publishing Group, 4255 W. Touhy Avenue, Lincolnwood, IL 60646-1975 (800) 323-4900 (p) or (708) 679-5500 (p); ntcpubz@aol.com (e)

How Do I Get Samples of My Product Into Trade Shows?

The most affordable, accessible shows with the highest return on investment are usually the U.S. Department of Commerce-sponsored shows. These government shows have excellent pavilion space for exhibiting and are cost-efficient. The government shows are reputable and have helped innumerable companies. These shows have many support services for first-time exhibitors, including information on how to exhibit and how to conduct meetings with potential buyers, travel arrangements, cultural differences to expect, and which shows will provide the greatest success rate for a particular product. The best way to become a trade show participant would be to contact the Trade Show Liaison office in the U.S Department of Commerce at (202) 482-5494. A local branch office of the Department of Commerce can also provide valuable insight.

If you decide to participate in a trade show, take the following steps:

- Create a list of all the shows in which the company is interested in participating
- Write to the show director or the government agency sponsoring the show to determine if that show is a valuable use of company time and resources
- Prioritize the list of trade shows
- Establish a budget
- Schedule the personnel who should attend (where appropriate)
- Make travel arrangements as far in advance as possible
- Check customs clearance requirements
- Design the program and demonstration booth while keeping in mind the targeted audience
- Have price quotes ready
- Produce literature in the language(s) of the target market

Many state international trade offices and the U.S. Department of Commerce offer catalogue trade shows where the company provides the literature and the government promotes the product. This is an inexpensive and lucrative way to generate sales without leaving the office!

The Illinois Trade Office of the Illinois Department of Commerce and Community Affairs assists Illinois companies participate in international trade shows and catalog shows around the world. Contact the Illinois Trade Office at (312) 814-7164 or visit web site www.commerce.state.il.us for a current list of state of Illinois sponsored trade programs.

RESOURCE

Trade Show Central: http://www.tscentral.com

Do I Need a License to Export My Product to a Particular Market?

The Bureau of Export Administration (BXA) administers export licenses and regulations. Most goods can be cleared by entering "NLR" (no license required) on the Shipper's Export Declaration. The Export Administration Regulations requires a license for certain activities and items (e.g., software and technology), subject to Export Administration Regulations if one of 10 general prohibitions applies, and the export or re-export is not eligible for a license exception.

Simply put, nearly 98 percent of all products shipped from the United States do not require an export license. An exporter can call BXA to determine if an export license is needed. BXA can be reached at (202) 482-4811 or fax at (202) 482-3617. BXA also maintains a web site which provides information on their regulations and procedures at http://www.bxa.doc.gov

Should a product not fall under a general licensing category, then a "validated license" must be obtained from the government. A validated license is a specific grant of authority issued by the U.S. government to a company regarding a particular product and its particular destination. This type of license is issued on a case-by-case basis and is valid for approximately two years. Products that fall under this type of licensing are usually those of a strategic nature, in short supply, or highly technical. Products that are destined for a country on which the U.S. government has placed an embargo or has foreign policy concerns are also subject to validated licensing.

There are three main questions to answer to determine if your product requires a validated license:

- What is the destination of the export? Check the schedule of country groups in the Export Administration Regulations
- What is being exported? Check the commodity control list
- Are there any special restrictions? A U.S. Department of Commerce trade specialist or the Bureau of Export Administration will advise a firm if a validated license is required.

For an application for a validated license, contact the Exporter Counseling Division at (202) 482-4811.

RESOURCES

Boycott Law Bulletin ($495/year) Nu-Tec Publishing, 4715 Strack Road, suite 211, Houston, TX 77069-1617 (713) 444-6562 (p); (713) 444-6564 (f); jkamalic@infohwy.com (e)

Export Administration Regulations ($88/year) SN #903-013-00000-7 U.S. Superintendent of Documents, P.O. Box 371954, Pittsburgh, PA 15250-7954 (202) 512-1800 (p); (202) 512-2250 (f); gpoaccess@gpo.gov (e)

Export Controls and Nonproliferation Policy ($5.50) S/N 052-003-01371 U.S. Superintendent of Documents, P.O. Box 371954, Pittsburgh, PA 15250-7954 (202) 512-1800 (p); (202) 512-2250 (f); gpoaccess@gpo.gov (e)

The Export License: How to Fill Out the Application: A step-by-step guide using Form BXA-622P (free) Export Seminar Staff, Office of Export Licensing, Bureau of Export Administration, U.S. Department of Commerce, Room 1608, Washington, DC 20230 (202) 482-8731 (p)

Handbook of Export Controls ($95) International Division Publications, U.S. Chamber of Commerce, 1615 H Street, NW, Washington, DC 20062-2000 (202) 463-5460 (p); member@uschamber.com (e)

What Is the Harmonized System Code and How Do I Use One?

The Harmonized System Classification (HS) is an international standardized numerical method of classifying traded products. The identifying number assigned to each product is used by customs officials around the world to determine the duties, taxes, and regulations that apply to the product.

The HS is a complete, multipurpose international goods classification system, organized in a ten-digit numbering system. The HS has replaced the old Tariff Schedule of the United States Annotated and the old Schedule B U.S. export code. The HS number must appear on the Shipper's Export Declaration and other documents in order for exports to leave the country.

The HS system was developed through the active participation of 60 countries, 23 public and private international organizations, and two national trade facilitation organizations. Most U.S. trading destinations were partner to the creation of this system to provide added exporting ease to businesses throughout the world.

The HS system is organized into 22 sections with 99 chapters. Each section generally covers an industry and the chapters cover the various products and materials of the industry (e.g., Section XI–Textiles and Textile articles, Chapter 50–Silk). The basic HS code contains a 4-digit heading and 6-digit subheading that builds upon the previous digits.

Using silk as an example, the HS code **5003.10.00** is "silk waste not carded or combed."

50 represents the chapter, "silk"

5003 is the heading, "Silk waste"

5003.10 is the subheading, "not carded or combed"

Digits seven through ten vary from country to country and are purely for statistical and tariff purposes. Sometimes an eleventh digit, a "check digit," is added as a protection measure. It ensures that the code is an authentic HS code. The first six digits are universal.

RESOURCE

Correct Way to Fill Out the Shipper's Export Declaration, The (free) U.S. Bureau of the Census, Washington, DC 20233 (301) 457-1086 (p); (301) 457-1159 (f); http://census.gov.foreign_trade (w)

How Can I Find My Schedule B Export Commodity Classification Number and Official Description of My Product?

To obtain your Schedule B Export Code number in the Harmonized System, call the Bureau of the Census Foreign Trade Division at (301) 457-1084. After pressing 1, select option #2 for pr oduct classification assistance. The Schedule B is available on the Internet in the U.S. Census Bureau Database. The web address is http://www.census.gov/foreign-trade/www/. The Schedule B can also be purchased on CD-ROM for $20 by call (301) 457-4100. Print version are available for $105 from the U.S. Government Printing Office. Contact the Government Printing Office at (202) 512-1800 to order by phone.

The U.S. Census Bureau Foreign Trade Division offers a database of over 9,000 official Schedule B export commodity numbers to locate export statistics or to complete the Shipper's Export Declaration. Both the CD-ROM and Internet site offer easy access to the database through searches using common names or key words in the official description of a product. To order the CD-ROM (Windows or DOS), call (301) 457-4100; fax at (301) 457-3842; or visit the Internet site at http://www.census.gov/foreign-trade/www.

RESOURCES

Export Compliance Guide ($577 plus monthly updates) Thompson Publishing Group, Subscription Service Center, P.O. Box 26185, Tampa, FL 33623-6185, (800) 925-1878 (p); (800) 759-7179 (f)

Schedule B: Statistical Classification of Domestic and Foreign Commodities Exported From The United States ($77) S/N 903-009-00000-4 U.S. Superintendent of Documents, P.O. Box 371954, Pittsburgh, PA 15250-7954 (202) 512-1800 (p); (202) 512-2250 (f); gpoaccess@gpo.gov (e)

Is Bribery Necessary to Export to Some Countries?

Bribery is not a normal business action in most foreign countries and U.S. firms seeking to do business in foreign markets must be familiar with the U.S. Department of Justice's Foreign Corrupt Practices Act (FCPA) of 1977. In general, the FCPA prohibits American firms from making illegal payments to foreign officials for the purpose of obtaining or keeping business. Investigations in the mid-1970s revealed that over 400 U.S. companies admitted making questionable or illegal payments in excess of $300 million to foreign government officials, politicians, and political parties. The abuses ranged from bribery of high foreign officials in order to secure some type of favorable action by a foreign government to so-called "grease" or "facilitating" payments that were made to government representatives for the purpose of obtaining or retaining business. Congress enacted the FCPA to bring a halt to the bribery of foreign officials and to restore public confidence in the integrity of the American business system. As a result, the FCPA makes it unlawful for any person or firm (as well as those acting on behalf of a firm) to offer, pay (or authorize such payment), or promise to pay money or anything of value to any foreign official, elected or otherwise. It is also unlawful to make a payment to any person while knowing that all or a portion of the payment will be offered, given or promised to any foreign official. Knowing is considered "conscious disregard" and "willful blindness."

Firms are subject to a fine of up to $2 million; officers, directors, employees, agents, and stockholders are subject to a fine up to $100,000 and imprisonment up to five years. Fines imposed on individuals may not be paid by the firm.

There is an exception to the antibribery prohibition for facilitating or expediting performance of "routine governmental action." A person charged with violating the FCPA antibribery provisions may assert as a defense that the payment was lawful under the written laws and regulations of the foreign country to which the payment was associated with demonstrating a product or performing a contractual obligation. Exemptions include obtaining permits, licenses or other official documentation; processing government papers such as visa and work orders; providing police protection; mail pick-up and delivery; providing phone service, power and water supply, loading and unloading cargo, or protecting perishable products; and scheduling inspections associated with contract performance or transit of goods across country.

The U.S. Department of Justice has an established Foreign Corrupt Practices Act Opinion Procedure by which any party is able to request a statement of the Justice Department's present enforcement intentions under the antibribery provisions of the FCPA regarding any proposed or intended business conduct. The Attorney General is required to issue an opinion in response to an inquiry from a person or firm within 30 days of the request. For more information, contact the U.S. Department of Justice Criminal Division, Fraud Section at (202) 514-7027.

RESOURCE

Doing Business Under The Foreign Corrupt Practices Act ($135) Practicing Law Institute, 810 Seventy Avenue, New York, NY 10019 (800) 260-4754 (p); (800) 321-0093 (f)

Are My Patents, Trademarks, Copyrights and Trade Secrets Protected Overseas?

U.S. patents, trademarks, copyrights, and trade secrets are recognized only within the 50 states and U.S. possessions and territories. There is no legally binding patent or trademark that is "international" or universal. Trademark and patent laws vary greatly from country to country, as does their enforcement. In order to receive patent protection within a foreign country, it is necessary to register with that foreign country.

Patent Laws

In the U.S., a patent must be applied for within a year from date of first public disclosure. In most other countries a patent application must be filed prior to the first public disclosure anywhere in the world. Fortunately, the U.S. has entered into treaties with most foreign countries that establishes a "priority date." This means that for a given product, a patent application filed in the U.S. on a given day allows for public disclosure of that product the next day and allows for a foreign patent application to still be filed within one year from the U.S. filing date. Failure to register for a foreign patent within that year results in a forfeit of any foreign patent rights.

To directly file in a particular foreign country, you will need to appoint a foreign agent, pay the government filing fees, and possibly pay fees for filing language translations. To make this easier, there are several regional patents including one for the EU, Arab, and African regions.

Another way to file a foreign patent is to file a Patent Cooperation Treaty (PCT) application in the U.S. The filing of a PCT application does not result in issuance of the actual patent, but it does extend the time limit from 12 months to 20-30 months under which the foreign patent must be filed. A PCT application is beneficial because it usually allows the company time to see whether a U.S. patent will be obtained, thus aiding the process of obtaining of a foreign patent. It can also reduce the overall expense of obtaining a foreign patent. Call (703) 308-9723 for patent information or call Public Affairs at (703) 305-8341.

Trademark Laws

These laws are different than the patent laws. A foreign trademark application filed within six months of the U.S. filing date is given the same effective date in the foreign country. But, unlike the patent laws, if you miss filing within this time period, you are not forever excluded from filing for trademark protection. Only the priority dating is forfeited.

In most countries, the first to register the trademark is the owner. In the United Kingdom, Canada, the United States, Ireland, Australia, New Zealand, India, and South Africa, the first to use the trademark in connection with the product is the owner, regardless of trademark registration. After registering a trademark, it must be maintained by renewing the trademark after the given term, usually ten years. It can be renewed an infinite number of times.

Be sure to talk with an experienced international trade attorney! There are too many stories of U.S. exporters who ended up not being able to sell their products by name in a particular market because they did not properly obtain trademark or copyright protection. Call (703) 308-9000 for trademark information or call Public Affairs at (703) 305-8341.

The Patent and Trademark Office's Office of Legislation and International Affairs assists in filing patent applications for other countries. Contact this office at U.S. Department of Commerce, 2011 Crystal Drive, Room 208B, Arlington, VA 22202; (703) 305-9300 or (703) 305-8341; (703) 308-9723 for patent information; (703) 308-9000 for trademark information; and (703) 305-8341 for publications information.

RESOURCES

Basic Facts About Patents, Basic Facts About Trademarks, Q&A About Trademarks (free), **Patent and Trademark Office** Office of Legislation and International Affairs, U.S. Department of Commerce, 2011 Crystal Drive, Room 208B, Arlington, VA 22202 (703) 305-9300 (p) or (703) 305-8341 (p)

World Patent Law and Practice Publication No. 622, Matthew Bender and Company, 2 Park Avenue, New York, NY 10001 (800) 223-1940 (p) or (212) 967-7707 (p); (212) 532-5737 (f); www.bender.com (w)

World Trade Mark Law and Practice Publication No. 425, Matthew Bender and Company, 2 Park Avenue, New York, NY 10001 (800) 223-1940 (p) or (212) 967-7707 (p); (212) 532-5737 (f); www.bender.com (w)

Copyrights
The term of copyright protection in the United States, for works created on or after January 1, 1987, is the life of the author plus 50 years after the author's death. Unlike patents and trademarks, which require filings in other countries in order to obtain protection, U.S. copyrighted works are automatically protected in all signatory countries to the Berne Convention for the Protection of Literary and Artistic Works. Berne Convention works that have a country of origin other than the United States are exempt from the requirement that copyrights be registered at the Copyright Office before an infringement suit can be brought. Works of U.S. origin continue to be subject to this requirement. To avoid problems, registration of a copyright is advisable. Register by filing copies of works with the Copyright Office at the Library of Congress, Washington, DC 20559 (202) 707-6800. Application forms are available at www.loc.gov/copyright.

Trade Secrets
In the United States, trade secrets are a creature of state, not federal law. Each state has its own body of law on trade secrets, although a number of states have adopted the Uniform Trade Secrets Act. Unlike patents, trade secrets do not convey exclusive rights for a specific number of years. Rather, the existence of trade secrets depends upon a continued ability to preserve their confidentiality (for example, through corporate security measures and confidentiality clauses in employment, technology licensing, distributorship, and joint venture agreements). Many countries, especially developing countries, do not have laws that provide protection against theft of trade secrets by third parties.

While there is no international treaty to protect trade secrets, there is no law to prohibit U.S. corporations from including a confidentiality provision in an international contract.

The Export Legal Assistance Network is a nationwide group of attorneys with experience in international trade who provide free initial consults to small business on export matters. Contact any Small Business Administration District Office or contact the National Coordinator of ELAN at (202) 778-3080 (p); (202) 778-3063 (f); jkessler@porterwright.com (e); http://www.miep.org/ELAN (w).

RESOURCES

How To Obtain Copyright, Trademark & Patent Protection (free) Department of Treasury U.S. Customs Service, Public Information Office, 1500 Pennsylvania Avenue, Washington, DC 20044 (202) 927-5580 (p); (202) 622-2599 (f)

International Copyright Laws and Practices ($360) Publication No. 399; Matthew Bender and Company, International Division, 2 Park Avenue, New York, NY 10001 (800) 223-1940 (p) or (212) 967-7707 (p); (212) 532-5737 (f); www.bender.com (w)

How Do I Find Out About International Tax Laws?

U.S. corporations are required to report to the U.S. government on their tax returns their income received worldwide, no matter what the source. Taxes are also imposed by foreign governments. There are certain exceptions and amendments to these rules. Foreign jurisdictions (cities, states, etc.) generally impose tax on income from sources within their jurisdiction. The rate of this taxation is generally dependent upon the permanence of establishment within the jurisdiction. Usually, income earned by a non-resident through a permanent establishment within the jurisdiction is taxed the same way as a resident taxpayer. Income earned by a non-resident from non-permanent establishments within the jurisdiction are subject to tax-based gross payment which must be withheld at the source. This source varies from jurisdiction to jurisdiction.

The United States is a co-signee of several bilateral tax treaties. With these treaties, income from the sale of merchandise is sourced to the country in which title passes. Sometimes the source is considered the payee's or the payer's country of residence. These treaties are most relevant to those companies with investments, sub-companies, branches, or joint-ventures abroad. Exporters will want to be aware of title transfers. Title transfers are provisions of the IRS foreign tax credits in which a foreign source income can reduce U.S. taxes. Title transfer involves allocating title and risk of loss to buyer outside the U.S. This makes income from export sales a foreign source income which can yield a tax reduction.

U.S. resident taxpayers who have incurred a tax from a foreign jurisdiction are entitled to relief from U.S. taxes on income taxes only. To avoid double taxation, tax treaties have been established stating exemptions, sourcing rules, and credits due to residents of either of the two contracting nations.

International tax laws are a very complex matter. If they are a concern for the business, it would be best to consult a lawyer or accountant with international taxation expertise.

RESOURCES

Corporate Taxes Worldwide Summary (free) Price Waterhouse, 1251 Avenue of the Americas, New York, NY 10020 (212) 819-5000 (p); (212) 790-6620 (f)

Ernst & Young International Business Series (free) Contact your local Ernst & Young office for the series. Also available from John Wiley and Sons, Inc. (800) 225-5945

Foreign Tax Credits Internal Revenue Service, U.S. Department of Treasury, 950 L'Enfant Plaza South, SW, Washington, DC 20024 (202) 622-7000 (p)

Income Taxation of Foreign-Related Transactions Pub. No. 337; Matthew Bender and Company, 2 park Avenue, New York, NY 10016 (800) 223-1940 (p) or (212) 967-7707 (p); (212) 532-5737 (f)

Tax Havens of the World ($350) Pub No. 722, Matthew Bender and Company, 1275 Broadway, Albany, NY 10224 (800) 223-1940 (p) or (212) 967-7707 (p)

What Is a Foreign Sales Corporation and How Can I Benefit?

A Foreign Sales Corporation (FSC) is a corporation set up in certain foreign countries or in U.S. possessions to obtain a corporate tax exemption on a portion of its earnings generated by the sale or lease of export property or the performance of some services. The FSC was created by the 1984 Tax Reform Act and amended by the Tax Reform Act of 1986 to allow U.S. executives to receive an exemption of up to 15 percent on their net export profits. A corporation initially qualifies as an FSC by meeting basic formation tests.

Forming an FSC

FSCs can be formed by manufacturers, non-manufacturers, or groups of exporters, such as export trading companies. An FSC can function as a principal, buying and selling for its own account, or as a commission agent. It can be related to a manufacturing parent or it can be an independent merchant broker.

There are ten common requirements to qualify as an FSC as stated in the IRS Code section 922: incorporation; location in an eligible foreign country or U.S. possession; not more than 25 shareholders; no preferred stock; office in qualifying country; maintenance of books of account and Internal Revenue Code section 6001 Records; a non-resident member of the Board of Directors; no domestic international sales corporation within the same group; and having an FSC election certificate on file.

- **Small FSCs** may be organized by a U.S. firm earning less than $5 million in international sales. To organize a small FSC, a firm must be incorporated in either the U.S. Virgin Islands, American Samoa, Guam, the Northern Mariana Islands or a qualifying foreign country. The company must also file with the Internal Revenue Service. One non-resident must serve on the Board of Directors. When export sales are made, a commission from the parent company to the FSC is computed using a statutory IRS formula. The commission to the FSC is claimed as a tax deduction by the parent company, which results in saving income taxes and an increase in the overall cash flow.

- **Large FSCs** may be organized by a U.S. firm that earns more than $5 million in international sales. The operating procedures are generally the same as a small FSC. However, the U.S. firm must hold annual meetings of the Board of Directors and shareholders outside the U.S. The principal bank of the FSC must also be located in a qualifying country.

- **Shared FSCs** are a group of up to 25 unrelated U.S. companies participating in international activities. These corporations offer the same tax benefits as the other FSCs but have lower marginal costs. Each exporter owns a separate class of stock and runs its own business as usual. Daily management and paperwork for the SFSC is handled by an independent firm. To receive tax credits, exporters pay a commission to the SFSC, which in turn, distributes the commission back to the exporter.

RESOURCE

For further information contact The Assistant Secretary for Trade Development at the U.S. Department of Commerce, 14th & Constitution Avenue, NW, Washington, DC 20230 or call (202) 482-1461. The Office of the Chief Counsel for International Commerce will also answer questions regarding the establishment and use of FSCs. The address is the same, but the phone number is (202) 482-0937. Another good contact for further information is the FSC/DISC Tax Association, Inc., FDR Station, P.O. Box 748, New York, NY 10150-0748.

What Are Tariffs and Quotas?

Tariffs

A tariff is a charge levied upon an imported product from a particular country, essentially to make the product more expensive in the foreign market to discourage consumers from buying that foreign product. The United States Customs Service may impose tariffs and quotas on products or services which are *imported into* the United States. Other countries may impose tariffs and quotas on products or services which are *imported from* the United States and other countries.

All goods manufactured in the United States destined for export to Canada are now duty free under the U.S.-Canada Free Trade Agreement (CFTA) signed in 1988. The North American Free Trade Agreement (NAFTA) offers U.S. businesses a decreasing tariff schedule reduction rate with Mexico. Approximately 50% of manufactured goods were given tariff elimination on January 1, 1994, and by the year 2003, all Mexican tariffs on U.S. industrialized products will be eliminated. Most products fall into one of four categories: A, B, C, or D. Categories A and D are now duty-free; Category B follows a 20% reduction in tariff rates per year for five years until 1999; and Category C products follow a 10% reduction per year for ten years until 2003. To determine where your product falls in the tariff schedule for Mexico, you must know your harmonized system commodity number which can be found on-line at http;//www.apectariff.org . Then, call (972) 574-4061 to obtain the tariff rate for your particular product. For other tariff rates, call the U.S. Department of Commerce Country Desk Officer of that respective country. Please refer to the Appendix for a listing of offices.

Quotas

A quota is a restriction on the quantity of certain goods that a country will allow to be imported during a specified time frame before imposing additional duties. For example, Japan may allow the importation of 5,000 U.S. cars at a reduced or waived duty. Once car number 5,001 enters, either no more can enter or a significantly increased duty rate will apply. A quota may also refer to a total restriction on a particular good entering a country. A product can be imposed both a quota and a tariff.

RESOURCE

Year In Trade ($14) U.S. Superintendent of Documents, P.O. Box 371954, Pittsburgh, PA 15250-7954 (202) 512-1800 (p); (202) 512-2250 (f); gpoaccess@gpo.gov (e)

Who Pays Duty on the Products I Export?

Traditionally, the seller pays the applicable duty charges unless another arrangement is agreed upon in advance. However, the seller may be able to obtain a refund on the duty paid through "drawback."

Export managers should investigate whether their export qualifies for duty drawback. Duty drawback is a term used for a situation in which a duty or tax lawfully collected is subsequently refunded, wholly or partially, because of a particular use that is made of the commodity. The rationale for duty drawback has always been to encourage U.S. trade. It permits U.S. manufacturers to compete in foreign markets without the handicap of including in their costs, and consequently in the sale price, the import duty paid on the merchandise.

The most common types of drawback include the following situations:

- If the export item was manufactured in the United States with imported materials, any duties paid on the imported materials may be refunded as drawback, less one percent, which is retained by customs to help defray costs.
- If both imported and exported materials of the same kind and quality are used to manufacture items, either retained in the United States or intended for export, 99 percent of the drawback which was paid on the imported materials is payable on the exports. This provision makes it possible for firms to obtain drawback without the hassle of maintaining separate inventories for domestic and imported materials.
- If an item is exported because it does not conform with specifications, or was shipped without the consent of the consignee, 99 percent of the duties paid on the items may be recovered.
- If imported materials are used to construct/equip vessels and aircraft built for a foreign account, 99 percent of the duties paid on the materials may be recovered, even though the vessels and aircraft are not truly exported.

The drawback procedure was designed give manufacturers assurance and protection to compete in foreign markets. However, the manufacturers must know, prior to making contractual agreements, that they will be entitled to drawback on their exports.

To obtain drawback, a drawback proposal must be filed with a Regional Commissioner of Customs and with the Entry Rulings Branch, Customs Headquarters. There are currently several general contracts available that eliminate the need for this proposal. They have been published in the Customs Bulletin, so check there first. A sample drawback proposal is available from your Regional Commissioner or the Entry Rulings Branch, U.S. Customs Service, Franklin Court, 1301 Constitution Avenue, NW, Washington, DC 20229; (202) 927-2077.

If the proposal is approved, the exporter will receive a letter from the Regional Commissioner or Customs Headquarters. To seek a change in the drawback rate, the applicant must repeat the process. Since there are several procedures to claim the drawback, the exporter is advised to speak with a local Customs Office prior to exporting.

RESOURCE

Drawback: A Duty Refund on Certain Imports (free) U.S. Custom's Service, P.O. 7407, Washington, DC 20044, (202) 927-6724, http://www.customs.ustreas.gov

How Can I Benefit From a Foreign Trade Zone?

Foreign Trade Zones (FTZs) are designated areas within the geographic boundary of the United States which are considered to be outside the Customs territory of the United States. Importers may bring foreign and domestic merchandise into FTZs without making formal Customs entry or paying Customs duties or excise taxes. One of the principal advantages of using an FTZ is the cash flow savings achieved by deferring the payment of Customs duties and excise taxes until the merchandise is shipped from the zone into the U.S. market. This advantage allows firms to warehouse goods in the U.S. at locations near their markets or distribution centers, while keeping inventory costs down. If the merchandise is exported from the zone, no duties or taxes are owed. In addition, the merchandise may be inspected, repaired, or destroyed prior to payment of Customs duties and excise taxes. No duties or taxes are owed when the merchandise is destroyed in the zone.

Firms which manufacture, manipulate, or assemble goods using components imported into an FTZ may be able to adjust the tariff classification from the imported merchandise to a different classification on the final product which carries a lower duty rate. Zone procedures allow firms to choose between the tariff classifications applicable to the components and the tariff classification applicable to the finished article. This zone procedure is particularly advantageous when the finished article has a duty rate lower than the rate on its components, the so-called "inverted tariff."

The FTZ program in the U.S. is intended to keep U.S.-based operations competitive with those offshore. Because FTZs offer companies the operational flexibility and cost savings that are vitally important to improving market positions, the only way foreign companies can benefit from the use of zones is by locating their operations in the United States, thereby employing domestic labor, which is a major program goal.

To encourage and facilitate international trade, more than 300 free ports, free-trade zones, and similar customs-privileged facilities are now in operation in some 75 foreign countries, usually in or near seaports or airports. Many U.S. manufacturers and distributors use free-trade zones for receiving shipments of goods that are reshipped in smaller lots to customers throughout the surrounding areas.

Questions regarding FTZ should be directed to the Foreign Trade Zones Board, International Trade Administration, U.S. Department of Commerce at (202) 482-2862 or contact the National Association of Foreign Trade Zones in Washington, D.C. at (202) 331-1950. In Michigan, contact W. Steven Olinek of the Greater Detroit Foreign Trade Zone, Inc. at (313) 331-3842.

RESOURCE

Foreign Trade Zones (free) U.S. Custom's Service, P.O. 7407, Washington, DC 20044 (202) 927-6724 (p) http://www.customs.ustreas.gov (w)

What Are Local Content Rules?

Rules of local content refer to regulations a nation adopts regarding the import of goods manufactured elsewhere (a.k.a. origin). Some governments mandate that a certain percentage of the goods must be produced within the country. Rules of origin are very important when exporting to a country in which the U.S. has an established trade agreement (e.g., NAFTA). Importing officials of countries that participate in bilateral or multilateral trade agreements need proof that the goods to which they are providing preferential treatment are truly goods of the exporting country.

The European Community (EC)
The EC has incorporated its rules of origin into one uniform customs code. It states that for products produced in more than one "non-preferential country" (e.g., United States), origin would be established where the last substantial process was performed to manufacture the product. Simple operations such as assembly or finishing do not apply to origin. U.S. firms can obtain binding origin determinations from EC customs authorities.

North American Free Trade Agreement (NAFTA) Countries
Canada and Mexico rules of origin stipulate that, with a few minor exceptions, all goods that desire preferential tariff treatment should be wholly produced in the United States, Canada or Mexico.

Country desk officers are a good source to consult regarding specific rules of content for various countries. Call (800) USA-TRADE to locate a country desk office.

RESOURCES

EC 1992: A Practical Guide for American Business update #4 ($21) International Division Publications, U.S. Chamber of Commerce, 1615 H Street, NW, Washington, DC 20062-2000 (202) 463-5460 (p); (202) 463-3114 (f)

EC 1992: The Effects of Greater Economic Integration Within the European Community on the United States U.S. International Trade Commission, Washington, DC 20436 (202) 205-1809 (p); (202) 205-2186 (f)

What Is ISO 9000?

The International Organization of Standardization (ISO) developed a series of five standards: 9000, 9001, 9002, 9003, and 9004. They describe quality assurance standards used by companies that supply goods and services to an international market. Other than ISO 9000, each document describes a quality model for use in different applications.

- ISO 9000 serves as an identifying and defining source for the rest of the series. It defines the five key quality terms.
- ISO 9001 is the most comprehensive document in the series. It applies to those operations that design and make products. It specifies a quality set-up to use when contracts dictate demonstration of a supplier's capability to design, produce, install, and service the product. ISO 9001 addresses topics including design, detection, and correction of problems during production, employee training, and record keeping.
- ISO 9002 applies to those commodity businesses with little design activity. It defines quality assurance in production and installation.
- ISO 9003 applies to all companies and outlines a quality system model for final testing and inspection.
- ISO 9004 studies the quality elements of the previous documents in greater detail. It lists "How-To" guidelines for quality management and the quality system elements needed to develop and implement a quality system.

The way to receive ISO certification is through a rigorous process of preparation, documentation, and inspection by an approved assessment body. The ISO 9000 series has become increasingly important in recent years as exporters discover that compliance, although not mandatory, has become imperative for success overseas. Customers worldwide are becoming more quality-conscious and demanding that these standards be met as a minimum requirement. In the near future, many predict that ISO will become the basic, internationally recognized quality standard.

Certification in ISO 9000 not only yields increased benefits in the international market, it also raises the quality standards for the company itself. This results in increased productivity and a decrease in the number of customer complaints. It is best to educate and familiarize yourself on ISO 9000 as early as possible. Suppliers of exporting companies should be aware that their customers may require them to be ISO certified as well. Many times, the ISO certification requirement has had a snowball effect: all suppliers of suppliers need to be certified.

To contact the ISO directly: ISO Central Secretariat; 1, rue de Varembe; Case postale 56, CH-1211; Geneve, 20, Switzerland; 41 22 749 01 11 (p); 41 22 733 34 30 (f).

RESOURCES

ISO 9000: Explained ($49) ISBN 1-882711-01-7; AQA Company 334 Crane Blvd., Los Angeles, CA 90065 (213) 222-3600 (p)

ISO 9000: Introduction for U.S. Business ($5) International Division Publications, U.S. Chamber of Commerce, 1615 H Street, NW, Washington, DC 20062-2000 (202) 463-5460 (p); (202) 463-3114 (f)

ISO 9000: In Your Company ($9) ISBN 1-882711-03-3 AQA Company 334 Crane Blvd., Los Angeles, CA 90065 (213) 222-3600 (p)

ISO 9000: Questions and Answers (free) National Institute of Standards and Technology, Standards Code Information Program, Office of Standards Service, Gaithersburg, MD 20899 (301) 975-4040 (p)

How Do I Become ISO Certified?

To become ISO certified, you must receive approval from an approved assessment group. American Society for Quality (ASQ) maintains the Registrar Accreditation Board that monitors and approves the activities of the various independent assessment groups nation wide. To obtain a list of approved assessors, contact ASQ, 611 E. Wisconsin, P.O. Box 3005, Milwaukee, WI 53201-3005; (414) 272-8575 (p); (414) 272-1734 (f); http://www.asq.org (e).

A common process in attaining ISO 9000 certification is first to establish a group which should include all company personnel (including lower and middle management) who will be affected by implementing the standard. One person should be designated as the point person who can answer questions and be responsible for developing, integrating, and writing the quality manual. The group then reviews company procedures and highlights revisions which will be appropriate for ISO 9000 requirements. After that process, the group creates a quality manual which establishes the company's quality assurance program. When new procedures are implemented, the internal group meets with the ISO qualifying team to present the manual and conduct a plant audit where each member of this team intensively and thoroughly inspects facilities, procedures, and company documentation. Their recommendation may or may not result in ISO certification.

Before beginning the process, make sure it is a wise decision to become certified! The process towards certification is expensive (in the range of $50,000-$100,000) and company preparation time usually requires six to nine months. However, many companies tend to view the expense as minimal compared to the gains involved with a presence in the international marketplace. <u>But ISO certification may not be required for your particular product.</u> It is critically important that you talk to colleagues or business owners in your field, several ISO 9000 consultants, and conduct research before deciding certification makes market sense for the business.

Remember, if a company supplies parts to an ISO-certified company, that company will most likely be required to obtain certification in order to remain on the supplier list. This is especially true with the automotive industry and its QS9000 process. QS is based on ISO but is specific to the auto industry. QS certification automatically ensures ISO certification but ISO certification does not necessarily guarantee QS certification. QS qualifications are more rigid, strict, and comprehensive than ISO.

RESOURCES

ISO 9000: Handbook and Guide to Registration ($85) McGraw Hill, 10521 Braddock Road, Fairfax, VA 22032-2236 (800) 745-5565 (p); (630) 789-5507 (f) www.mcgrawhill.com (w)

ISO 9000: An Implementation Guide for Small to Mid-sized Businesses ($51.90) ISBN: 1-884015-10-7, St. Lucie Press, 100 E. Linton Blvd., Suite 403B, Delray Beach, FL 33483 (407) 274-9906 (p); (407) 274-9927 (f)

ISO 9000: The 90-Day Manual ($184.95) ISBN: 1-884015-11-5 St. Lucie Press, 100 E. Linton Blvd., Suite 403B, Delray Beach, FL 33483 (407) 274-9906 (p); (407) 274-9927 (f)

ISO 9000 Registered Company Directory ($195/yr) Irwin Professional Publishing, 11150 Main Street, Fairfax, VA 22030-5066 (800) 353-4809 0p) or (703) 591-9008 (p); (703) 591-0971 (f)

Where Can I Obtain Copies of ISO 9000 Standards?

The following organizations provide standards information, copies of standards, draft international standards, publications, and related documents and materials:

AMERICAN NATIONAL STANDARDS INSTITUTE (ANSI)
(U.S. member body for ISO)
11 West 42nd Street, 13th Floor
New York, NY 10036
(212) 642-4900
(212) 398-0023 (f)
This group will provide copies of ISO drafts and final standards, information on all standards and creditation programs.

DOCUMENTS CENTER
1504 Industrial Way, Unit 9
Belmont, CA 94002
(415) 591-7600
(415) 591-7617 (f)
This center sells the ISO documents and will notify customers of updates and changes.

GLOBAL ENGINEERING DOCUMENTS
15 Inverness Way East, P.O. Box 1154
Englewood, CO 80150-1154
(800) 854-7179 -or- (303) 792-2181
(303) 792-2192 (f)
This group will distribute standards.

STANDARDS SALES GROUP
20025 Highway 18
Apple Valley, CA 92307
(619) 946-0500
This group sells the ISO documents. They are not a service provider.

U.S DEPARTMENT OF COMMERCE
National Institute of Standards and Technology (NIST)
National Center for Standards and Certification Information (NCSCI)
TRF Building, Room A163
Gaithersburg, MD 20899
(301) 975-4040
(301) 975-2128 (f)
This U.S. government agency provides information on the ISO 9000 standards.

RESOURCES

ISO 9000: Quality Systems ($69) ISBN 1-882711-04-1; AQA Company 334 Crane Blvd., Los Angeles, CA 90065 (213) 222-3600 (p)

ISO 9000: Self-Study Guide ($130) American Management Association, P.O. Box 319, Saranack Lake, NY 12983 (518) 891-5510 (p); (518) 891-0368 (f); cust_serv@amanet.org (e); www.amanet.org (w)

ISO 9000 Videos ISO 9000: Making Your Company Competitive ($139); Employee Introduction to ISO 9000 ($129); A Practical Guide to Documenting and Implementing ISO 9000 ($379); Internal Auditing for ISO 9000 ($379) The Media Group, Inc., 18 Blair Park Road, Suite 100, Williston, VT 05495 (802) 879-5403 (p) or (800) 678-1003 (p); (802) 879-2702 (f)

QS 9000 Handbook ($66.90) ISBN 1-57444-011-X, St. Lucie Press, 100 E. Linton Blvd., Suite 403B, Delray Beach, FL 33483 (407) 274-9906 (p); (407) 274-9927 (f)

What Is ISO 14000?

The main purpose of the ISO 14000 series is to promote more effective and efficient environmental management in organizations — ones that are cost-effective, systems-based, and flexible. However, compliance with the standards may bring a competitive advantage to exporting firms. The documents listed below relate specifically to the steps service businesses and manufacturers take to meet internationally-accepted environmental management criteria.

For firms in developing countries, the ISO 14000 series represents an opportunity for technology transfer and a source of guidance for introducing and adopting an environmental management system based on universal practices. Following are the core documents that will guide firms on establishing, maintaining, auditing, and continually improving the firm's environmental management system.

Environmental Management Systems
ISO 14001 - Specifications with guidance and use
ISO 14004 - General guidelines on environmental management principles, systems, and supporting techniques

Guidelines for Environmental Auditing
ISO 14010 - General principles
ISO 14011 - Audit procedures for environmental management systems
ISO 14012 - Qualification criteria for environmental auditors

Work in progress on other standards include:
Environmental Labels and Declaration
ISO 14020 - Basic principles of all environmental labeling
ISO 14021 - Self declaration, environmental claims, terms and definitions
ISO 14022 - Symbols
ISO 14023 - Testing and verification methodologies
ISO 14024 - Practitioner programmes and guiding principles, practices, certification procedures
ISO 14031 - Environmental performance evaluation

Life-Cycle Assessment
ISO 14040 - Guiding principles and framework
ISO 14041 - Goals and definition/scope and inventory assessment
ISO 14042 - Impact assessment
ISO 14043 - Life cycle interpretation
ISO 14050 - Terms and definitions, guide 64 environmental aspects of product standards

Further information on the development of the ISO 14000 series is available from the ISO Secretariat. The ISO publication "The ISO 14000 Environment: ISO Guideline for Environmental Management System Standards" is a useful guide that can be obtained through ISO member bodies or from ISO headquarters: ISO Central Secretariat, Case Postale 56, 1211 Geneva 20, Switzerland.

RESOURCE

Environmental Management Kit ($215) and **Guide to ISO 14001** (free) and **ICC Business Charter for Sustainable Development** (free), ICC Publishing, 156 Fifth Avenue, Suite 305, New York, NY 10010 (212) 206-1150, iccpub@interport.net

What Is Eco-Labeling?

Environmental labelling or "eco-labelling" is fundamentally different from the setting of minimum product standards or requirements. The key difference is that environmental labelling is intended to reward environmental leadership. An eco-label on a product is a guide for consumers who wish to choose products and services causing less damage to the environment. An environmental label makes a positive statement for a company in that it identifies products and services as less harmful to the environment than similar products or services used for a specific function.

Eco-labelling programs may be industry-driven or government mandated. However, participation in eco-labelling programs is voluntary. If a firm decides not to participate, it will not be able to display an eco-label on its product, but it will still have the same access to the market as those corporations which do participate in the program and meet the standards necessary to display the eco-label.

Currently, there are 28 eco-labelling programs in existence worldwide, including Germany's Blue Angel eco-label, the Green Seal program in the United States, the independently awarded eco-labels in many European countries, Japan, and the Republic of Korea, and Thailand's Thai Green Label.

To illustrate a typical eco-labelling program, the following describes Thailand's Green Label program. The Green Label uses life-cycle analysis and stresses certain high-priority national goals such as waste reduction and energy and water conservation. Product selection and criteria are developed with regard to local capability to conduct necessary testing and monitoring. Product categories for which criteria have been developed include recycled plastics, energy-saving fluorescent lamps, low-energy refrigerators, low pollutant emulsion paints, water-economizing flush toilets, and batteries with no mercury. Other product categories will include office and sanitary/household recycled paper, CFC-free sprays, detergents, and low-energy air-conditioners. Preliminary costs of application for a company is 1000 Baht (US$ 40). If approved, use of the Thai Green Label costs 5000 Baht (US$ 200) and is valid for two years.

The Centre for Environmental Labelling located at the University of British Columbia in Vancouver, B.C., Canada has established a knowledge base concerning environmental labelling (EL) programs worldwide, their use as an environmental policy instrument, and the marketing advantages that exist for companies using environmental labels. The center is active in the dissemination of information and research, specifically the trends occurring in environmental labelling worldwide and the promotion of mutual recognition of labelling programs. The center is studying the possibilities of the harmonization of environmental labelling criteria in all countries either with or presently developing labelling programs. For more information, view the Center's web site at http://unixg.ubc.ca:780/~ecolabel/cel.html, or contact via e-mail at ecolabel@unixg.ubc.ca, phone (604) 822-3132, or fax (604) 822-9106.

Other related organizations and associations include the International Standardisation Organisation Environmental Labelling Standards in Strathfield, Australia. Call 61 2 746 4700 or fax 61 2 746 4766 for more information. The Organisation for Economic Cooperation and Development in France can be contacted by calling 33-1-4524 9870 or faxing 33-1-4524 7876. The United Nations Task Force on Environmental Labelling in New York City can be reached by calling (212) 963-8210 or faxing (212) 963-7341.

RESOURCES

Environmental Guidelines, Criteria, And Standards In Developed Countries

- Brasil - Departmento de Certificacocao Gerente
- Canada - Environmental Choice Program
- Greece - ASAOS
- Israel - Green Label Program
- Japan - Ecomark
- Luxembourg - Ministere de L'Environment
- Norway - Nordic Swan Label
- Spain - AENOR
- Sweden and Norway - Nordic Swan Label
- (ROC) Taiwan - Green Mark Program
- United Kingdom - European Union Ecolabel Award Scheme
- U.S.A. - Green Seal

What Is the CE Mark Certification Process?

In order to harmonize the consumer protection laws of the member states of the European Union, the European Council issues common policies called the "New Approach Directives" which apply to products that pose a potential threat to consumer health and safety. CE stands for Conformite European (European Conformity). Once the CE mark is applied to a product, it is considered to meet the regulatory requirements for all countries of the European Union as well as the European Free Trade Area countries.

It is important to note that a product may be required to meet the essential requirements of more than one directive. The CE mark is not required on products that will be temporarily imported to the EU for exhibition in trade shows. However, upon the date it becomes mandatory for a certain product to have the CE mark, the product must meet all requirements and have all documentation in place or risk severe penalties.

Aside from customs officials, others are monitoring firms compliance with directives. Your competitors may alert EU authorities to misuse of the mark. Directives outline essential requirements for products in each category.

There are eight different ways to obtain the CE mark, ranging from the simplest method of self-certification to the more complicated methods involving third party audits. The eight different paths are called modules which cover both the design and production phases of manufacturing.

Certification that a product meets all applicable directives is issued by a notified or competent body. Please call the European Desk of the U.S. Department of Commerce at (202) 482-5279 to obtain the most current list of notified bodies for each applicable directive. They should also have a list of CE Notified Body contacts located in the U.S.

The difference between ISO and CE is the following: CE is applied to the product; ISO is applied to the process.

Excerpts from *A Beginner's Guide to the CE Mark Certification Process* by Kristen Jones, Indiana Department of Commerce, International Trade Division, One North Capitol, Suite 700, Indianapolis, IN 46204-2288 (317) 233-3762 (p); (317) 232-4146 (f).

For information via the Internet, search for "testing and certification" at www.eurunion.org

RESOURCES

Guide to Europe ($130) ISBN 0-8103-2139-4; Gale Research Company, Book Tower, Dept. 77748, Detroit, MI 48226 (800) 223-GALE (p)

Implementing the European Community Single Market (free) USITC Publication 2723 Secretary to the Commission, United States International Trade Commission, Washington, DC 20436

Where Can I Obtain Information From Standards Bodies, Quality Associations, and Inspection Bodies?

Following are key national and international organizations from which to obtain information on standards, technical regulations, certification, eco-labeling, and quality management schemes:

- American National Standards Institute, 11 West 42nd Street, 13th Floor, New York, NY 10036, (212) 642-4900
- American Society for Quality, 611 East Wisconsin Avenue, P.O. Box 3005, Milwaukee, WI 53201, (414) 272-8575
- Codes Alimentarius Commission, Joint FAO/WHO Food Standards Programme, Via delle Terme di Caracalla, 00100 Rome, Italy, (396) 579-4476
- Department of Agriculture, Food, Safety, and Inspection Services, Accredited Lab Program, Science, Chem, Plan. Rev., Washington, D.C. 20250 USA, (202) 447-5850
- Department of Health and Human Services, Food and Drug Administration, Toxic Lab Monitoring Program, Room 12A-55 Parklawn, 5600 Fishers Lane, Rockville, MD 20857 USA, (301) 443-2390
- European Organization for Testing and Certification, Secretary General's Office, rue de Stassart 36, B-1050 Brussels, Belgium (322) 519-6825; www.eurunion.org (w)
- Global Environmental Management Initiative, 2000 L Street, NW, Suite 710, Washington, D.C. 20037-1101 USA, tel.: (202) 296-7449
- International Commission on Microbiological Specifications for Foods, ICMSF Secretary, 2022 La Vista Circle, Tucker, GA, (404) 938-8094.
- International Electrical Commission, 3 rue de Varembe, P.O. Box 131, 1211 Geneva 20, Switzerland, (4122) 919-0211.
- International Office of Epizootics (Animal Health), 12 Rue de Prony, 75017 Paris, France, (331) 227-4574.
- National Center for Standards and Certification Information, U.S. Department of Commerce, TRF Building, Room A163, Gaithersburg, MD 20899, (301) 975-4040
- WTO-TBT & SPS Enquiry Point, Standards Code and Information Program, Office of Standards Services, National Institute of Standards and Technology, TRF Building, Room A-163, Gaithersburg, MD 20899, (301) 975-4040

RESOURCE

For a copy of the "World Directory of Information Sources on Standards, Technical Regulations, Certification, Eco-labelling, and Quality Management Schemes," contact the International Trade Centre UNCTAD/WTO, 54-56 rue de Montbrillant, CH-1202, Geneva, Switzerland. (4122) 730 01 11 (p); (4122) 733 44 39 (f); e-mail: itcreg@intracen.org

How Do I Determine if My Price is Competitive?

Determine if a price for a given product is competitive by simply looking at similar products within a particular market, then checking the selling prices of the domestic and imported brands. How does the price compare with your price? Is it higher or lower? What is the image in the marketplace? Are the products considered "top of the line" or "deep discount?" Understanding the competition in a global market will establish some guidelines for your company's pricing policy. Good sources of information to help determine foreign market competition are trade associations identified with the product.

A high-pricing strategy should be utilized if a company is selling a unique or new product, or if the company wishes to establish a high-quality image for the product. A benefit of this approach is high profit margins. Conversely, selecting a high-price strategy can also limit the product's marketability and will probably attract competition to that market.

A low-price strategy is ideal if you want to dispose of excess or obsolete inventory. The low- price strategy is generally considered a short-term strategy. Although it tends to discourage new competition and might reduce the competition's market share, the result will be low profit margins. Moreover, you risk giving the wrong impression to the market (i.e., that you are not serious about a long-term commitment to an international market or that you possess a low-quality product).

A moderate price strategy is a safe alternative to the previous high- and low-price strategies. It enables a company to meet the competition and at the same time retain an adequate margin and develop market share. Moderate pricing can lead to a long-term position in the market. The disadvantage is that it might encourage existing suppliers to present tough price competition. For this reason, it is important to know your competitors' prices prior to market entry.

While the final price of the purchased item often is thought to be the principal focus of negotiation, there are many other elements of the contract that a buyer and supplier can negotiate. Buyers in the United States were surveyed by the National Association of Purchasing Management, Inc. to rate the relative importance of various contractual elements for international negotiation. Respondents ranked quality assurance and timely delivery schedules as being significantly more important elements for negotiation than price. In other words, buyers realize that both quality and time can be more important than price as the key determinant when deciding to buy from one supplier or another.

In rank order from 1-14, the following factors contribute to the decision to buy: 1) quality; 2) delivery schedule; 3) price; 4) warranties; 5) liability for claims/damages; 6) patents and infringement protection; 7) technical assistance; 8) confidentiality; 9) changes in drawings/specifications; 10) price revisions; 11) packaging; 12) terms of payment; 13) mode of transportation; and 14) progress reports.

RESOURCES

U.S. Global Trade Outlook, 1995-2000 ($19) S/N 003-009-00650-3 U.S. Superintendent of Documents, P.O. Box 371954, Pittsburgh, PA 15250-7954 (202) 512-1800 (p); (202) 512-2250 (f); gpoaccess@gpo.gov (e)

Weekly Roundup of World Production and Trade (free) U.S. Department of Agriculture, Information Division, Room 5920, S. Building, Foreign Agriculture Service, Washington, DC 20250-1000 (202) 447-7937 (p)

How Should I Prepare to Discuss Price?

If the buyer indicates that the initial price quoted is too high and a substantial drop is required, ask on what basis the price should be dropped; stress product quality and benefits before discussing price.

If the buyer indicates that better offers have been received from other exporters, ask for more details. Convince the buyer that your firm has a better offer.

If the buyer makes a counter-offer or requests a price discount, avoid making a lower offer without asking for something in return, but without jeopardizing interest. Make a specific suggestion, such as "If I give you a 5% price discount, would you arrange for surface transport including storage costs?"

Avoid "last offers" presented by the buyer. First find out the quantities involved, determine if there will be repeat orders, and negotiate who pays for storage, promotion, and after-sales service, etc.

If the buyer indicates the product is acceptable but the price is too high, agree to discuss details of the cost, and promote the product's benefits, your reliability as a regular supplier, and promise of timely delivery.

If the buyer accepts the price quoted, find out why the importer is so interested in the offer. Recalculate the cost, check competitor prices, contact other potential buyers to get more details on market conditions, review the pricing strategy, and agree to the order as a trial order only.

RESOURCES

Dynamics of Successful International Business Negotiations ($27.50) ISBN: 0-87201-196-8 Gulf Publishing Company, P.O. Box 2608, Houston, TX 77252-2608 (713) 520-4444 (p) or (800) 231-6275 (p)

U.S. Trade Shifts in Selected Industries ($15) U.S. Superintendent of Documents, P.O. Box 371954, Pittsburgh, PA 15250-7954 (202) 512-1800 (p); (202) 512-2250 (f); gpoaccess@gpo.gov (e)

How Do I Price My Product?

In their negotiations, exporters too often limit their discussions to pricing issues. Although pricing is a key factor in any business transaction, a number of other questions need to be clarified before any realistic business proposal can be considered. Price is only one of many issues that need to be discussed during negotiations with buyers. Yet too often, new exporters tend to compromise on price at the start of discussions, thereby bypassing other negotiating strengths (e.g., product's benefits, firm's business experience). The subject of price should be postponed until other aspects of the transaction have been agreed upon.

In addition to customers' preferences, an exporter should assess competition from both domestic and foreign suppliers and be familiar with the prices they quote. The distribution channels used for the products and the promotion tools and messages required should also be examined. Making counter-proposals also requires detailed information on the costs of the exporter's production operations, freight insurance, packing, and other related expenses.

To promote itself as a partner committed to long-term business relationships, the exporter can stress these aspects of its operations: management capability; production capacity and processes; quality control systems; technical cooperation; structure for handling orders; export experience, including types of companies dealt with; and financial standing and links with banks. After covering these issues, the exporter can shift the discussion in the final phase of the talks to financial matters bearing on the price quotation. This is the time to come to an agreement on issues such as credit terms, payment schedules, currencies of payment, insurance, commission rates, warehousing costs, after-sales servicing responsibilities, and costs of replacing damaged goods. Agreement on these points constitute the price package.

Price depends on the competitive situation, the level of demand for the product in the foreign market, and the total costs necessary to bring the product to market. Depending upon the distance and other factors, a 5% to 50% price increase may be necessary. To calculate the cost of a good for a foreign market, consider all factors for which the exporter will be responsible. Remember that the foreign customer should only be charged for the expenses incurred that are applicable to the exports and not those used for domestic production. Consider the costs of direct materials and labor for the production of the goods; proportional share of factory overhead expenses; international insurance, legal fees and travel expenses; market demand; and domestic and foreign competitive prices.

Completing the Export Pricing Worksheet on page 69 will be helpful for a manager trying to determine a foreign sale price. Be sure to remain consistent in your pricing schedule for all export markets. It is amazing to see how quickly the global buyer network knows what someone is paying for products in Asia, Latin America, and the United States. Buyers will aggressively question pricing discrepancies. If a buyer is not satisfied with your rationale, an alternate supplier may be sought.

RESOURCES

A Short Course In International Business Negotiating ($19.95) World Trade Press, 1505 Fifth Avenue, San Rafael, CA 94901 (800) 833-8586 (p); (415) 453-7980 (f)

A Short Course In International Entrepreneurial Trade ($19.95) World Trade Press, 1505 Fifth Avenue, San Rafael, CA 94901 (800) 833-8586 (p); (415) 453-7980 (f)

Export Pricing Worksheet

The following is a sample export pricing worksheet which the firm should utilize when attempting to competitively price a product for export. Prices can be quoted FOB Factory ($1,150); FOB, Port City – Export Packed ($1,550); FAS Vessel or Airplane ($1,680); and CIF, Port of Destination (at $2,000, this essentially assures that the exporter incurs all charges). Since the price at CIF essentially doubles the exporter's initial costs, it is important to accurately complete this worksheet when quoting prices.

Customer Information

Name ____________________
Address ____________________
City, State, Zip____________________
Country____________________

Cable Address____________________
Telex No.____________________
Fax No.____________________
E-mail address ____________________

Product Information

Product____________________
Dimensions______x_______x________
Net Weight____________________
Total Measure____________________

SIC/HS Numbers____________________
No. of Units ____________________
Cubic Measure____________(sq.inches)
Gross Weight ____________________

Product Charges		
Cost per unit $10 x units $100	A.	$1000
Profit or markup (A. multiplied by x %) 10%	B.	100
Sales Commissions (A. multiplied by x%) 5%	C.	50
FOB Factory	**D.**	**$1150**

Fees-Packing, Marking, Processing Charges:		
Freight Forwarder processing	E.	$ 50
Financing Costs on production loan (A multiplied by x%) 8%	F.	80
Other charges (including letter of credit processing fee)	G.	20
Export Packing Charges	H.	100
Labeling/Marking for 100 units	I.	50
Inland Freight Charges to ____________	J.	100
FOB, Port City (Export Packed) (D plus E, F, G, H, I, J)	**K.**	**$1550**

Port Charges/Documents		
Unloading (heavy lift)	L.	$ 50
Terminal	M.	50
Consular Document (if required) ___________	N.	10
Certificate of Origin (if required)___________	O.	10
Export License (if required)	P.	10
FAS Vessel (Or Airplane) (K plus L, M, N, O, P)	**Q.**	**$1680**

Freight and Insurance Charges based on:		
Weight___Measure___Ocean___Air___Ondeck_____Underdeck___		
Rate_____Minimum_____ Amount	R.	$ 300
Insurance Coverage based on ______________at ___________ rate	S.	20
CIF, Port of Destination: (Q plus R, S)	**T.**	**$2000**

How Do I Prepare an Accurate Quote?

To facilitate a greater understanding of the product and its delivery, describe the product in detail in a quotation. State the price for the product, set the time of shipment, specify the terms of sale, and terms of payment. On the price quotation, it is crucial to state explicitly that the prices are subject to change without notice.

A proforma invoice may or may not be requested along with the quotation. It is wise to acquire the habit of sending both a proforma invoice and a quote together, regardless if both were requested. For more detailed information regarding a proforma invoice, consult page 72. It is important to make sure that the proforma invoice is clearly labeled as such. The proforma is not in any way a contract. Labeling the documents as such will alleviate any potential problems.

To establish a quote, the seller will need to be familiar with several international INCOTERMS such as: FOB, CIF, C&F. Pages 83 through 85 explain common INCOTERMS and how you can obtain a copy of these terms from the International Chamber of Commerce in New York or Paris. A word of caution: using nebulous terms such as FOB PLANT and FOB DOMESTIC PORT pricing leaves the foreign buyer uninformed as to the actual price they would have to pay for the product, as there are more transportation and incidental charges for the foreign buyer to consider from such a point.

Many foreign buyers come from countries much smaller in size than the continental U.S. and they cannot fathom how large the U.S. really is. A buyer trying to figure out the shipping costs from your plant in Kansas City may assume that Kansas City is close to the Los Angles port and not realize the true distance and increased cost involved. It would be easier for an American company to quote inland freight prices and port charges etc. A foreign buyer may be so grateful that the American company is handling these details that, despite a higher quote, the foreign buyer will offer that American company the contract. Proper usage of the INCOTERMS will show you as a professional and adept exporter. Therefore, it is wise to educate yourself on the most commonly used terms.

An export manager may wish to consider adding a 10-percent buffer in the pricing due to fluctuating transportation costs or other incidentals, but make sure the foreign buyer understands that only the actual costs will be charged. This strategy allows the U.S. company to offer a realistic quote.

RESOURCES

Business America ($53/year) ISSN 0190-6275 U.S. Superintendent of Documents, P.O. Box 371954, Pittsburgh, PA 15250-7954 (202) 512-1800 (p); (202) 512-2250 (f); gpoaccess@gpo.gov (e)

What Is a Purchase Order?

The main purpose of a purchase order is to act as a confirmation to the seller that his product or service is desired and that the terms of sale set forth in the proforma invoice are agreeable. The purchase order also acts as an internal control on spending. Payment is made when a commercial invoice is provided by the seller. Essential elements of a purchase order include a description of the goods or services, the cost of goods or services, name and address of seller and buyer, the term of sale, the method of transportation and designated port, and date in which the goods are required. Prior to the manufacture of goods, you will want to make certain you possess the proper information derived from the purchase order or other correspondence. If the information has not been made available to the American manufacturer, increased inventory costs may accrue to the manufacturer over some length of time.

Purchase Order

ABC Company, Inc.
5278 S. Auto Street
Detroit, MI 48201
(313) 555-1234

Ship To: *XYZ Company, Inc.*
25 Sushi Way
Tokyo, Japan

Forwarding Agent: Speedy Transport, LTD

Via: Ocean Freight   Country of Origin: USA

P.O. No: *1234-5678*

Invoice No: *98765*

Date: *20-Feb-94*

Terms of Payment
L/C-First Bank of Japan
#AB1290

International Markings

Quantity	Part Number	Description of Goods	Price
			U.S. $
20,000	*AZX23*	*Motorized Toothbrushes @ $10.00 per unit*	*$200,000.00*
		Total: 10 packages	
		Estimated Gross WT: 500 lbs.	
		Dimensions: 2.0 cu ft each	
		Other Charges:	
		Freight	*$2,100.00*
		Insurance	*$1,800.00*
		Total CIF	*$203,900.00*

Prepared By: ______________________
Export Manager
ABC Company, Inc.

What Is a Proforma Invoice?

A proforma invoice is provided by the seller prior to the shipment of merchandise to inform the buyer of the types and quantities of goods to be sent, value of the goods, and other important specifications. A proforma invoice is a binding agreement that can protect against currency fluctuations, apply for foreign exchange, or open a letter of credit. A proforma is not a sales invoice, although the two documents may look identical. A proforma invoice includes insurance and shipping costs, delivery point, terms of payment, volumes and shipping weights, prices, product descriptions, and a list of requested products.

Quoting the price in U.S. dollars will protect the U.S. company from risk associated with currency fluctuations. The sample provided indicates the typical components of a proforma invoice. While this serves as a general illustration, individuals preparing the proforma must draft the document according to the specific needs and nuances of each transaction. You can use a typical invoice clearly marked "Proforma" on each copy.

Proforma Invoice

ABC Company, Inc.
5278 S. Auto Street
Detroit, MI 48201
(313) 555-1234

Proforma

Purchase Order No. 1234-5678	Invoice No. 98765
Import License No.	Invoice Date: 20-Feb-94
Terms of Payment L/C First Bank of Japan #AB1290	
International Markings	

Country of Origin: USA

Invoice to: XYZ Company, Inc.
25 Sushi Way
Tokyo, Japan

Ship to:

Forwarding Agent: Speedy Transport LTD

VIA: ocean freight
FOB San Francisco

Quantity	Part Number	Description	Unit Price	Total Price
			$U.S.	$U.S.
20,000	AZX23	Motorized Toothbrushes	$10	$200,000
		Additional Charges:		
		FOB	$200,000	
		Cartage		
		Freight	$2,100	
		Any Fees		
		Insurance	$1,800	
		Total CIF	$203,900	
Total: 10 pkgs Estimated Gross WT: 500 lbs Dimensions: 2.0 cu ft each				
		Total U.S. $		$203,900

Export License No.
Expires:

Signature: ______________________
Domestic Export Manager

How Do I Ensure That I Will Get Paid?

There are many ways to receive payment from an overseas buyer that represent low-to-no risk to the U.S. supplier, therefore ensuring payment. As a brief overview, following is a listing of the traditional methods of payment and the amount of risk involved:

Advance Payment - no risk to the seller. The buyer pays up front. This is not a very attractive offer for the buyer. Advance payment policies lack competitiveness and a U.S. company adopting this method of payment may lose customers.

Letter of Credit - low risk to the seller. The letter of credit is issued by the buyer's bank to the seller's bank verifying payment to be made immediately upon the shipment of goods. With this method, both the buyer and the seller are happy: the buyer is assured of the shipment of goods prior to releasing payment, and the seller is assured of prompt payment when releasing goods.

Credit Cards - low risk to the seller. By accepting a charge payment, payment barriers are avoided and currency fluctuations are monitored by the credit card company (usually on an hourly basis).

Foreign Bank Checks - medium risk to the seller. A check can be drawn on either a U.S. or foreign bank. Usually a fee is involved in processing foreign checks and most large banks process them on a daily basis.

Open Account - high risk to the seller. The buyer is not required to pay until goods are received. This arrangement is good for the customer but bad for the U.S. business because there is no guarantee of payment. If no payment is received, the only recourse is legal action within the foreign country. If proper documents are missing, legal action will be difficult to pursue. If you must offer open account terms, check the buyer's credit thoroughly. See page 77.

Non-traditional methods of payment include:
Direct Debit - low risk to the seller. The seller directly debits the buyer's account without prior notification as long as the buyer receives the lowest price possible at that moment. Direct debt requires the seller to open a bank account in the foreign country.

Bank Transfers - low risk to the seller. The foreign buyer transfers funds directly to the seller's bank. Bank transfers may be difficult to track with multiple order and reorder payments.

Consignment - high risk to the seller. The seller does not receive payment until the goods are actually sold overseas, not merely purchased by the buyer. The seller may have to wait a long time for payment and if goods cannot be sold, the seller must pay to have goods shipped back to the United States.

Unfortunately, there is little statistical information available regarding length of time that U.S. exporters wait for payment. Most financiers will tell you that length of time to receive payment is related to the state of the economy in that country, but sometimes it is just the nature of that culture to make payments in a rather untimely fashion.

Detailed information about methods of payments and what option is best for a particular company can be obtained from the international department of a bank.

RESOURCES

Financing and Insuring Exports: A User's Guide to Eximbank and FCIA Programs ($50) Export Import Bank of United States, 811 Vermont Avenue, N.W., Washington, DC 20571 (202) 565-3900; http://www.exim.gov (w)

Guide to Uniform Rules for Collections ($39.95) ICC Publishing, 156 Fifth Avenue, Suite 305, New York, NY 10010 (212) 206-1150 (p), iccpub@interport.net (e)

Palgrave Dictionary of Money & Finance ($595 = 3 vol.) ISBN 1-56159-041-X Stockton Press, 345 Park Avenue, 10th Floor, New York, NY 10110 (212) 689-9200 (p); (212) 212-689-9711 (f); grove@grovestocktn.com (e)

What Is a Letter of Credit?

A letter of credit is a document issued by a bank, per instructions of the buyer of the goods, committing itself to honor drafts drawn for the seller in accordance with the specified terms and conditions. With this method of payment, the risk lies on the bank, not the buyer. Letters of credit afford one of the highest degrees of protection and assurance of payment ***if*** the proper documents are presented in strict conformity with the terms and conditions of the letter of credit and all documentation details agree perfectly. The letter of credit is rapidly becoming the preferred method of payment in the exporting community due to its low risk factor for buyer and seller. A letter of credit travels through certain, specific steps which are:

1. The buyer and seller agree upon the terms of purchase.
2. The buyer applies at the buyer's bank for a letter of credit to cover the transaction.
3. The buyer's bank will then prepare the letter of credit for the seller's bank, whereupon the seller receives the letter of credit.
4. The goods are shipped.
5. The seller delivers the proper documentation to his/her bank, which then transmits the documentation to the issuing bank.
6. The buyer, now assured that the goods have been shipped, makes a payment to the issuing bank.
7. The issuing bank, in turn, pays the seller's bank.
8. The proper documents are then released to the buyer, in order to receive the goods from the transporter which assures payment to the seller before the buyer ever sees the goods.

It is important to remember that a letter of credit is not a sales contract and should never be considered a sales contract. A letter of credit can remain valid even if a sales contract becomes null and void. The letter of credit is to assure the importer (buyer) that the goods are shipped prior to payment and likewise assure the exporter (seller) of payment prior to shipment.

An export manager making all quotes in U.S. dollars will not have to worry about losing money due to price fluctuations. In newly emerging foreign markets, or any country without full currency convertibility, it would be wise to ask for payment in U.S. dollars, because their currency is of no value in the open market. Other payment options include trading in the country's inconvertible hard currency, countertrade, or barter. Always quote in U.S. Dollars to protect yourself from currency fluctuations.

RESOURCES

Export Letters of Credit and Drafts ($69.50) International Trade Institute, 5055 North Main St., Dayton, Ohio 45415 (800) 543-2453; (937) 276-5920 (f)

Letters of Credit ($185) Matthew Bender and Co., International Division, 1275 Broadway, Albany, NY 12204 (800) 424-4200 (p) or (518) 487-3584 (p)

Standby/Commercial Letters of Credit ($159.95) ICC Publishing, 156 Fifth Avenue, Suite 305, New York, NY 10010 (212) 206-1150 (p), iccpub@interport.net (e)

UCP 500/1993 Revision ($10.95); **Uniform Rules: Bank-to-Bank Requirements** ($10.95); **Uniform Rules: Contract Guarantee** ($15.95) ICC Publishing, 156 Fifth Avenue, Suite 305, New York, NY 10010 (212) 206-1150 (p); iccpub@interport.net (e)

Confirmed Irrevocable Letter Of Credit

International Banking Group
Jack and Jill Bank Corp.
P.O. Box 1234
Detroit, MI 48201

Advice Number: BA000000094
Advice Date: 21 Apr 94
Issue Bank Ref: 1234/LMC/5678
Expiry Date and Place: 21 July 94, Tokyo

Amount: US$
Two hundred three thousand
nine hundred only
$203,900

Beneficiary:
ABC Company, Inc.
5278 S.Auto Street
Detroit, MI 48201

Applicant:
XYZ Company, Inc.
25 Sushi Way
Tokyo, Japan

We have been requested to advise you that the following letter of credit was issued by:

First Bank of Japan
123 Saki Drive
Tokyo, Japan

Please be guided by its terms and conditions and by the following:

Credit is available by negotiation of your draft(s) in duplicate at sight for 100% of invoice value drawn on us accompanied by the following documents:

1. Signed commercial invoice one (1) original and three (3) copies.
2. Full set of ocean bills of lading cosigned to the order of First Bank of Japan, Japan, and marked: "notify applicant" and "freight collect."
3. Packing list, two (2) copies.
4. Certificate of origin in duplicate.
5. Insurance certificate for 110% of value covering Institute Cargo Clause "A" and War and Strike Risks.

Evidencing Shipment of: 20,000 motorized toothbrushes
FOB San Francisco

Shipment from: Detroit, MI to San Francisco, CA **To:** Tokyo, Japan
Latest Shipping Date: 01 Jul 94

Partial Shipments: not allowed.

All banking charges outside Japan are for beneficiary's account.

Documents must be presented within 21 days from B/L date, but within the validity of the credit.

At the request of our correspondent, we confirm this credit and also engage with you that all drafts drawn under and in compliance with the terms of this credit will be duly honored by us.

Please examine this instrument carefully. If you are unable to comply with the terms or conditions, please communicate with your buyer to arrange for an amendment.

This is page 1 of _____ signed page(s).

Signature

International Banking Group, Jack & Jill Bank Corp.

Where Can I Obtain Financial Assistance?

U.S. Small Business Administration (SBA). The U.S. Small Business Administration (SBA) offers loan guarantees through the *Export Working Capital Program* (EWCP) for up to 90% of the amount of a loan up to $833,333. In 1997, SBA assisted small business exporters with 401 EWCP loans worth more than $141.3 million. The average size of loans requested by exporters has been in the $350,000 range, to finance foreign market development or labor and materials needed to manufacture or wholesale for export. The loan can take the form of a revolving line of credit or it can be structured for a single transaction. Loans typically mature in 12 months or less. *The International Trade Loan Guarantee Program* is offered to small businesses who can significantly expand existing export markets or develop new export markets. It also is available to companies adversely affected by import competition. Loans are guaranteed up to $1.2 million for facilities and equipment and up to $750,000 for working capital. Maturities of loans may extend up to 25 years. SBA also offers *Export Express* which provides domestic lenders with the information they need to assess an exporter's loan package and guarantees up to $250,000 on a single transaction requiring six or less months of financing. Through streamlined paperwork and an interactive web site, Export Express transactions have an authorized three-day turnaround time. To locate your local SBA office, call SBA headquarters at (800) 827-5722. Visit the SBA web site at http://www.sba.gov/oit.

Export-Import Bank (Ex-Im Bank). Dealing with transactions greater than $750,000, Ex-Im Bank has programs which provide trade financing and other assistance including insurance, working capital guarantee programs, and direct loans to foreign buyers. The *Working Capital Guarantee Program* helps small businesses obtain critical pre-export financing from commercial lenders. Ex-Im Bank will guarantee 90% of the principal and a limited amount of interest on loans or revolving lines of credit extended to eligible exporters. The funds may be used for such pre-export activities as buying raw materials or foreign marketing. Ex-Im Bank's *Certified Bank List* provides a list of banks and contacts that are knowledgeable about Ex-Im Bank's programs. The list is free. For more information, call Ex-Im's export finance hotline at (202) 565-3946. Visit its web site at http://www.exim.gov.

Overseas Private Investment Corporation (OPIC). Medium- to long-term financing for overseas investment projects is made available through loan guaranties and direct loans. Loans generally range up to $6 million and are reserved exclusively for projects involving U.S. small businesses. Final maturities range from five to twelve years or more. Contact the Overseas Private Investment Corporation Office of Public Affairs at (202) 457-7087. *OPIC also offers a fax retrieval system with a variety of information including OPIC programs, forms, country and area reports, and regional reports.*

Alternative Sources. Although a number of financing programs exist, not all meet the individual needs of U.S. exporters. Alternative financing services have emerged to fill the unconventional needs of U.S. exporters. The *Guide To Alternative Trade Finance Options* may be obtained through the Trade Information Center, U.S. Department of Commerce, HCHB 7424, Washington, D.C. 20230; (800) USA-TRADE. Listings include basic trade finance, pre-export finance, factoring services, forfeiting services, investment services, financial consultation services, countertrade, foreign exchange, debt collection services, export receivables financing, credit reporting services, and environmental project financing.

Many state governments provide export financing through their international trade offices. A list of all state trade offices is available through the Trade Information Center at (800) USA TRADE. The Bankers Association for Foreign Trade, a non-profit association of approximately 450 banks, matches exporters in need of trade financing with interested banks. It can be contacted at (202) 452-0942 or visit its web site at http://www.miep.org/axcap/index.html. The Export Finance Hotline operates 24-hours-a-day to answer your finance questions; call (800) 424-5201.

RESOURCES

Bankable Deals: A Question & Answer Guide to Trade Finance (free) U.S. Small Business Administration Office of International Trade (202) 205-6720 (p); (202) 205-7272 (f)

Export and Project Financing ($449) Thompson Publishing Group, Subscription Service Center, P.O. Box 26185, Tampa, FL 33623-6185 (800) 925-1878 (p); (800) 759-7179 (f)

International Trade Finance Handbook ($15) The Journal of Commerce, 445 Marshall Street, Phillipsburg, NJ 08865-9984 (800) 221-3777 (p); haddock@interport.net (e); http://www.joc.com (w)

Multilateral Development Banks: Increasing U.S. Exports and Creating U.S. Jobs ($8.50) U.S. Superintendent of Documents, P.O. Box 371954, Pittsburgh, PA 15250-7954 (202) 512-1800 (p); (202) 512-2250 (f); gpoaccess@gpo.gov (e)

How Can I Check a Buyer's Credit?

Extending credit greatly increases the risk to the U.S. company. While trying to gain a foothold in a foreign market, cash in advance or a letter of credit is best to insure payment. The manager will be dealing in an unfamiliar territory and may not have access to traditional means of checking a new buyer's credit. It is best to proceed with caution. Once management feels comfortable and has established a relationship with the foreign buyers, it may be advantageous to offer credit.

If the customer the U.S. company is targeting already has a practice of dealing with credit, offering credit may be necessary to obtain the order. If the U.S. company has secured some type of U.S. governmental loan/ payment guarantee (see page 76) then it could "afford" to extend credit to the foreign buyers. Remember that if offering credit is not necessary for your initial entry into the market, do not offer it. However, if credit is necessary, before it is offered, make sure you are confident that you will receive payment for your goods. Otherwise, only ship what you can afford to lose.

Before you agree to any deal, it is essential that a potential buyer, distributor, or partner's credit be checked. Bad debts are more easily avoided than rectified. If a U.S. company has a problem with collecting money from a foreign entity after the products have been delivered overseas, the only way for that U.S. company to collect payment is to prosecute the buyer through the foreign legal channels. This process can take years to resolve and can be very costly.

Check a foreign buyer's credit the same way you check out your domestic customer's credit. Consider trade associations, trade reference services, and credit reporting agencies, such as America's Business Information Association (404) 933-4142; Dun and Bradstreet Information Services (800) 932-0025; J I International (203) 589-1698; Graydon International (212) 633-1434; Owens on-line, Inc. (800) 745-4656; Piguet International, Inc. (800) 766-9922; LIDA Credit Agency, Inc. (800) 423-0026; Standard and Poor's Rating Service (212) 208-1146; and Veritas (800) 929-8374.

Among the best sources are international departments of large U.S. banks. These people make it their business to know overseas creditors. They routinely respond to letters of credit, know "who's who" in overseas banking and many have their own branches overseas. Ex-Im Bank uses its repayment records to provide credit information for U.S. exporting firms and provides information useful in the financing of export sales to a specific country or company abroad. Finally, the U.S. Department of Commerce offers International Company Profiles which are a method for checking the reputation, reliability, and financial status of a prospective trading partner. These International Company Profiles also provide recommendations from the U.S. Embassy as to the suitability of the foreign entity as a trading partner. This service costs $100. Contact a local U.S. Department of Commerce or District Export Assistance Center for assistance.

Make sure you are not trading with a U.S.-prohibited individual or business. Check out the Bureau of Export Administration's Table of Denial Orders at http://www.fedworld.gov (file named 1.denial.txt).

RESOURCES

Restricted International Traders ($69) International Division Publications, U.S. Chamber of Commerce, 1615 H Street, NW, Washington, DC 20062-2000 (202) 463-5460 (p); (202) 463-3114 (f); http://www.uschamber.org (w)

A Short Course In International Contracts ($19.95) World Trade Press, 1505 Fifth Avenue, San Rafael, CA 94901 (800) 833-8586 (p); (415) 453-7980 (f)

A Short Course In International Economics ($19.95) World Trade Press, 1505 Fifth Avenue, San Rafael, CA 94901 (800) 833-8586 (p); (415) 453-7980 (f)

Where Can I Obtain Referrals for Banks Located Abroad?

Most exporters will not need to use an overseas bank, but an overseas bank may be a useful contact. The exporter may need a foreign bank to speed collections, obtain information about a foreign bank if your buyer wants to make payments utilizing a letter of credit, or the importer may need to make payments through a direct deposit at a local bank. A wire transfer of funds by the foreign bank to a U.S. bank would then be necessary unless the exporter uses the foreign funds to pay off local debtors.

Make sure the sponsoring bank is financially sound, even if it has a major presence in the big cities of the countries where you do business. A wide variety of resources are available to assist a company find foreign banks, including international departments of large U.S. banks. The men and women who work in these departments deal with overseas banks on a daily basis. They know which foreign banks are reputable and financially sound. Their information also typically comes from Polk's Directory or the Banker's Almanac.

Because OPIC deals with many overseas banks in its work with foreign direct investments, it may be able to provide recommendations on foreign banks. Contact: Overseas Private Investment Corporation, Public Affairs Office, 1613 M Street N.W., Washington, DC 20537; (800) 424-6742. To locate a credit reporting agency operating in foreign countries, contact a U.S. Department of Commerce Country Desk Officer.

RESOURCES

Export Credit Insurance: The Competitive Edge (free) Export-Import Bank of the United States, 811 Vermont Avenue, NW, Washington, DC 20571-0999 (202) 566-4490 (p)

Exporter's Guide to Foreign Sources for Credit Information Trade Data Reports, 6 West 37th Street, New York, NY 10018 (212) 563-2772 (p)

Managing Foreign Exchange Risk ($29.95) ICC Publishing, 156 Fifth Avenue, Suite 305, New York, NY 10010 (212) 206-1150 (p), iccpub@interport.net (e)

How Does Countertrade Work?

Countertrade is another way to conduct business in the global economy. In some cases, it represents an alternative to no trade at all. Countertrade is a practice whereby a supplier contractually commits to making a purchase from the other party and/or undertaking certain specified commercial initiatives. Quite simply, countertrade is an exchange of goods or services. Under countertrade, a company may exchange physical goods or intangibles in lieu of payment in currency. For example, a U.S. business may agree with a Russian entrepreneur to export 500 pairs of designer blue jeans in exchange for 1,500 bottles of premium vodka. However, if the blue jean manufacturer does not want to sell this vodka, it may cut a deal with a business in Europe that has the need for this product. In exchange, the European firm will take the vodka and pay the U.S. firm in hard currency. According to U.S. Department of Commerce statistics, more than 100 nations have required some form of countertrade as part of their foreign procurement practices.

A need for countertrade developed in late 1970s due to the decreasing ability of many developing nations to finance their imports adequately. Nations of low credit-worthiness, like the former Soviet republics, could not secure bank loans and relied on many forms of assistance from the western nations. Businesses that are receptive to countertrade have a competitive advantage in these marketing environments.

There are several limitations to countertrade. Policies that are aimed at short-term solutions that ignore risks and cost sharing with the foreign partner could backfire on one or both parties. Unpredictable approval processes and regulatory shifts cause difficulties in some countries. Inflexible attitudes may result when bureaucracies engage in unique ways of conducting and facilitating business transactions. And difficulties in isolating foreign exchange earnings from the domestic sale of countertraded goods may confuse the accounting structure of the U.S. company. Countertrade is surely not appropriate for all types of export transactions.

Countertrade practices will probably continue to be favored in troubled economies. Because debt is increasing in developing countries, financing based on countertrade arrangements may become increasingly accepted and used. Countertrade can be viewed as a strong fallback or supplemental feature to traditional financing methods.

Although the U.S. government does not look favorably upon countertrade activities, it will not oppose the participation of U.S. companies in such activities unless it could have a negative affect on U.S. national security. U.S. governmental agencies review applications for countertrade on a case-by-case basis. All goods imported into or exported from the United States, regardless of method, are subject to the same tariff and quota laws.

The U.S. Department of Commerce provides advisory assistance on countertrade to U.S. exporters and is perhaps the best source to consult about countertrade. The Financial Services and Countertrade Division within the International Trade Administration will be the department to consult. Call (202) 482-4471.

RESOURCE

Countertrade Handbook ($55) ISBN 0-89930-320-X Greenwood Publishing, 88 Post Road West, Box 5007, Westport, CT 06881 (203) 226-3571 (p)

What Forms of Countertrade Exist?

The primary forms of "compensatory trade arrangements" are offset, barter, buyback/compensation, counterpurchase, and umbrella countertrade.

Offset Barter is a term used for a broad range of industrial and commercial compensation practices required as a condition of purchase in commercial or government sales of military or high-cost civilian hardware. Offset arrangements may include demands for overseas coproduction, licensed production, sub-contractor production, overseas investment, technology transfer, and countertrade initiatives.

Barter is a one-time transaction bound under a single contract that specifies the direct exchange of selected goods and another of equivalent value. There is no monetary exchange involved with barter. Barter is the oldest form of reciprocal trade.

Buyback/Compensation is an agreement whereby the original exporter accepts products derived from the original exported product as full or partial repayment. Buyback arrangements may include leasing and production sharing agreements, long-term coproduction ventures, and equity ventures.

Counterpurchase is an agreement whereby the original exporter accepts products unrelated to the original exported product as full or partial repayment. Common counterpurchase goods include agricultural commodities, fertilizers, chemicals, minerals, consumer goods, and low-technology components. Counterpurchase is generally utilized in conjunction with separate import/export contracts.

Umbrella Countertrade Agreements are bilateral trade agreements between public agencies of two countries, or between a public entity and a foreign private enterprise. Umbrella contracts are convenient because they provide for the inclusion of multiple trading parties. These arrangements are reviewed on an annual basis.

Although the words may sometimes be used interchangeably, barter and countertrade are not the same. There are four major distinctions:

1) Bartering involves an exchange of goods only. No exchange of money is involved. Under countertrade, there is partial or full compensation with money;

2) Bartering requires one contract. Countertrade requires two or more contracts. One contract is for the sale to the foreign customer and the other is for the exporter to agree to purchase goods from the foreign customer;

3) Barter transactions usually require one year or less to complete while countertrade transactions can require much longer, thus requiring a greater commitment of the company's resources; and

4) Barter does not require much of a commitment or involve much of a risk for the U.S. company. Countertrade can become very involved and risky, sometimes even requiring great amounts of foreign capital investment.

RESOURCE

World Payment Systems Handbook ($39.95) ICC Publishing, 156 Fifth Avenue, Suite 305, New York, NY 10010 (212) 206-1150 (p), iccpub@interport.net (e)

What Is the Best Way to Ship My Products?

In export transactions, it will be advantageous for both you and your customer to keep freight costs to a minimum while still meeting the customer's needs. But the decision regarding the best way to ship a product is not solely based on cost. The following example will help illustrate the issues involved in considering shipping alternatives.

Company A and Company B produce widgets in the United States for the same cost. Company A air ships its widgets to Germany for $42. Company B ocean ships its widgets to Germany for $37. Which company has the competitive advantage? At first glance, one might be tempted to answer that Company B has the advantage because it can sell its product at a cheaper rate. But, consider that air freight gets the product to its destination within one week whereas ocean freight takes three weeks. What happens to the competitive advantage if the foreign customer needs the product promptly? Would the answer change? Because of this, there is no one standard or best way to ship a product. While price is definitely a key consideration, it is not the only one. Because of the competitiveness of the shipping industry, a company should always request quotes from more than one shipper on more than one method of shipping.

Ocean freight rates are usually based on cubic measure, not actual weight. Rates also depend upon destination, the amount of traffic going to that area, and the frequency of trips made to that area.

Air freight rates are calculated differently. The goal of airlines is to fill the plane to capacity with as much weight as permissible and, because of this, they can offer better rates than freight forwarders for dense, heavy cargo. Rates also vary depending on destination, amount of traffic, and frequency of trips made to that area.

Remember that the plane or ship will make its scheduled trips even if it is not at full capacity. Because the shippers prefer a full load, forwarders can sometimes offer a cheaper rate by combining shipments of several exporters headed for the same destination.

Though freight forwarders are increasingly incorporating all facets of transportation within their organizations, there are some companies that exclusively specialize in either ocean or air freight. A forwarder may offer consolidated air services which allow him to sell less expensive rates based on combining shipments to the same destination from a variety of shippers.

For ocean freight, a forwarder may utilize a Non-Vessel Owning Company Carrier (NVOCC) to sell rates which have been filed with the Federal Maritime Commission. The forwarder is able to do this because the containers are purchased from a steamship line at a single cost based on a mixed commodity rate.

The major difference between the air and ocean industries in the U.S. can be attributed to deregulation. The deregulation of the airline industry has caused rates to fluctuate in comparison to the more consistent ocean rates.

The costs of transportation are paid by the buyer or the seller. The designated party should be predetermined in the terms of sale (see INCOTERMS, page 83). Most often, the seller pays for transport to the foreign port and the buyer pays for any inward shipping thereafter.

Freight forwarders are professionals knowledgeable in all aspects of transportation and logistics management.

RESOURCES

Distribution ($65/year) Distribution Department, P.O. Box 2106, Radnor, PA 19089-9206 (610) 964-4386 (p); (610) 964-5029 (f)

Export Shipping ($69.50) International Trade Institute, 5055 North Main St., Dayton, Ohio 45415 (800) 543-2453 (p); (937) 276-5920 (f)

National Highway and Airway Carriers Directory ($170/2 issues) National Highway Carriers, P.O. Box 6099, Buffalo Grove, IL 60089 (708) 634-0606 (p)

What Functions Does a Freight Forwarder Perform?

Because of the variety of considerations involved in the physical export process, most exporters, both new and experienced, rely on an international freight forwarder to perform these services. The international freight forwarder acts as an agent for the exporter in moving cargo to the overseas destination. These agents are familiar with the import rules and regulations of foreign countries, methods of shipping, government export regulations, and the documents connected with foreign trade.

Freight forwarders can assist with an order from the start, by advising the exporter of the freight costs, port charges, consular fees, cost of special documentation and insurance, as well as their handling fees — all of which help in preparing price quotations. Freight forwarders may also recommend the type of packing for best protecting the merchandise in transit; they can arrange to have the merchandise packed at the port or containerized. They also reserve the necessary space on board an ocean vessel or airplaine, if the exporter desires. The cost for their services is a legitimate export cost that should be figured into the price charged to the customer.

When the order is ready to ship, freight forwarders should be able to review the letter of credit, commercial invoices, packing list, etc., to ensure that everything is in order. They may also prepare any special required documentation.

Once the cargo arrives at the port of export, freight forwarders may make the necessary arrangements with customs brokers to ensure that the goods comply with customs export documentation regulations. In addition, they may have the goods delivered to the carrier in time for loading. After shipment, they forward all documents directly to the customer or to the paying bank, if desired.

The National Customs Brokers & Forwarders Association of America, Inc. is a national trade association of U.S.-licensed international freight forwarders that will assist in locating a local freight forwarder. Call (212) 432-0050 for more information.

RESOURCES

Directory of Freight Forwarders and Custom House Brokers ($30) International Wealth Success, Inc., 24 Canterbury Road, Rockville Centre, NY 11570 (800) 323-0548 (p)

Guide To INCOTERMS ($19.95) ISBN 92-842-1088-7 The Chamber of Commerce of the United States, 1615 H Street, NW, Washington, DC 20062 (202) 659-6000 (p)

Intermodal Freight Transportation ($35) Eno Foundation for Transportation, P.O. Box 2055, Westport, CT 06880 (703) 729-7200 (p); (703) 729-7219 (f)

What Are INCOTERMS?

International Commercial Terms (INCOTERMS) are acronyms used in shipping documentation which provide a clear international understanding for the parties involved regarding terms of sale, point of origin, destination, and the party responsible given a certain condition. Thirteen INCOTERMS specify exactly which party has responsibility for the cargo, at what point that responsibility transfers from the buyer to the seller, and define seller and buyer costs. Incoterms are developed by the International Chamber of Commerce (ICC). The 13 Incoterms currently in use are:

Group E - Departure Terms - Buyer Possession at Seller's Premises

EXW-Ex Works: the seller makes the goods available at his named premises.

Group F - Carriage Unpaid - Main Carriage Freight Prepaid - Seller Selects Carrier

FCA-Free Carrier: seller hands over the goods, cleared for export, into the custody of the first carrier (named by the buyer) at the named place. This term is suitable for all modes of transport, including carriage by air, rail, road, and containerised / multi-modal transport.

FAS-Free Alongside Ship: Seller must place the goods alongside the ship at the named port. The buyer must clear the goods for export. Suitable for maritime transport only.

FOB-The classic maritime trade term, Free On Board: Seller must load the goods on board the ship nominated by the buyer, the cost and risk being divided at ship's rail. The seller must clear the goods for export. Maritime transport only.

Group C - Carriage Paid - Main Carriage Freight Prepaid - Seller Selects Carrier

CFR-Cost and Freight: Seller must pay the cost and freight to bring the goods to the port of destination. However, risk is transferred to the buyer once the goods have crossed the ship's rail. Maritime transport only.

CIF-Cost, Insurance and Freight: Exactly the same as CFR except that the seller must, in addition, procure and pay for the insurance for the buyer. Maritime transport only.

CPT-Carriage Paid To: General/containerised/multimodal equivalent of CFR. The seller pays for carriage to the named point of destination, but risk passes when the goods are handed over to the first carrier.

CIP-Carriage and Insurance Paid: Containerised transport/multimodal equivalent to CIF. Seller pays for carriage and insurance to the named destination point, but risk passes when the goods are handed over to the first carrier.

Group D - Arrival Terms - Seller Delivers to Destination Point

DAF-Delivered At Frontier: Seller makes the goods available, cleared for export, at the named place on the frontier. Suitable for rail/road transport.

DES-Delivered Ex Ship: Seller makes the goods available to the buyer on board the ship at the port of destination, uncleared for import.

DEQ-Delivered Ex Quay: One step further than DES: the goods must be unloaded onto quay at the port of destination, and import clearance must be obtained by the seller.

DDU-Delivered Duty Unpaid (new in Incoterms 1990): Seller must deliver the goods all the way to a named place in the country of destination. However, the buyer must clear the goods for import and pay the necessary duties.

DDP-Delivered Duty Paid: Maximum obligation for the seller: seller pays for all costs, charges, and official formalities up to destination.

RESOURCES

Comprehensive Guide To Trade Terms ($36.50) U.S. Department of Commerce, Washington, DC 20230, (800) STAT-USA (p); (202) 482-2164 (f); stat-usa@doc.gov (e); http://www.stat_usa.gov (w)

Dictionary of International Trade ($16.50) World Trade Press, 1505 Fifth Avenue, San Rafael, CA 94901 (800) 833-8586 (p); (415) 453-7980 (f)

Export Reference Glossary ($99.95) International Trade Institute, 5055 North Main Street, Dayton, OH 45415 (800) 543-2453 (p); (937) 276-5920 (f)

INCOTERMS - 1990 ($29.95) ISBN 92-842-0087-3; International Chamber of Commerce, 38 Cours Albert, 75008, Paris, France (212) 206-1150 (p); (212) 633-6025 (f)

How Do I Obtain International Insurance?

Insurance is necessary in international trade because of the risks that are present in any export transaction. A company can use insurance as a risk management tool. Insurance is available against shipping risks, commercial risks, and political risks.

- Shipping risk coverage is generally purchased from warehouse to warehouse and policies are purchased on a shipment-by-shipment basis. This type of insurance is usually available through the freight forwarder. Shipping risk insurance can also be purchased from an insurance agent. The agent will base the cargo insurance on the value of the entire shipment including freight. Rates will vary due to product, client, destination, etc. Air cargo generally costs less than ocean cargo because of the length of time, distance and hazards involved.

- Commercial risk insurance covers losses due to nonpayment by the buyer. By having such an insurance plan, you can extend credit to foreign buyers, which enhances your competitive position.

- Political risk refers to such situations as war, currency inconvertibility, and expropriation which is the seizing of property without permission.

The Export-Import Bank's New-to-Export Policy is available to firms just beginning to export or with average annual export sales of less than $2,000,000 for the past two years and who meet the SBA definition of a small business. The policy offers enhanced coverage at a lower premium than usually found in regular insurance policies. An Umbrella Policy is available to commercial lenders, state agencies, export trading companies, and similar organizations to insure export receivables of their small to medium-sized clients. Short-Term Single-Buyer Policies and Medium-Term Single-Buyer Policies allow exporters to insure their receivables against loss due to commercial and specified political risks on a selective basis. Lease Insurance Policies offer a lessor opportunity to expand an overseas leasing program, by providing comprehensive insurance for both the stream of lease payments and the fair market value of the leased products.

The Foreign Credit Insurance Association (FCIA) is a private insurance group which operates as Ex-Im Bank's agent. It offers insurance to cover political and commercial risks on exports mentioned earlier.

Either the buyer or seller may pay for the cargo insurance. The proper party should be predetermined in the terms of sale. If the terms of sale make the buyer responsible for the insurance, the exporter should not assume that adequate insurance has been obtained. Improper or too little coverage may result in a loss for the exporter should inclement weather, rough handling in transit, or any other unforeseen hazard arise. To be safe, the exporter may want to agree to provide the insurance in order to guarantee that the proper level and type of coverage is obtained.

RESOURCE

A Short Course In International Payments ($19.95) World Trade Press, 1505 Fifth Avenue, San Rafael, CA 94901 (800) 833-8586 (p); (415) 453-7980 (f)

Where Can I Find a Reliable Source of Information to Ensure My Shipments Comply With Export and Import Regulations?

Editor's Note: Although Unz and Company is a commercial enterprise, firms should know about the varied services of this excellent and highly reputable export services company. The following information is on how Unz & Co. can assist exporters.

A 116-year-old firm which specializes in providing products and services that simplify and standardize compliance with export regulations for its 50,000 clients, Unz & Co. provides exporters with the forms required to clear shipments worldwide as well as the information and training to complete them properly. In addition, it offers documentation software, CD-ROMs, and numerous publications. A newly created consulting division assists export companies in developing expertise and procedures to handle export compliance, including L/C Expeditor™ — a service designed to reduce discrepant letter of credit documents and to speed payments to exporters.

Unz & Co. maintains close ties with customs services around the world. It is an active participant in key initiatives to automate trade data, including AES, the U.S. Customs Service's Automated Export System. (The AES is the first phase of a U.S. government initiative to effect trade data exchange among countries worldwide.)

Unz & Co. enjoys a valued reputation in the trade community as a premier source for complete, accurate, and up-to-date trade documentation based on both product quality and timeliness of product introductions. For example, when the NAFTA legislation was being drafted in 1994, Unz & Co. worked closely with both Revenue Canada and Mexican Hacienda officials to supply U.S. exporters with approved certificates within weeks of the Agreement's passage, months before they were available from any other commercial source.

Unz & Co. is actively involved in a number of leading associations, including the National Association of Customs House Brokers and Freight Forwarders, National Council on International Trade Development, American Association of Importers and Exporters, National Association of Exporting Companies, U.S. Council on International Banking, FCIB-NACM Corporation, and Bolero Association. In 1994, Unz & Co. received the President's prestigious E-Star Award for Excellence in Export Service, and the "E" Award in 1989.

For more information or to obtain Unz's free Sourcebook, call (800) 631-3098, e-mail at unzco@unzexport.com, or visit its web site at http://www.unzexport.com.

RESOURCE

Who's Who of American Customs Brokers and International Freight Forwarders ($12) National Customs Brokers and Forwarders Association of America, One World Trade Center, Suite 1153, New York, New York 10048 (212) 432-0050 (p)

What Export Forms Do I Need to Fill Out?

Some common government-required document forms are listed below. The seller normally prepares his or her commercial documents and the freight forwarder normally prepares the transportation documents. Some freight forwarders will do all the paperwork.

Bill of Lading. These documents are contracts between the owner of the goods and the carrier. There are two types: a straight bill of lading which is non-negotiable and the negotiable/shipper's order bill of lading which can be bought, sold, or traded while goods are in transit and is used for letter-of-credit transactions. The customer usually needs a copy as proof of ownership to take possession of the goods.

Certificate of Origin. Certain nations require a signed statement as to the origin of the export item in order to monitor import tariffs and quotas. Such certificates are usually obtained through a semiofficial organization such as a local chamber of commerce, and must be certified by the chamber of commerce. A certificate may be required even though the invoice contains all the necessary information. Documentation that requires a notary stamp or chamber of commerce stamp can be handled by a freight forwarder.

Commercial Invoice. As in a domestic transaction, the commercial invoice is a bill for the goods from the buyer to the seller. A commercial invoice should include a description of the goods, address of the shipper and seller, and the delivery and payment terms. The buyer needs the invoice to prove ownership and arrange payment. Some government agencies use the invoice to assess customs duties.

Consular Invoice. Consular invoices are required by certain nations and used to identify goods. This type of invoice is purchased from the consulate of the country into which the goods are shipped and must be prepared in the language of that country. Call the foreign embassy in the U.S. to request the number of the consular's office closest to your business.

Destination Control Statement. This statement appears on the commercial invoice, ocean or air waybill of lading, and SED to notify the carrier and all foreign parties that the item may be exported only to certain destinations.

Export Packing List. An export packing list itemizes the material in each individual package, and shows the individual net, legal, tare and gross weights in U.S. and metric. Package markings should be shown along with the shipper's and buyer's references. The packing list is attached to the outside of the package in a clearly marked waterproof envelope. The list is used to determine the total shipment weight and whether the correct cargo is being shipped. Customs officials may use it to check the cargo at inspection points.

Inspection Certificate. Some purchasers and countries may require a certificate of inspection attesting to the specifications of the goods shipped. The inspection is usually performed by a third party, such as an independent testing organization.

Insurance Certificate. If the seller provides insurance, the insurance certificate states the type and amount of coverage.

Shipper's Export Declaration (SED). The SED authorizes the export of freight. It is used by the U.S. government to control exports and compile trade statistics. It must be prepared and submitted to the customs agent for shipments by mail valued at more than $500 and all other shipments, by any other means, valued at more than $2,500. An SED must be prepared for all Individual Validated License (IVL) shipments, regardless of value. Call (202) 482-4811 if you have any questions regarding the SED.

RESOURCES

Correct Way to Fill Out the Shipper's Export Declaration, The (free) U.S. Bureau of the Census, Washington, DC 20233 (301) 457-1086 (p); (301) 457-1159 (f); http://census.gov.foreign_trade (w)

Export Documentation ($69.50) International Trade Institute, 5055 North Main Street, Dayton, OH 45415 (800) 543-2453 (p); (987) 276-5920 (f)

Sourcebook of International Trade (free) UNZ & Co., 190 Baldwin Avenue, Jersey City, NJ 07306 (800) 631-3098 (p); (908) 665-7866 (f); unzco@unzexport.com (w); http://www.unzexport.com (w)

Shipper's Export Declaration

FORM **7525-V**

U.S. DEPARTMENT OF COMMERCE - BUREAU OF THE CENSUS - INTERNATIONAL TRADE ADMINISTRATION

SHIPPER'S EXPORT DECLARATION

OMB No. 0607-0018

1a. EXPORTER *(Name and address including ZIP code)*

ZIP CODE

2. DATE OF EXPORTATION

3. BILL OF LADING/AIR WAYBILL NO.

b. EXPORTER EIN (IRS) NUMBER

c. PARTIES TO TRANSACTION

☐ Related ☐ Non-Related

4a. ULTIMATE CONSIGNEE

b. INTERMEDIATE CONSIGNEE

5. FORWARDING AGENT

6. POINT (STATE) OF ORIGIN OR FTZ NO.

7. COUNTRY OF ULTIMATE DESTINATION

8. LOADING PIER (VESSEL ONLY)

9. MODE OF TRANSPORT *(Specify)*

10. EXPORTING CARRIER

11. PORT OF EXPORT

12. PORT OF UNLOADING *(vessel and air only)*

13. CONTAINERIZED *(vessel only)*

☐ Yes ☐ No

14. SCHEDULE B DESCRIPTION OF COMMODITIES

15. MARKS, NOS. AND KINDS OF PACKAGES

(Use columns 17-19)

D/F (16)	SCHEDULE B NUMBER (17)	CHECK DIGIT	QUANTITY - SCHEDULE B UNIT(S) (18)	SHIPPING WEIGHT *(Kilos)* (19)

21. VALIDATED LICENSE NO/GENERAL LICENSE SYMBOL

22. ECCN *(When required)*

23. Duly Authorized officer or employee

The exporter authorizes the forwarder named above to act as forwarding agent for export control and customs purposes

24. I certify that all statements made and all information contained herein are true and correct and that I have read and understand the instructions for preparation of this document, set forth in the **"Correct Way to Fill Out the Shipper's Export Declaration."** I understand that civil and criminal penalties including forfeiture and sale, may be imposed for making false or fraudulent statements herein, failing to provide the requested information or for violation of U.S. laws of exportation (13 U.S.C. Sec. 305, 22 U.S.C. Sec. 401, 18 U.S.C. Sec. 1001, 50 U.S.C. Sec. 24 10).

Signature	Confidential - For use solely for official purposes authorized by the Secretary of Commerce.
Title	Export shipments are subject to inspection by U.S.. Customs Service and/or Office of Export Enforcement
Date	25. AUTHENTICATION *(When required)*

Bill Of Lading

Speedy Transport, LTD.

BILL OF LADING

DATE

SHIPPER	BILL OF LADING NO.
	FORWARDING AGENT
CONSIGNEE	ROUTING INSTRUCTIONS
SHIP/AIR — PORT OF LADING	METHOD OF PACKING
PORT OF DISCHARGE — PLACE OF DELIVERY	COUNTRY OF ORIGIN

Numbers	No. of Pkgs.	Description of Goods	Gross Weight	Measurements
		Invoice No. & Date Export License No. Import License No.		

BILLS OF LADING Page of Page(s)	PLACE OF ISSUE	PLACE OF PAYMENT

Dated at:______________ on______________ Speedy Transport, LTD. By:______________________________ Signature	LADED ON BOARD Date:______________________________ By:______________________________ Signature

Commercial Invoice

ABC Company, Inc.
5278 S. Auto Street
Detroit, MI 48201
(313) 555-1234

Purchase Order No. 1234-5678	Invoice No. 98765
Import License No.	Invoice Date: 20-Feb-94
Terms of Payment L/C First Bank of Japan #AB1290	
International Markings	

Country of Origin: USA

Invoice to: XYZ Company, Inc.
25 Sushi Way
Tokyo, Japan

Ship to:

Forwarding Agent: Speedy Transport LTD

VIA: ocean freight
FOB San Francisco

Quantity	Part Number	Description	Unit Price	Total Price
			$U.S.	$U.S.
20,000	AZX23	Motorized Toothbrushes	$10	$200,000
		Additional Charges:		
		FOB	$200,000	
		Cartage		
		Freight	$2,100	
		Any Fees		
		Insurance	$1,800	
		Total CIF	$203,900	
Total: 10 pkgs Estimated Gross WT: 500 lbs Dimensions: 2.0 cu ft each				
		Total U.S. $		$203,900

Export License No.
Expires:

Signature: ____________________
Domestic Export Manager

Consular Invoice

<table>
<tr><td colspan="4">THE GOVERNMENT OF JAPAN

Date:
Invoice No:
Issued At:</td><td colspan="2">Port of Loading
Port of Discharge
Date of Departure
Carrier</td></tr>
<tr><td colspan="3">EXPORTER</td><td colspan="3">CONSIGNEE</td></tr>
<tr><td>Marks and Numbers</td><td>Quantity</td><td colspan="3">Description of Goods</td><td>Value of Shipment</td></tr>
<tr><td></td><td></td><td colspan="3"></td><td>U.S.$</td></tr>
<tr><td colspan="6">Total (FOB, C&F, or CIF)</td></tr>
<tr><td colspan="5">Other Charges</td><td>Amount of Charges</td></tr>
<tr><td colspan="5">Total</td><td>U.S.$</td></tr>
<tr><td colspan="5">Certified Correct By:
Witnessed By:
Fee Paid: U.S.$</td><td></td></tr>
</table>

Certificate Of Insurance

U.S.$ __________ __________ Date:

(Amount Insured)

CERTIFICATE OF INSURANCE

Rest-A-Sure Insurance Corp.
1999 Safe Way
Detroit, MI 48201

This is to certify that on the day of Rest-A-Sure Insurance Corp. insured under Policy No: limited in the sum of U.S. $ Valued at sum insured. Shipped via B/L dated at and from to loss, if any, payable to on surrender of this certificate which conveys the right of collecting any such loss as fully as if the property were covered by a special policy direct to the holder hereof, and free from any liability for unpaid premiums. This certificate is issued subject to the standard REST-A-SURE INSURANCE CORP. open cargo policy, which is incorporated herein by reference. To the extent that any terms or conditions in this certificate are inconsistent with the standard policy, the standard policy shall govern the rights and duties of all parties subject to the contract of insurance. Copies of this standard policy are available upon request from REST-A-SURE INSURANCE CORP.

SPECIAL CONDITIONS	MARKS AND NUMBERS *(same as on Bill of Lading)*
TERMS AND CONDITIONS	

Countersigned By: ______________________________

(Insurance Agent)

What Is a Certificate of Origin, When Is One Required, and Where Can I Get One?

A certificate of origin is a document required by certain foreign countries for tariff purposes, signed by the exporter, and witnessed by a semi-official agency. It indicates that the country originating the specified goods is indeed the exporter's country. An exporter can obtain a certificate of origin from several sources including a local U.S. Department of Commerce office, a freight forwarder, or a local chamber of commerce. Chambers of commerce are often viewed by many foreign companies as having more authority and function than is actually the case in the United States. A freight forwarder or foreign consulate office of that particular country can provide advice on the actual need for a certificate of origin.

There is no uniform rule as to when a certificate of origin is required. The requirement is left to the discretion of each country. Proof of origin is critically important to those countries in which the U.S. has a reciprocal trade agreement, especially the North American Free Trade Agreement (NAFTA). Exporters must prove that the goods they are exporting are entitled to receive the preferential tariff reduction or elimination. In brief, goods produced entirely in the United States qualify for NAFTA tariff treatment. In some cases, at least fifty percent of the product must be produced in the United States. Goods processed outside of the U.S., Mexico, or Canada regardless of the original content do not qualify for NAFTA tariff treatment.

Certificate of Origin

DEPARTMENT OF THE TREASURY
UNITED STATES CUSTOMS SERVICE

Approved through 12/31/96
CMBNO. 1515-0204
See back of form for Paperwork Reduction Act Notice.

NORTH AMERICAN FREE TRADE AGREEMENT
CERTIFICATE OF ORIGIN

19 CFR 181.11,181.22

PLEASE PRINT OR TYPE

1. EXPORTER NAME AND ADDRESS TAX IDENTIFICATION NUMBER:	2. BLANKET PERIOD *(DD/MM/YY)* FROM TO
3. PRODUCER NAME AND ADDRESS TAX IDENTIFICATION NUMBER:	4. IMPORTER NAME AND ADDRESS TAX IDENTIFICATION NUMBER:

5. DESCRIPTION OF GOODS	6. HS TARIFF CLASSIFICATION NUMBER	7. PREFERENCE CRITERION	8. PRODUCER	9. NET COST	10. COUNTRY OF ORIGIN

AIR OR OCEAN CARRIER: ....
NUMBER OF PACKAGES: ....
SHIPMENT WEIGHT IN KILOS: ....
INVOICE NUMBER: ....
PURCHASE ORDER NUMBER: ....

AUTHORIZED CHAMBER OF COMMERCE SIGNATURE:

I CERTIFY THAT:

• THE INFORMATION ON THIS DOCUMENT IS TRUE AND ACCURATE AND I ASSUME THE RESPONSIBILITY FOR PROVING SUCH REPRESENTATIONS. I UNDERSTAND THAT I AM LIABLE FOR ANY FALSE STATEMENTS OR MATERIAL OMISSIONS MADE ON OR IN CONNECTION WITH THIS DOCUMENT;

• I AGREE TO MAINTAIN, AND PRESENT UPON REQUEST, DOCUMENTATION NECESSARY TO SUPPORT THIS CERTIFICATE, AND TO INFORM, IN WRITING, ALL PERSONS TO WHOM THE CERTIFICATE WAS GIVEN OF ANY CHANGES THAT COULD AFFECT THE ACCURACY OR VALIDITY OF THIS CERTIFICATE;

• THE GOODS ORIGINATED IN THE TERRITORY OF ONE OR MORE OF THE PARTIES, AND COMPLY WITH THE ORIGIN REQUIREMENTS SPECIFIED FOR THOSE GOODS IN THE NORTH AMERICAN FREE TRADE AGREEMENT, AND UNLESS SPECIFICALLY EXEMPTED IN ARTICLE 411 OR ANNEX 401, THERE HAS BEEN NO FURTHER PRODUCTION OR ANY OTHER OPERATION OUTSIDE THE TERRITORIES ON THE PARTIES; AND

• THIS CERTIFICATE CONSISTS OF ☐ PAGES, INCLUDING ALL ATTACHMENTS.

11.	11a. AUTHORIZED SIGNATURE		11b. COMPANY	
	11c. NAME *(Print or Type)*		11d. TITLE	
	11e. DATE *(DD/MM/YY)*	11f. TELEPHONE NUMBER ▷	*(Voice)*	*(Facsimile)*

Customs Form 434 (121793)

Packing List

PACKING LIST

SOLD TO	SHIP TO

Date	Invoice No.

Quantity	Part No.	Description	No. of Pkgs.	Net Wt. Each	Total Gross Wt.	Dimensions
		Totals:				

Marks:

Numbers:

Method of Packing:

Page of page(s)

Certificate Of Inspection

Certificate of Inspection

Date: 23-Mar-94

Tests performed for: *ABC Company, Inc.*
5278 S. Auto Street
Detroit, MI 48201

This letter certifies that goods at Pier 33, San Francisco, U.S.A. on shipment described as:

Markings include:

Samples taken, tests performed and results:

Analysis and additional comments:

Inspected By: Inspectors-R-Us
365 S. Fisherman's Wharf
San Francisco, CA 89007
(819) 555-3456

Signature: ____________________________

Inspectors-R-Us

Where Can I Obtain Export Processing Forms?

Most of the forms necessary for export are available from a Government Printing Office store, business supply stores and mail order services or a freight forwarder. Most of the forms are regulated by the U.S. Department of Commerce. If you are having difficulty locating forms, call the U.S. Department of Commerce's Trade Information Center at (800) USA-TRADE to obtain copies of necessary forms. Or contact the National Council on International Trade Documentation (NCITD) at (212) 925-1400 for several low-cost publications that contain information on specific documentation commonly used in international trade. NCITD provides a free listing of its publications.

Because of the vast amount of documentation that can be required, it is best to enlist the expertise of a freight forwarder whose job is to know documentation required with exporting. The necessary documentation varies from order to order and country to country. All documents must be fully completed with information precisely the same on each. Slight discrepancies may prevent the merchandise from being exported, precipitate its being seized by the United States or a foreign government, and delay payment. Collection documents are subject to a time limit and may not be honored if out of date. With so much at stake, an export manager can see why it is best to consult a freight forwarder to help insure accuracy. After gaining some export experience, management may be able to do it by themselves, but they should learn from a freight forwarder or a trade specialist until comfortable doing it solo.

Filing a Shipper's Export Declaration (SED) is easier and less costly than ever before due to the Census Bureau and U.S. Customs Service's Automated Export System which automates the export process. Small exporters will benefit from substantially reducing processing costs by filing the SED electronically and eliminating the handling of paper. For more information call (202) 927-0280; fax at (202) 927-3555; or visit the Internet site at www.customs.ustreas.gov/AES.

The following firms offer software for comprehensive management of export documentation, transportation, and other processes:

	Phone	Web Site or E-mail address
Integrated Trade Systems	630-261-9740	www.tradesolutions.com
Shipping Solutions - $250	888-890-SHIP	www.shipsolutions.com
Automated Logistics Suite	888-564-6246	info@joinagm.com
International Software Marketing	800-773-9476	www.ismworld.com
Quick Assistant - $895	203-396-0022	www.exitsinc.com
Unz and Co. Export Software - $529	800-631-3098	www.unzexport.com
FedEx Document Prep - free	800-781-3076	www.fedex.com
DHL Worldwide Express Guide - free	800-225-5345	

RESOURCES

Export/Import Procedures and Documentation ($75), ISBN 0-8144-0035-0, American Management Association, P.O. Box 169, Saranack Lake, NY 12983, (518) 891-5510 (p); cust_ser@amanet.org (e); http://www.amanet.org (w)

International Trade Forms: Shipper's Export Declaration; Canada Customs Invoice; and NAFTA Certificate of Origin (each $60 for 500) International Trade Institute, 5055 North Main St., Dayton, Ohio 45415 (800) 543-2453 (p); (937) 276-5920 (f)

New Standard Export Forms ($29.95) ICC Publishing, 156 Fifth Avenue, Suite 305, New York, NY 10010 (212) 206-1150 (p); iccpub@interport.net (e)

Are Special Certificates Required to Export Agricultural Goods?

The federal government offers highly specialized information and services for businesses dealing in agricultural products through the U.S. Department of Agriculture Foreign Agricultural Service (FAS). The FAS is a full-service agency offering the exporter everything from marketing assistance and information to technical assistance to export programs. The *AgExport Action Kit* provides detailed information on all services available and the appropriate contacts. For your free kit contact: AgExport Connection, U.S. Department of Agriculture-FAS, Washington, DC 20250-1000; (202) 720-7103; (202) 690-4374 (f).

Licensing/Inspections: Most agricultural exports fall under the general export license granted by the U.S. Government , however, some foreign countries require a special import license. These countries require U.S. products be certified to certain standards. An inspection of the goods at the point of embarkation will usually suffice. The Agricultural Market Service will certify products for a fee. Contact the USDA Room: 3510, South Building, Washington, DC 20250-1000; (202) 720-8998. Information on foreign requirements of livestock fruits and vegetables can be obtained from the Animal and Plant Health Inspection Service (APHIS), Department of Agriculture, National Center for Import-Export, 4700 River Road Unit 40, Riverdale, MD 20737-1231; (301) 734-8537. Grain Inspections are provided by the Federal Grain Inspection Service, USDA, Room 1095, South Building, Washington, DC 20250-0226; (202) 720-0226. Meat and Poultry inspections are provided by the Food Safety and Inspection Service, USDA, Room 341-E, Administrative Building, Washington D.C. 20250-1000; (202) 720-3473.

Shipping: Shipping livestock and fresh produce requires special attention. Freight forwarders are a good source of information to help ensure your products arrive safely and in a timely fashion. Livestock may be shipped by air or by sea. Air is more expensive and you must ship in smaller quantities but it is also faster (usually within 24 hours) so food and water stores are usually not required to be shipped along with the animals. The faster transport also places less stress on the animals. Perishable food items that are being shipped via air or water require careful packaging to prevent spoilage. The USDA Information Desk provides many informative handbooks addressing shipping concerns.

Marketing: AgExport Services also provides Foreign Buyer Lists and U.S. Supplier Lists to help match prospective buyers and sellers. Both of these services charge $15 per list, and lists are available by country or by commodity. They also maintain U.S. pavilions at foreign trade shows and initiate special trade missions.

For help tracking down any USDA-FAS services, call the USDA locator: (202) 720-USDA.

Books from the Information Division Include: "Transportation Tips" on livestock; "Protecting Perishable Foods During Transport by Truck" (AH669); "Export Handbook for U.S. Agricultural Products" (AH593); "Tropical Products Transportation Handbook" (AH668); "Dictionary on International Agricultural Trade" covers terms one may encounter in exporting and descriptions of domestic and foreign programs. The Information Division may be reached at U.S. Department of Agriculture, Information Division, Room 5920, S. Bldg., Washington, DC 20250-1000; (202) 720-7937.

RESOURCES

AgExporter ($51/year) ISSN SUB 9737 5285 Port Royal Road, Springfield, VA 22161 (703) 487-4630 (p)

Buyer Alert Advertising for Exporters ($15 per announcement) AgExport Services Connections Division, AgBox 1052, USDA/FAS/AGX, Washington, D.C. 20250-1052 (202) 690-3416 (p); (202) 690-4374 (f)

Foreign Agricultural Circular U.S. Department of Agriculture, 12th Street and Jefferson Drive, SW, Washington, DC 20250 (202) 447-7937 (p)

Foreign Agricultural Service Country Reports (free) U.S. Department of Agriculture-Information Division, Reports Office, 14th and Independence Avenue, S.W., Room 6072-S, Washington, DC 20250-1000 (202) 720-6343 (p); (202) 690-0193 (f)

Foreign Buyer List ($15 for each) AgExport Services Connections Division, AgBox 1052, USDA/FAS/AGX, Washington, D.C. 20250-1052 (202) 690-3416 (p); (202) 690-4374 (f)

What Is an ATA Carnet?

An ATA carnet (pronounced *car-nay*) is an international customs document or a "merchandise passport" issued by a member country in the ATA (Admission Temporoire) Carnet System. The carnet permits the holder to carry or send merchandise for one year into other member countries for display or demonstration without paying duties, posting bonds, or submitting the normal customs documents.

The advantages of using an ATA Carnet include a reduced cost to the exporter, by eliminating value-added taxes and other fees at the time of importation; simplified Customs procedures, by allowing a single document to be used for all customs transactions; and the facilitation of reentry into the United States, by eliminating the need to register the goods with Customs at the time of departure.

Virtually all personal, durable and professional goods are covered by an ATA Carnet. The Carnet does not cover consumable goods, such as food, disposable goods, or postal traffic. The ATA Carnet is valid in approximately 50 countries throughout Europe, North America, Asia, and Africa. New countries are added to the system periodically.

The U.S. Treasury Department established the U.S. Council for International Business in 1968 to manage the ATA Carnet system in the United States. Typically, the Council issues over 11,000 Carnets a year covering goods valued at over one billion dollars. Call the U.S. Council for International Business at (212) 354-4480 to check whether the country to which you are traveling is covered, call the Carnet Application Hotline at (800) 5-DUTYFREE, or visit its web site at http://www/uscib.org. Or, contact the National Carnet Service Center, 118 Barrington Commons Court, Suite 236; Barrington, IL 60010; (847) 381-1558 (p); (847) 381-3857 (f); information@atacarnet.com (e); http://www.atacarnet.com (w) for questions regarding temporary importation of goods.

The cost of an ATA Carnet varies. The processing fee is determined by the value of the shipment.

Shipment Value	**Basic Processing Fee**
Under $5,000	$120
$5,000-14,999	$150
$15,000-49,999	$175
$50,000-199,999	$200
$200,000-499,999	$225
$500,000 and over	$250

RESOURCE

Carnet: Move Goods Duty Free Through Customs (free) U.S. Council for International Business, 1212 Avenue of the Americas, New York, NY 10036 (212) 354-4480 (p) or (800) 5-DUTY FREE (p); (212) 944-0012 (f); atacarnet@uscib.org (e); http://uscib.org

How Should I Package My Products?

When packaging a product for export there are four major factors to keep in mind: breakage, weight, moisture and pilferage. How a product should be packaged also depends upon the destination and the method of transportation. Typical types of packages include cartons or fiberboard boxes, plastic or fiberboard containers, drums and tubing, or styrofoam.

Aside from the normal handling encountered in domestic transit, the exporter must consider the stress on the package due to repeated loading and unloading. Goods can be stacked, shoved, processed on a conveyer belt, sent down a chute, pushed, dragged or dropped. Many foreign ports may have less sophisticated equipment than in the United States. Cargo can be unloaded and stored in the rain.

If a buyer does not give any packaging specifications, be sure to remember to pack in strong containers that are adequately sealed and filled, ensure the weight is evenly distributed within the container, pack goods on pallets if possible to ensure greater ease in handling, and ensure that packages and filler are made of moisture-resistant material.

To avoid pilferage in foreign ports, it is best to use plain boxes devoid of logos and name brands. Such blatant "advertising" of the goods inside the package will be a dead giveaway to thieves and make the package more susceptible to tampering. A determined thief can penetrate any type of packaging, even metal.

Normally, air shipments require lighter packaging than ocean shipments. For both ocean and air shipments, freight forwarders and carriers can provide the best information on packaging.

Also note that because transportation costs are determined by volume and weight, special reinforced and lightweight packing materials have been devised for exporting. Careful packing of goods to minimize volume and weight, while giving strength, may well save money as well as ensuring that goods are properly packed.

RESOURCE

Export Packing List: A Guide ($6) National Council on International Trade and Documentation, 350 Broadway Suite 205, New York, NY 10013 (212) 925-1400 (p)

What Kind of Labeling Is Required to Ship Overseas and In What Language Should I Prepare the Labels?

Labeling is used on export shipping containers to meet shipping regulations, ensure proper handling, conceal the identity of the contents, and help receivers identify shipments. It should not be used for advertising purposes.

The overseas buyer specifies export marks that must appear on the cargo for easy identification. Markings needed for the actual shipment include:

- Shipper's mark
- Country of origin
- Weight marking
- Number of packages and size of cases
- International handling marks
- Cautionary markings
- Port of entry
- Labels for hazardous materials

To prevent misunderstandings and shipping delays, legibility is extremely important. Letters and symbols are generally stenciled on the package in water-proof black ink on three sides of the carton. To avoid any confusion, remove old markings.

Exporters may find that customs regulations regarding labeling are strictly enforced. Most freight forwarders and export packing specialists can provide the necessary information regarding specific regulations.

Unless otherwise instructed by the buyer, label the goods in English. However, the U.S. manufacturer may wish to put cautionary markings in both English and the language of the port of destination. There are many internationally recognized symbols that may be used. Any freight forwarder should be able to provide or instruct you on the appropriate symbols for your shipments. An example of a correctly labeled package is found below:

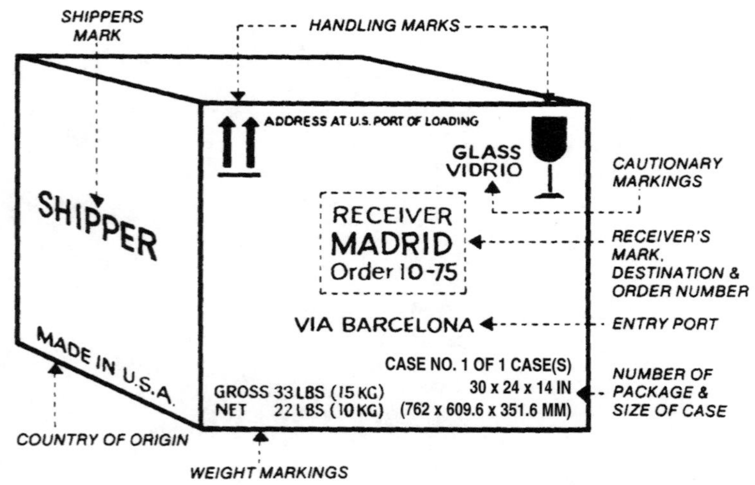

LARGE PACKAGES SHOULD HAVE MARKINGS ON TWO SIDES

What Should I Know About the Metric System?

Metrication can be considered a new business "language." Learning this "language" as quickly as possible and making the proper adjustments within the company now will provide a competitive advantage over firms who do not use metric as yet. Certainly, using metrics will allow you easier market access. Being the first to convert to the metric system allows quick cost recovery. Every country except the United States (and two small countries) officially uses the metric system. Metrication is not a complicated process, but it will take careful planning to make it most cost effective and as efficient as possible.

The National Institute of Standards and Technology (NIST) offers an excellent metric program which provides information on foreign metric import regulations and on matters relating to the U.S. transition to the metric system. It provides referrals to metric coordinators in other federal agencies, metric related organizations, and state metric contacts. For information on metric standards, assistance with metric transition, and to order a free metric kit, call (301) 975-3690 for more information .

ENGLISH TO METRIC

To Convert:	Into	Multiply By:
Acres	Hectares	0.4047
Bushels	Cubic Meters	0.03524
Cubic Feet	Cubic Meters	0.02832
Cubic Inches	Cubic Centimeters	16.39
Feet	Meters	0.3048
Inches	Centimeters	2.54
Inches	Millimeters	25.4
Yards	Meters	0.9144
Miles	Kilometers	1.609
Gallons	Liters	3.785
Ounces	Grams	28.3495
Ounces (fluid)	Liters	0.02957
Pints	Liters	0.4732
Pounds	Kilograms	0.4536
Square Feet	Square Meters	0.0929
Square Inches	Square Centimeters	6.452
Square Miles	Square Kilometers	2.950
Square Yards	Square Meters	0.8361
Tons	Tons (metric)	0.9078

METRIC TO ENGLISH

To Convert:	Into	Multiply By:
Centiliters	Ounces (fluid)	0.3382
Liters	Pints	2.113
Liters	Gallons	0.2642
Grams	Ounces	0.03527
Kilograms	Pounds	2.205
Centimeters	Inches	0.3937
Kilometers	Miles	0.6214
Meters	Feet	3.281
Meters	Yards	1.094
Millimeters	Inches	0.03937
Cubic Centimeters	Cubic Inches	0.06102
Cubic Meters	Bushels	28.37
Cubic Meters	Cubic Feet	35.31
Hectares	Acres	2.471
Square Centimeters	Square Inches	0.155
Square Kilometers	Square Miles	0.3861
Square Meters	Square Feet	10.76
Square Meters	Square Yards	1.196
Tons (metric)	Tons	1.10156

TEMPERATURE

To convert:

Centigrade to Fahrenheit, multiply by 9/5 and add 32
Fahrenheit to Centigrade, subtract 32 and multiply by 5/9

How Has NAFTA Affected the U.S. Economy?

The North American Free Trade Agreement went into effect on January 1, 1994, despite much political debate over the predicted positive and negative effects. Three years later, conventional wisdom is that NAFTA resulted in neither a significant net loss nor net gain of jobs overall. In terms of trade, NAFTA is an important vehicle which will foster increased trade between the nations. Within ten years, all tariffs will be eliminated on North American industrial products traded between the U.S., Canada, and Mexico. Within fifteen years, many tariffs on agricultural goods will be phased out. As well, non-tariff barriers, which include import licenses, quotas, Mexican local content, and production rules will be eliminated. Under NAFTA, the U.S. will be afforded the same access to the Mexican market that it has allowed Mexico to possess in the U.S. market, and the U.S. will also possess a competitive advantage in the Mexican market because tariffs will still be levied upon European and Asian goods exported to Mexico.

Included in the October, 1997 *Clearinghouse on State International Policies,* Carol Conway reported findings from the "Study on the Operation and Effects of the North American Free Trade Agreement" from the Office of the President which included:

- Growth in U.S. Export Volumes. The peso crisis hit December 20, 1994, a few days shy of NAFTA's first anniversary. U.S. exports to Mexico, especially consumer products, plummeted in 1995. Conditions improved considerably in 1996. As a result, U.S. exports to Mexico actually registered an increase of 36.5 percent between 1993 and 1996.
- U.S. Income Growth. A recent study estimated that NAFTA alone boosted U.S. exports to Mexico by $12 billion in 1996, compared to a smaller real increase in Mexican imports of $5 billion. If accurate, the NAFTA-induced exports would have contributed $13 billion to U.S. income.
- An Increase In Jobs Supported By Exports. U.S. exports to Canada and Mexico supported an estimated 2.3 million jobs in 1996, an increase of 311,000 jobs over 1993. Of the increase, 189,000 jobs were attributed to sales to Canada, and the other 122,000 to sales to Mexico.
- Mexican Tariff Concessions. Before NAFTA was signed, Mexico's tariffs on imports were significantly higher than those imposed by the U.S. As a result of NAFTA, Mexico's average applied tariffs on U.S. goods have fallen from 10 percent to 2.9 percent. U.S. import tariffs have fallen from 2.1 to 0.6 percent.
- U.S. Suppliers Dominate Many of Mexico's Import Markets. Before NAFTA, the U.S. supplied an average of 69.3 percent of Mexico's imports. Today, 75.5 percent of Mexican imports come from the U.S.

The Office of NAFTA and Inter-American Affairs helps U.S. exporters take advantage of U.S. trade opportunities in Canadian and Mexican markets within the framework of the NAFTA. The office analyzes Western Hemisphere trade trends, regional agreements, negotiations, and priorities for the Free Trade of the Americas (FTAA). Trade specialists provide business counseling, regulations, investment opportunities, Customs and rules of origin issues, and product standards. Visit its web site at http://www.itaiep.doc.gov.

For more information on NAFTA, call the NAFTA Flash Fax Hotline at (202) 482-4464. Order document #0101 for a complete menu. This document will arrive within minutes on your fax machine.

RESOURCES

NAFTA: Clinton Administration Statement ($1.25) U.S. Superintendent of Documents, P.O. Box 371954, Pittsburgh, PA 15250-7954 (202) 512-1800 (p); (202) 512-2250 (f); gpoaccess@gpo.gov (e)

NAFTA: Documentation and Procedures ($88.00) International Trade Institute, 5055 North Main St., Dayton, Ohio 45415 (800) 543-2453 (p); (937) 276-5920 (f)

NAFTA: Full Text (Volumes I and II) ($40) S/N 041-001-00407-6 U.S. Superintendent of Documents, P.O. Box 371954, Pittsburgh, PA 15250-7954 (202) 512-1800 (p); (202) 512-2250 (f); gpoaccess@gpo.gov (e)

NAFTA: Guide to Customs Procedures (free) U.S. Custom's Service, P.O. 7407, Washington, DC 20044 (202) 927-6724 (p), http://www.customs.ustreas.gov (w)

NAFTA: Visiting the Accord ($15.95) James Doyle, Inc., International Trade Research Center, 574 McBride Point Drive, St. Louis, MO 63011 (314) 458-0727 (p); (314) 532-5750 (f)

What Is the North American Industrial Classification System?

A new classification system for NAFTA countries came into play in 1997. The Standard Industrial Classification (SIC codes) has been replaced with the North American Industrial Classification System (NAICS, pronounced "knacks") which essentially harmonizes the three countries' classification systems.

Whereas the worldwide Harmonized System classifies transportable goods and commodities through a series of common numbers, the NAICS classifies industries, not particular products. It is important that exporters understand the concept of NAICS because U.S. exporters can now conduct market research on industries in the United States, Mexico, and Canada.

A practical application for exporters is the ease with which they can now develop mailing lists for these countries. To obtain a current NAICS code which replaces the old SIC code, either obtain a copy of the April 9, 1997 *Federal Register*, go to the U.S. Census Bureau's web site at http://www.census.gov (go to Subjects A-Z and then click on "N"), or call (301)-457-2672.

RESOURCES

NAFTA: Guide To U.S. Implications for U.S. Business ($15.95) International Division Publications, U.S. Chamber of Commerce, 1615 H Street, N.W. Washington, DC 20062-2000 (202) 463-5460 (p); (202) 463-3114 (f)

NAFTA: Industry Sector Reports ($24) U.S. Superintendent of Documents, P.O. Box 371954, Pittsburgh, PA 15250-7954 (202) 512-1800 (p); (202) 512-2250 (f); gpoaccess@gpo.gov (e)

NAFTA: An Overview ($40) U.S. Superintendent of Documents, P.O. Box 371954, Pittsburgh, PA 15250-7954 (202) 512-1800 (p); (202) 512-2250 (f); gpoaccess@gpo.gov (e)

NAFTA: Supplemental Agreements ($6.50) S/N 041-001-00411-4 U.S. Superintendent of Documents, P.O. Box 371954, Pittsburgh, PA 15250-7954 (202) 512-1800 (p); (202) 512-2250 (f); gpoaccess@gpo.gov (e)

What Is the World Trade Organization, Formerly Known As GATT?

The World Trade Organization (WTO) oversees major tariff reductions, of approximately 38% on manufactured goods in 177 countries, that were negotiated during the final (Uruguay) round of the General Agreement on Tariffs and Trade (GATT).

This worldwide trade agreement will:

- reduce barriers to global commerce and expand U.S. trade, through the total elimination of foreign tariffs as of 2004, on goods produced in hundreds of major markets in the pharmaceutical, medical equipment, construction equipment, agricultural equipment, steel, beer, distilled spirits, paper/pulp and printed matter, and toys industries
- create deep cuts in other foreign tariffs affecting most U.S. exports, averaging a 1/3 cut across the board
- simplify and harmonize customs procedures, which yields a reduction in paperwork costs
- foster stronger intellectual property protection
- open foreign markets for U.S. services
- create more open market access to rapidly-growing and developing nations
- enforce full recognition of U.S. health and environmental standards

In sum, the Uruguay Round tightened controls on tariffs and non-tariff barriers and extended those on subsidies and regional group preferences. It established a framework for regulating services trade, which includes rules on capital and labor movement. It added protection of intellectual property through regulation of copyright and patent law. Finally, it greatly strengthened and refined the system for monitoring and enforcement through the new powers assigned to the WTO, the formalized successor organization to GATT.

The ability of industries and business enterprises to benefit fully from the rule-based system of the Uruguay Round depends on their knowledge and understanding of the detailed rules. Detailed rules give industries and business enterprises certain right vis-a-vis their own governments. Exporting industries also have, in certain cases, the right to defend their interests in export markets against the imposition of measures affecting their trade.

New Uruguay Round policy is to review anti-dumping actions. Dispute settlements all depend on countries' use of them. Unlike other international organizations, the WTO has no authority to take action itself against violations of the rules. It is the damaged party who must bring a complaint to Council and, where permitted, take retaliatory action to enforce a judgment. Limited forms of collective complaint and action will now be permitted. Dispute settlement reform is now undertaken by a framework of automatic procedures. Under the new rules, time limits are laid down for each stage, giving a maximum time from complaint to Council adoption of about a year. Adoption is automatic, unless voted down by the Council.

As a tool for understanding rules and regulations under the new Uruguay Round, the International Trade Centre of UNCTAD/WTO and the Commonwealth Secretariat have jointly issued a new publication, *Business Guide to the Uruguay Round* which explains in clear, nonlegal terms the results of the Round. Call the International Trade Centre in Geneva, Switzerland at 011-22-730-02-51 to order.

RESOURCES

NAFTA: Tariff Schedules of Canada, Mexico & U.S. (($33) S/N 041-001-00409-2, ($38) S/N 041-001-00410-6, ($37) S/N 041-001-00408-4 respectively) U.S. Superintendent of Documents, P.O. Box 371954, Pittsburgh, PA 15250-7954 (202) 512-1800 (p); (202) 512-2250 (f); gpoaccess@gpo.gov (e)

North American Trade Guide ($329) Global Trade Publishing Group, 401 North Broad Street, Philadelphia, PA 19108 (800) 777-8074 (p); (215) 238-5412 (f)

EIU Guide to the New GATT ($225) ISBN: 0 85058 800 6 The Economist Intelligence Unit, 111 West 57th Street, New York, NY 10019 (212) 554-0600 (p); (212) 586-1181 (f)

What Does the Uruguay Round Mean for My Product?

The improved rule-based system developed by the Uruguay Round is expected to promote an orderly development of international trade among the 183 signatory nations by ensuring that enterprises can trade with countries on a fair and equitable basis. The intent is to foster a freer trade environment which is not interrupted by sudden or arbitrary imposition of trade restrictions. Rules covering agricultural products and textiles will help ensure that the use of quantitative restrictions are followed in practice by all countries. The Uruguay Round has also resulted in binding the tariff rates by all countries which allows enterprises to make decisions based on firm rules. Following is a summary of implications of the Round as they relate to specific sectors.

Manufactured Products. Under GATT and WTO rules for trade in manufactured products, tariffs on imports discriminate by sector, not by country. Current tariffs levels are bound and registered with GATT/WTO. Tariffs can be lowered, but not raised except through further negotiation or compensation. According to the Overseas Development Institute in London, the Uruguay Round saw an average fall for industrial country Most Favored Nation tariffs on goods exported by developing countries of 2.4 points, from 6.3% to 3.9%. Given existing Generalized System of Preferences advantages, however, actual tariff reductions were negligible. Tariff reductions for least developed countries, were smallest because many of their exports are already exempt from tariffs.

Textiles and Clothing. Negotiations regarding tariff rates on textiles and clothing were removed from GATT in 1962, and instead were subject to a series of quota systems under the Multi-Fiber Arrangement (MFA) through which tariffs remained high. The study by the Overseas Development Institute in London found that MFA quotas were imposed by individual importers on individual exports and products, at a very detailed level, with provisions to add new countries and products as they reached significant shares or trade growth rates. As each new country became successful, it attracted quotas. The effect was to disperse trade from the original successful exporters (principally the large countries of Asia) to a series of other suppliers with cheap labor, until they also had quotas. Under the Uruguay Round, the MFA will be phased out by 2006 by increasing and eliminating all quotas, in four stages. For textiles and clothing, tariffs will remain at about 12%.

Agriculture. The principal reform in agriculture is the substitution of tariffs for a system of quotas, controls, and variable tariffs which will be reduced to a level on average 36% below 1986-88 levels. The settlement also requires reductions in domestic and export subsidies and in the quantity of subsidized exports. These changes mainly affect developed countries, but middle-level developing countries must reduce subsidies by 24%; the least developed are exempt.

Services. Developing countries are expected to benefit from the Uruguay Round as it relates to the service industry as a result of low labor costs, more modern structures in sectors such as air, shipping, construction, computing, and communications. It appears that the sectors which have "opened up" the most include tourism, business, and finance, with distribution and education the least "open." An analysis of the Uruguay Round, as it relates to services, shows greater freedom in foreign investment, little freedom for professional workers to migrate to provide services, and little or no opening for unskilled labor. Overall, the establishment of the principle that services are subject to international regulation and the new availability of information on the national systems of control represent a significant gain for all countries. The agreement also explicitly requires in several services a reopening or continuation of negotiations.

RESOURCES

Import Quotas (free) U.S. Custom's Service, P.O. 7407, Washington, DC 20044 (202) 927-6724 (p); http://www.customs.ustreas.gov (w)

Uruguay Round of Multilateral Trade Negotiations, General Agreement on Tariffs and Trade ($40) U.S. Superintendent of Documents, P.O. Box 371954, Pittsburgh, PA 15250-7954 (202) 512-1800 (p); (202) 512-2250 (f); gpoaccess@gpo.gov (e)

How Do I Import?

Any merchandise entering the United States must be cleared through the United States Customs Service which has offices located at ports of entry throughout the United States. Clearance through U.S. Customs typically involves entry, inspection, appraisal, classification, or liquidation of the goods. Principle forms of entry include formal, informal, temporary, in-transit, special duty-free, or warehouse. This answer explains the formal entry process.

Entry. Entry of goods must be made by the owner or purchaser of the goods or by a licensed customshouse broker. Right to entry requires the filing of several documents to determine whether the goods can be released from customs custody and the applicable duty to be levied, if any. These documents include:

- Entry Manifest (Customs Form 7533) or Special Entry Permit (Customs Form 3461)
- Evidence of right to make entry: bill of lading/airway bill/carriers certificate to prove ownership
- Commercial invoice/proforma obtained from the seller to show value and describe the items
- Packing list if applicable
- Evidence of surety bond to cover any potential duties, etc.

Entry documents must be presented to the U.S. Customs officer at the U.S. port of entry within five days of arrival of goods within a customs territory (excluding foreign trade zones). If the documents are not filed within five days of arrival, the goods may be placed in a warehouse with storage costs to be incurred by the importer. Importers of perishable items may apply for immediate delivery using the Special Entry Permit Form 3461.

Inspection. Inspection is an encompassing step involving appraisal and classification. During inspection, goods must be valued for duty status, checked for proper country of origin markings, for the shipment of prohibited items, and counted in total. U.S. Customs officials also check the invoice for accuracy. The customs invoice is perhaps the most important document, and should be in English. An invoice should be included with each shipment.

Appraisal. The objective of the appraisal is to determine the value of the goods in order to levy tariffs or duties. Two primary methods of appraisal include utilizing the actual transaction price or utilizing a known formula that is used to calculate daily commodity market prices.

Duties. Customs duties are categorized as *ad valorem,* which can be a percentage of the customs value of the merchandise; a specific rate, a rate based on weight or quantity; or a compound rate, which is a combination of *ad valorem* and a special rate. Duty charges may also vary according to the country of origin. Reduced rates apply to those countries with which the United States has signed trade agreements.

Classification. All goods are classified via the Harmonized System. The initial classification should be designated by the importer. Tariff and classification changes also occur without warning, especially with the influx of new trade agreements. To avoid a costly mistake based on ignorance of these changes, consult a licensed customshouse broker.

Liquidation. U.S. Customs makes the final decision on whether or not to accept the goods and what duties are to be imposed. At this point the entry process is normally completed and the notice of entry is posted electronically via the Customs Automated Commercial System (ACS).

RESOURCES

Customs Bonded Warehouses (free) U.S. Custom's Service, P.O. 7407, Washington, DC 20044, (202) 927-6724, http://www.customs.ustreas.gov

Customs Bulletin and Decisions ($128/52 issues) U.S. Superintendent of Documents, P.O. Box 371954, Pittsburgh, PA 15250-7954 (202) 512-1800 (p); (202) 512-2250 (f); gpoaccess@gpo.gov (e)

Import Procedures ($69.50) International Trade Institute, 5055 North Main St., Dayton, Ohio 45415 (800) 543-2453; (937) 276-5920 (f)

Do I Need a License To Import Goods?

The U.S. Customs Service does not require import licenses for goods brought into the United States. It is important to realize that other agencies may require a license or form of certification for importing certain regulated commodities. Some of these items and their approval agency include:

IMPORT	REGULATING AGENCY	TELEPHONE
Agricultural commodities	Food and Drug Administration	(800) 532-4400
Consumer goods	Department of Energy	(202) 955-5060
Currency	Department of Justice	(202) 514-2000
Food, drugs, and beverages	Dept. of Health & Human Services	(202) 619-0257
Toxic and hazardous substances	Environmental Protection Agency	(202) 260-2090
Textiles	Federal Trade Commission	(202) 326-2222
Wildlife	Department of the Interior	(202) 208-3100

Look in your local federal blue pages of your telephone book for federal agencies which may regulate the import of other types of goods.

How Do I Find Information Regarding Quotas Placed on Imported Goods?

The U.S. Customs Service has responsibility for enforcing import quotas on goods entering the United States. It has a staff available to answer questions on quotas for the countries that are subject to them (China, India, Indonesia, Japan, Korea, Macau, Malaysia, Pakistan, Philippines, Romania, Singapore, Sri Lanka, Taiwan, Thailand, and Turkey). You can reach them at (202) 927-5396, http://www.customs.ustreas.gov

What Are the Key Contacts for Importing Goods?

U.S. Customs Service Contact Information	(202) 927-6724
To Obtain a Harmonized System Number to Assess Duty	(202) 466-5618
To Pay Duty on Products Mailed into the United States	(202) 927-0540
To Register Imported Goods	(202) 927-0540
To Obtain Proper Import Forms	(202) 622-2111
To Obtain Documentation for Foreigners to Travel to the U.S.	(202) 514-4316
To Obtain An Advanced Ruling on Duty Rates of Imported Goods	(202) 927-2244
For Information on Intellectual Property Rights Protection	(202) 927-2330
For Information on the Automated Broker Interface System	(202) 927-1210
For Information on U.S. Import Quotas	(202) 927-5850
To File a Complaint with the U.S. Customs Service	(202) 927-2931
To Obtain Duty Rates On Imported Goods	(212) 466-5618
U.S. Customs Service Trade Ombudsman	(202) 927-1440
Import/Export Statistics	(301) 457-2800 x2242

RESOURCES

Global Trade Talk ($11) U.S. Superintendent of Documents, P.O. Box 371954, Pittsburgh, PA 15250-7954 (202) 512-1800 (p); (202) 512-2250 (f); gpoaccess@gpo.gov (e)

Importer's Manual USA ($87) World Trade Press; 1505 Fifth Avenue; San Rafael, CA 04901 (415) 454-9934 (p); (415) 453-7980 (f); worldpress@aol.com (e)

U.S. Import Requirements (free) U.S. Custom's Service, P.O. 7407, Washington, DC 20044, (202) 927-6724 (p); http://www.customs.ustreas.gov (w)

What Is a Customshouse Broker?

A customshouse broker is a licensed, private sector service provider who coordinates the activities of all parties involved in the import transaction. Customshouse brokers are to importing what freight forwarders are to exporting. These individuals are licensed by the U.S. Department of Treasury and follow instruction under the U.S. Customs Bureau. Their mission is to facilitate imports while protecting U.S. tax revenues. All client relationships are confidential, but because brokers must keep detailed entry and accounting records and act on behalf of the importer, a power of attorney must be signed.

Customshouse services tend to be highly competitive. Therefore it is best to gather several quotes before selecting your broker. Always look for an ABI broker, which indicates that the broker is using the Automated Broker Interface (ABI) with the U.S. Customs Service Automated Commercial System (ACS) to transact business. Use of the Customs computer system facilitates transactions and allows brokers to check the status of a client's shipment awaiting Customs clearance.

Using a customshouse broker can be beneficial for several reasons. Customshouse brokers usually receive a discounted shipping rate. Brokers have access to the ACS system to facilitate customs clearance. A broker is an import expert and can save you from making costly errors. Customshouse brokers may also use their bond to cover goods which saves the hassle of personally obtaining a bond. Most importers find it easier to pay the nominal customshouse broker fee than attempting to import on their own. Your local yellow pages will have a listing of the customshouse brokers.

RESOURCES

Global Trade ($45/year) North American Publishing, 401 North Broad Street, Philadelphia, PA 19108 (215) 238-5300 (p); (215) 238- 5457 (f)

U.S. Custom House Guide ($399) North American Publishing Company, 401 North Broad Street, Philadelphia, PA 19108 (800) 777-8074 (p); (215) 238-5412 (f)

Besides Formal Entry, Are There Any Other Ways to Import Goods?

There are several legal ways to enter goods through U.S. customs. The most familiar methods include informal entry, temporary import, in-transit entry, special duty free entry, and warehouse entry.

Informal. The following items are not subject to formal Customs entry: Shipments of limited value (less than $1,250); household/personal effects entitled to duty-free entry as outlined in Chapter 98 of HS Code; household/personal effects used abroad and not intended for sale; some books and library artifacts as outlined in Chapter 98 of HS Code; theatrical scenery; travelers' samples; professional instruments; and tools (with exceptions).

Shipments of an informal nature need only have an invoice, attached to the packaging, giving an accurate description of the contents and value. This invoice form is available from the post office.

Temporary Importation Bond. Covered by a bond of double the duty, temporary goods are admitted duty-free for one year, not to exceed three years. The articles must be then exported under Customs supervision to cancel the bond. Prior to export, the exporter must advise the Customs office in writing. Customs will then designate a time and place for inspection of the export items.

In-transit Entries. In-transit entries are imports that are allowed to move from initial port of entry to another district to have the goods cleared in the new district (e.g., the geographical location of the company). Shipments are moved by bonded carrier. Use the entry on Customs form 7512 to designate intent. An example of an in-transit entry would be a Kansas City company importing from Germany asking that goods shipped to New York then be transported to Kansas City for entry processing.

Special Duty-Free Entries. Special duty-free entries are Chapter 98 allowances such as articles of U.S. origin that are repaired abroad or assembled then returned to the U.S. These items are relieved from any tax burden. To receive this benefit, a company should register the goods at the time of exportation with customs and Customs Form 4455.

Warehouse Entries. Imports designated for warehouse entry are placed in a bonded warehouse upon entering a U.S. port. No duties are paid until the goods are removed from the warehouse for entry into the marketplace. The goods are subject to the duties in existence at the time of removal from the warehouse. There are a variety of different warehouses that an importer may use, ranging from those owned by the government to those maintained by the importer per customs regulations. Customs Form 7505, Warehouse Withdrawal for Consumption, must be completed.

RESOURCES

Foreign Assembly of U.S. Components (free) U.S. Custom's Service, P.O. 7407, Washington, DC 20044, (202) 927-6724 (p), http://www.customs.ustreas.gov (w)

Importing Into United States (4.50) U.S. Government Printing Office, Superintendent of Documents, Washington, DC 20402 (202) 512-1530 (p); gpoaccess@gpo.gov (e); http://www.customs.ustreas.gov (w)

Marking of Country of Origin Brochure U.S. Customs Service, Public Information Office, Department of Treasury, P.O., Box 7407, Washington, DC 20044 (202) 927-5580 (p)

Appendix

Special Insert for International Business Educators, Consultants, and Researchers

U.S. EXPORT ASSISTANCE CENTER LOCATIONS

Birmingham, Alabama
Anchorage, Alaska
Phoenix, Arizona
Little Rock, Arkansas
Los Angeles, California
Long Beach, California
Newport Beach, California
Ontario, California
San Diego, California
San Francisco, California
Santa Clara, California
Denver, Colorado
Middletown, Connecticut
Miami, Florida
Clearwater, Florida
Orlando, Florida
Tallahassee, Florida
Atlanta, Georgia
Savannah, Georgia
Honolulu, Hawaii
Boise, Idaho
Chicago, Illinois
Highland Park, Illinois
Peoria, Illinois
Rockford, Illinois
Wheaton, Illinois
Indianapolis, Indiana
Des Moines, Iowa
Wichita, Kansas
Louisville, Kentucky
Somerset, Kentucky
New Orleans, Louisiana
Portland, Maine
Baltimore, Maryland
Gaithersburg, Maryland
Boston, Massachusetts
Marlborough, Massachusetts
Ann Arbor, Michigan
Detroit, Michigan
Minneapolis, Minnesota
Jackson, Mississippi
St. Louis, Missouri
Grand Rapids, Michigan
Pontiac, Michigan
Kansas City, Missouri
Omaha, Nebraska
Reno, Nevada
Portsmouth, New Hampshire
Trenton, New Jersey
Newark, New Jersey
Santa Fe, New Mexico
Albany, New York
Buffalo, New York
Harlem, New York
Long Island, New York
Rochester, New York
Manhattan, New York
Westchester, New York
Greensboro, North Carolina
Charlotte, North Carolina
Cincinnati, Ohio
Cleveland, Ohio
Columbus, Ohio
Toledo, Ohio
Oklahoma City, Oklahoma
Tulsa, Oklahoma
Portland, Oregon
Eugene, Oregon
Philadelphia, Pennsylvania
Harrisburg, Pennsylvania
Pittsburgh, Pennsylvania
San Juan, Puerto Rico
Providence, Rhode Island
Columbia, South Carolina
Charleston, South Carolina
Greenville, South Carolina
Sioux Falls, South Dakota
Nashville, Tennessee
Memphis, Tennessee
Knoxville, Tennessee
Dallas, Texas
Austin, Texas
Houston, Texas
San Antonio, Texas
Salt Lake, City Utah
Montpelier, Vermont
Richmond, Virginia
Seattle, Washington
Tri-Cities Washington
Charleston, West Virginia
Wheeling, West Virginia
Milwaukee, Wisconsin

SMALL BUSINESS DEVELOPMENT CENTER STATE OFFICES

ALABAMA
University of Alabama/SBDC Consortium, Medical Towers Building, 1717 11th Avenue, Suite 419, Birmingham, AL 35294, (205) 934-7260, (205) 934-7645 (F)

ALASKA
Alaska SBDC, University of Alaska Anchorage, 430 W. Seventh Avenue, Suite 110, Anchorage, AK 99501, (907) 274-7232, (907) 274-9524 (F)

ARIZONA
Arizona SBDC Network, 2411 W. 14th St, Ste 132, Tempe, AZ 85281, (602) 731-8720, (602) 731-8729 (F)

ARKANSAS
Arkansas SBDC, University of Arkansas at Little Rock, 100 South Main, Suite 401, Little Rock, AR 72201, (501) 324-9043, (501) 324-9049 (F)

CALIFORNIA
California SBDC, California Trade/Commerce Agency, 801 K St., Suite 1700, Sacramento, CA 95814, (916) 324-5068, (916) 322-5084 (F)

COLORADO
Colorado SBDC, Colorado Office of Business Development, 1625 Broadway, Suite 1710, Denver, CO 80202, (303) 892-3809, (303) 892-3848 (F)

CONNECTICUT
Connecticut SBDC, University of Connecticut, 368 Fairfield, U-41, Room 422, Storrs, CT 06269-2041, (203) 486-4135, (203) 486-1576 (F)

DELAWARE
Delaware SBDC, University of Delaware, Purnell Hall, Suite 005, Newark, DE 19716-2711, (302) 831-1555, (302) 831-1423 (F)

DISTRICT OF COLUMBIA
District of Columbia SBDC, Howard University, 2600 Sixth St., Room 128, Washington, DC 20059, (202) 806-1550, (202) 806-1777 (F)

FLORIDA
Florida SBDC, 19 W. Garden Street, Pensacola, FL 32501, (904) 444-2060, (904) 444-2070

GEORGIA
Georgia SBDC, University of Georgia, 180 East Broad St., Chicopee Complex, Athens, GA 30602-5412, (706) 542-6762, (706) 542-6776 (F)

HAWAII
Hawaii SBDC, University of Hawaii at Hilo, 200 W. Kawili Street, Hilo, HI 96720-4091, (808) 933-3515, (808) 933-3683 (F)

IDAHO
Idaho SBDC, Boise State University, 1910 University Drive, Boise, ID 83725, (208) 385-1640, (208) 385-3877 (F)

ILLINOIS
Illinois SBDC, Dept of Commerce & Community Affairs, 620 E. Adams St., 3rd Floor, Springfield, IL 62701, (217) 524-5856, (217) 785-6328 (F)

INDIANA
Indiana SBDC, Economic Development Council, One North Capitol, Suite 420, Indianapolis, IN 46204, (317) 264-6871, (317) 264-3102 (F)

IOWA
Iowa SBDC, Iowa State University, 137 Lynn Avenue, Ames, IA 50014, (515) 292-6351, (515) 292-0020 (F)

KENTUCKY
University of Kentucky SBDC, College of Business & Economics Building, 225 Business & Economics Building, Lexington, KY 40506-0034, (606) 257-7668, (606) 258-1907 (F)

LOUISIANA
Northeast Louisiana University SBDC, College of Business Administration, 700 University Ave., Adm. 2-57, Monroe, LA 71209-6435, (318) 342-5506, (318) 342-5510 (F)

MAINE
Maine SBDC, University of Southern Maine, 96 Falmouth St., Portland, ME 04103, (207) 780-4420, (207) 780-4810 (F)

MARYLAND
Maryland SBDC, Dept. of Economic & Employment Dev., 217 E. Redwood St., Ste 936, Baltimore, MD 21202, (410) 333-6995, (410) 333-4460 (F)

MASSACHUSETTS
Massachusetts SBDC, University of Massachusetts-Amherst, School of Management, Room 205, Amherst, MA 01003, (413) 545-6301, (413) 545-1273 (F)

MICHIGAN
Michigan SBDC, 2727 Second Ave., Room 197, Detroit, MI 48201, (313) 964-1798, (313) 964-3648 (F)

MISSISSIPPI
Mississippi SBDC, University of Mississippi, Old Chemistry Building, Suite 216, University, MS 38677, (601) 232-5001, (601) 232-5650 (F)

MISSOURI
Missouri SBDC, University of Missouri, 300 University Place, Columbia, MO 65211, (314) 882-0344, (314) 884-4297 (F)

MONTANA
Montana SBDC, Montana Dept. of Commerce, 1424 Ninth Avenue, Helena, MT 59620, (406) 444-4780, (406) 444-1872 (F)

NEBRASKA
Nebraska SBDC, University of Nebraska at Omaha, 60th & Dodge Sts., CBA Room 407, Omaha, NE 68182, (402) 554-2521, (402) 554-3747 (F)

NEVADA

Nevada SBDC, University of Nevada, Reno, College of Business Admin.-032, Rm. 411, Reno, NV 89557-0100, (702) 784-1717, (702) 784-4337 (F)

NEW HAMPSHIRE

New Hampshire SBDC, University of New Hampshire, 108 McConnell Hall, Durham, NH 03824, (603) 862-2200, (603) 862-4876 (F)

NEW JERSEY

New Jersey SBDC, Rutgers Univ Grad School of Mgmt., 180 University Avenue, Newark, NJ 07102, (201) 648-5950, (201) 648-1110 (F)

NEW MEXICO

New Mexico SBDC, Sante Fe Community College, P.O. Box 4187, Santa Fe, NM 87502-4187, (505) 438-1362, (505) 438-1237 (F)

NEW YORK

New York SBDC, State University of New York, SUNY Central Plaza, S-523, Albany, NY 12246, (518) 443-5398, (518) 465-4992 (F)

NORTH CAROLINA

North Carolina SBDC, University of North Carolina, 4509 Creedmoor Road, Suite 201, Raleigh, NC 27612, (919) 571-4154, (919) 571-4161 (F)

NORTH DAKOTA

North Dakota SBDC, University of North Dakota, 118 Gamble Hall, Box 7308, Grand Fork, ND 58202-7308, (701) 777-3700, (701) 777-3225 (F)

OHIO

Ohio SBDC, 77 South High Street, 28th Floor, P.O. Box 1001, Columbus, OH 43226, (614) 466-2711, (614) 466-0829 (F)

OKLAHOMA

Oklahoma SBDC, Southeastern Oklahoma State University, P.O. Box 2584, Station A, Durant, OK 74701, (405) 924-0277, (405) 924-7071

OREGON

Oregon SBDC, Lane Community College, 99 W. 10th Avenue, Suite 216, Eugene, OR 97401, (503) 726-2250, (503) 345-6006 (F)

PENNSYLVANIA

Pennsylvania SBDC, The Wharton School, University of Pennsylvania, 423 Vance Hall, 3733 Spruce Street, Philadelphia, PA 19104-6374, (215) 898-1219, (215) 573-2135 (F)

PUERTO RICO

Puerto Rico SBDC, University of Puerto Rico, P.O. Box 5253 College Station, Mayaguez, PR 00681, (809) 833-5822, (809) 832-5550 (F)

RHODE ISLAND

Rhode Island SBDC, Bryant College, 1150 Douglas Pike, Smithfield, RI 02917, (401) 232-6111, (401) 232-6416 (F)

SOUTH CAROLINA

Small Business Development Center, University of South Carolina, College of Business Administration, Columbia, SC 29201-9980, (803) 777-4907, (803) 777-4403 (F)

SOUTH DAKOTA

South Dakota SBDC, University of South Dakota, 414 E. Clark Street, Vermillion, SD 57069, (605) 677-5498, (605) 677-5272 (F)

TENNESSEE

Tennessee SBDC, Memphis State University, Building 1, South Campus, Memphis, TN 38152, (901) 678-2500, (901) 678-4072 (F)

TEXAS-DALLAS

North Texas-Dallas SBDC, Bill J. Priest Institute for Economic Dev., 1402 Corinth Street, Dallas, TX 75215, (214) 565-5835, (214) 565-5813 (F)

TEXAS-HOUSTON

University of Houston SBDC, University of Houston, 1100 Louisiana, Suite 500, Houston, TX 77002, (713) 752-8444, (713) 756-1500 (F)

TEXAS-LUBBOCK

N.W. Texas SBDC, Texas Tech University, 2579 S. Loop 289, Suite 114, Lubbock, TX 79423, (806) 745-3973, (806) 745-6207 (F)

TEXAS-SAN ANTONIO

UTSA South Texas Border SBDC, 1222 N. Main St., Ste 450, San Antonio, TX 78212, (210) 558-2450, (210) 558-2464 (F)

UTAH

Utah SBDC, University of Utah, 102 West 500 South, Suite 315, Salt Lake City, UT 84101, (801) 581-7905, (801) 581-7814 (F)

VERMONT

Vermont SBDC, Vermont Technical College, P.O. Box 422, Randolph, VT 05060, (802) 728-9101, (802) 728-3026 (F)

VIRGIN ISLANDS

UVI Small Business Development Center, University of the Virgin Islands, 8000 Nisky Center, Ste 202, Charlotte Amalie, VI 00802-5804, (809) 776-3206, (809) 775-3756 (F)

VIRGINIA

Virginia SBDC, 1021 East Cary Street, 11th Floor, Richmond, VA 23219, (804) 371-8253, (804) 371-8185 (F)

WASHINGTON

Washington SBDC, Washington State University, 245 Todd Hall, Pullman, WA 99164-4727, (509) 335-1576, (509) 335-0949 (F)

WEST VIRGINIA

West Virginia SBDC, 350 Kanawha Boulevard, East, Charleston, WV 25301, (304) 558-2960, (304) 558-0127 (F)

WISCONSIN

Wisconsin SBDC, University of Wisconsin, 432 North Lake St., Room 423, Madison, WI 53706, (608) 263-7794, (608) 262-3878 (F)

U.S. SMALL BUSINESS ADMINISTRATION DISTRICT OFFICES

ALABAMA
2121 Eighth Avenue North Ste 200, Birmingham, AL 35203-2398, (205) 731-1338, (205) 731-1404 (F)

ALASKA
222 West Eighth Avenue Ste 67, Anchorage, AK 99513-7559, (907) 271-4838, (907) 271-4545 (F)

ARIZONA
2828 North Central Avenue Ste 800, Phoenix, AZ 85004-1025, (602) 640-2315, (602) 640-2360 (F)

ARKANSAS
2120 Riverfront Drive Ste. 100, Little Rock, AR 72202, (501) 324-5278, (501) 324-5199 (F)

CALIFORNIA
REGION IX OFFICE, 71 Stevenson St., San Francisco, CA 94105-2939, (415) 744-6432, (415) 744-6435 (F)

COLORADO
999 18th Street Suite 701, Denver, CO 80202, (303) 294-7072, (303) 294-7153 (F)

CONNECTICUT
330 Main Street Second Floor, Hartford, CT 06106, (203) 240-4700, (203) 240-4659 (F)

DELAWARE
920 North King Street Ste. 412, Wilmington, DE 19801, (302) 573-6295, (302) 573-6060 (F)

DISTRICT OF COLUMBIA
1110 Vermont Avenue N.W., Ste. 900, P.O. Box 34500, Washington, DC 20005, (202) 606-4000, (202) 606-4225 (F)

FLORIDA
501 East Polk Street Ste 104, Tampa, FL 33602-3945, (813) 228-2594, (813) 228-2111 (F)

GEORGIA
1375 Peachtree Street N.E., Fifth Flr., Atlanta, GA 30367-8102, (404) 347-2797, (404) 347-2355 (F)

GUAM
U.S. Small Business Administration, 238 Archbishop F.C Flores Street, Room 508, Agana, GU 96910, (671) 472-7277, (671) 550-7365 (F)

HAWAII
300 Ala Moana Blvd. Room 2213, P.O. Box 50207, Honolulu, HI 96850, (808) 541-2973, (808) 541-2976 (F)

IDAHO
1020 Main Street Suite 290, Boise, ID 83702, (208) 334-1782, (208) 334-9353 (F)

ILLINOIS
300 South Riverside Plaza, Ste. 1975, Chicago, IL 60606-6617, (312) 353-5000, (312) 353-3426 (F)

INDIANA
429 North Pennsylvania Street, Room 100, Indianapolis, IN 46204-1873, (317) 226-7269, (317) 226-7259 (F)

IOWA
210 Walnut Street, Ste. 749, Des Moines, IA 50309, (515) 284-4026, (515) 284-4572 (F)

KANSAS
100 East English Street Ste. 510, Wichita, KS 67202, (316) 269-6273, (316) 269-6499 (F)

KENTUCKY
600 Martin Luther King Jr. Place, Room 188, Louisville, KY 40202, (502) 582-5971, (502) 582-5009 (F)

LOUISIANA
1661 Canal Street Ste. 2000, New Orleans, LA 70112, (504) 589-6685, (504) 589-2339 (F)

MAINE
40 Western Avenue Rm. 512, Augusta, ME 04330, (207) 622-8378, (207) 622-8277 (F)

MARYLAND
10 South Howard Street Rm. 608, Baltimore, MD 21202, (410) 962-2235, (410) 962-1805 (F)

MASSACHUSETTS
155 Federal Street Ninth Flr., Boston, MA 02110, (617) 451-2023, (617) 565-5598 (F)

MICHIGAN
477 Michigan Avenue Room 515, Detroit, MI 48226, (313) 226-6075, (313) 226-4769 (F)

MINNESOTA
U.S. Small Business Administration, 100 North Sixth Street Ste. 610-C, Minneapolis, MN 55403, (612) 370-2343, (612) 370-0179 (F)

MISSISSIPPI
101 West Capital Street Ste. 400, Jackson, MS 39201, (601) 965-4384, (601) 965-4294 (F)

MISSOURI
REGION VII OFFICE, 911 Walnut Street 13th Flr., Kansas City, MO 64106, (816) 426-7762, (816) 426-5559 (F)

MONTANA
301 South Park Rm. 528, Drawer 10054, Helena, MT 59626, (406)449-5381, (406)449-5474 (F)

NEBRASKA
1145 Mill Valley Road, Omaha, NE 68154, (402) 221-3604, (402) 221-3680 (F)

NEVADA
50 South Virginia Street Rm. 238, Reno, NV 89505-3216, (702) 784-5268, (702) 784-5069 (F)

NEW HAMPSHIRE
143 North Main Street Ste. 202, Concord, NH 03301-1257, (603) 225-1400, (603) 225-1409 (F)

NEW JERSEY
Military Park Building. Fourth Flr., 60 Park Place, Newark, NJ 07102, (201) 645-2434, (201) 645-6265 (F)

NEW MEXICO
U.S. Small Business Administration, 625 Silver Avenue S.W. Third Flr., Albuquerque, NM 87102, (505) 766-1870, (505) 766-1057 (F)

NEW YORK
REGION II OFFICE, 26 Federal Plaza Room 31-08, New York, NY 10278, (212) 264-1450, (212) 264-0900 (F)

NORTH CAROLINA
200 North College Street, Ste. A2015, Charlotte, NC 28202-2137, (704) 344-6587, (704) 344-6769 (F)

NORTH DAKOTA
657 Second Avenue North Rm. 218, P.O. Box 3086, Fargo, ND 58108, (701) 239-5131, (701) 239-5645 (F)

OHIO
2 Nationwide Plaza Suite 1400, Columbus, OH 43215-2542, (614) 469-6860, (614) 469-2391 (F)

OKLAHOMA
200 Northwest Fifth Street Ste. 670, Oklahoma City, OK 73102, (405) 231-4301, (405) 231-4876 (F)

OREGON
222 S. W. Columbia Street Ste. 500, Portland, OR 97201-6605, (503) 326-2682, (503) 326-2808 (F)

PENNSYLVANIA
REGION III OFFICE, 475 Allendale Road Ste. 201, King of Prussia, PA 19406, (215) 962-3700, (215) 962-3743 (F)

PUERTO RICO
Carlos Chardon Avenue Rm. 691, Hato Rey, PR 00918, (809) 766-5572, (809) 766-5309 (F)

RHODE ISLAND
380 Westminister Mall Fifth Flr., Providence, RI 02903, (401) 528-4561, (401) 528-4539 (F)

SOUTH CAROLINA
1835 Assembly Street Rm. 358, P.O. Box 2786, Columbia, SC 29201, (803) 765-5298, (803) 765-5962 (F)

SOUTH DAKOTA
101 Main Avenue Ste. 201, Sioux Falls, SD 57102, (605) 330-4231, (605) 330-4215 (F)

TENNESSEE
50 Vantage Way Ste. 201, Nashville, TN 37228-1504, (615) 736-5039, (615) 736-7232 (F)

TEXAS
8625 King George Drive, Building C, Dallas, TX 75235-3391, (214) 767-7659, (214) 767-7870 (F)

UTAH
125 South State Street Rm. 2237, Salt Lake City, UT 84138-1195, (801) 524-3215, (801) 524-4160 (F)

VERMONT
87 State Street Rm. 205, Montpelier, VT 05602, (802) 828-4422, (802) 828-4485 (F)

VIRGIN ISLANDS
Federal Office Building Rm. 210, Veterans Drive, St. Thomas, VI 00802, (809) 774-8530, (809) 774-2312 (F)

VIRGINIA
400 North Eighth Street, Rm. 3015, P.O. Box 10126, Richmond, VA 23220, (804) 771-2400, (804) 771-2312 (F)

WASHINGTON
2615 Fourth Avenue Rm. 440, Seattle, WA 98121, (206) 553-5676, (206) 220-6570 (F)

WEST VIRGINIA
550 Eagan Street Suite 309, Charleston, WV 25301, (304) 347-5220, (304) 347-5350 (F)

WISCONSIN
212 East Washington Avenue, Rm. 213, Madison, WI 53703, (608) 264-5542, (608) 264-5541 (F)

WYOMING
100 East B Street Rm, 4001, P.O. Box 2839, Casper, WY 82602-2839, (307) 261-5761, (307) 261-5499 (F)

VERMONT
87 State Street Rm. 205, Montpelier, VT 05602, (802) 828-4422, (802) 828-4485 (F)

US AND FOREIGN COMMERCIAL SERVICE DISTRICT OFFICES

Lauri J. Fitz-Pagado, Assistant Secretary and Director General, U.S. and Foreign Commercial Service, HCHB 3802, 14th & Constitution Avenue NW, Washington, DC 20230, (202) 482-5777, (202) 482-5013 (F)

Robert S. LaRussa, Principal Deputy Assistant Secretary, U.S. and Foreign Commercial Service, HCHB 3802, 14th & Constitution Avenue NW, Washington, DC 20230, (202)482-0725, (202)482-5013 (F)

Daniel J. McLaughlin, Deputy Ass't. Secretary, Domestic Oper. , U.S. and Foreign Commercial Service, HCHB 3810, 14th & Constitution Avenue NW, Washington, DC 20230, (202)482-4767, (202)482-0687 (F)

ALABAMA
Medical Forum Building, 7th Floor, 950 22nd Street, N, Birmingham, AL 35203, (205) 731-1331, (205) 731-0076 (F)

ALASKA
Suite 319, World Trade Center Alaska, 4201 Tudor Centre Drive, Anchorage, AK 99508, (907) 271-6237, (907) 271-6242 (F)

ARIZONA
Tower One, Suite 970, 2901 N. Central Avenue, Phoenix, AZ 85012, (602) 640-2513 , (602) 640-2518 (F)

ARKANSAS
TCBY Tower Building, Suite 700, 425 West Capitol Avenue, Little Rock, AR 72201, (501) 324-5794, (501) 324-7380 (F)

CALIFORNIA
11000 Wilshire Blvd., Room 9200, Los Angeles, CA 90024, (904) 487-1407, (310) 235-7220 (F)

COLORADO
1625 Broadway, Suite 680 , Denver, CO 80202, (303) 844-6622, (303) 844-5651 (F)

CONNECTICUT
Room 610B, 450 Main Street, Hartford, CT 06103, (203) 240-3630, (203) 240-3473 (F)

DELAWARE
Served by the Philadelphia District Office

DISTRICT OF COLUMBIA
Served by the Gaithersburg Branch Office

FLORIDA
P.O. Box 590570, 5600 Northwest 36th St., Suite 617, Miami, FL 33166, (305) 526-7425, (305) 526-7434 (F)

GEORGIA
Plaza Square North, 4360 Chamblee Dunwoody Road, Suite 310, Atlanta, GA 30341, (404) 452-9101, (404) 452-9105 (F)

HAWAII
P.O. Box 50026, 300 Ala Moana Blvd., Room 4106, Honolulu, HI 96850, (808) 541-1782, (808) 541-3435 (F)

IDAHO
700 West State Street, 2nd Floor, Boise, ID 83720, (208) 334-3857, (208) 334-2783 (F)

ILLINOIS
Xerox Center, 55 West Monroe St., Suite 2440, Chicago, IL 60603, (312) 353-8040, (312) 353-8098 (F)

INDIANA
Penwood One, 11405 N Pennsylvania Street, Suite 106, Carmel, IN 46032, (317) 582-2300, (317) 582-2301 (F)

IOWA
Federal Building, 210 Walnut Street, Room 817, Des Moines, IA 50309, (515) 284-4222, (515) 284-4021 (F)

KANSAS
Kansas City District Office, 151 N Volutsia, Wichita, KS 67214, (316) 269-6160, (316) 683-7326 (F)

KENTUCKY
601 W Broadway, Room 6368, Louisville, KY 40202, (502) 582-5066, (502) 582-6573 (F)

LOUISIANA
Hale Boggs Federal Building, 501 Magazine Street, Room 1043, New Orleans, LA 70130, (504) 589-6546, (504) 589-2337 (F)

MAINE
Boston District Office, 187 State Street, Augusta, ME 04333, (207) 622-8249, (207) 626-9156 (F)

MARYLAND
World Trade Center, 401 Pratt Street, Suite 2432, Baltimore, MD 21202, (410) 962-4539, (410) 962-4529 (F)

MASSACHUSETTS
World Trade Center, 164 Northern Avenue, Suite 307, Boston, MA 02210, (617) 424-5950, (617) 424-5992 (F)

MICHIGAN
477 Michigan Ave., 1140 McNamara Building, Detroit, MI 48226, (313) 226-3650, (313) 226-3657 (F)

MINNESOTA
110 South 4th Street, 108 Federal Building, Minneapolis, MN 55401, (612) 348-1638, (612) 348-5386 (F)

MISSISSIPPI
201 W. Capitol Street, Suite 310 , Jackson, MS 39201, (601) 965-4388, (601) 965-5386 (F)

MISSOURI
8182 Maryland Avenue, Suite 303, St. Louis, MS 63105, (314) 425-3302, (314) 425-3381 (F)

MONTANA
Served by the Boise Branch Office

NEBRASKA
Des Moines District Office, 11335 "O" Street, Omaha, NB 68137, (402) 221-3664, (402) 221-3668 (F)

NEVADA
1755 East Plumb Lane, Room 152, Reno, NV 89502, (702) 784-5203, (702) 784-5343 (F)

NEW HAMPSHIRE
Boston District Office, 601 Spaulding Turnpike, Suite 29, Portsmouth, NH 03801, (603) 334-6074, (603) 334-6110 (F)

NEW JERSEY
3131 Princeton Pike, Bldg. #6, Suite 100, Trenton, NJ 08648, (609) 989-2100, (609) 989-2395 (F)

NEW MEXICO
Dallas District Office , NM Dept. of Economic Development, 1100 St Francis Drive, Santa Fe, NM 87503, (505) 827-0350, (505) 827-0263 (F)

NEW YORK
26 Federal Plaza, Room 3718, New York, NY 10278, (212) 264-0634, (212) 264-1356 (F)

NORTH CAROLINA
400 West Market Street, Suite 400, Greensboro, NC 27401, (910) 333-5345, (910) 333-5158 (F)

NORTH DAKOTA
Served by the Minneapolis District Office

OHIO
550 Main Street, Room 9504, Cincinnati, OH 45202, (513) 684-2944, (513) 684-3200 (F)

OKLAHOMA
440 South Houston Street, Tulsa, OK 74127, (918) 581-7650, (918) 581-2844 (F)

OREGON
One World Trade Center, 121 SW Salmon Street, Suite 242, Portland, OR 97204, (503) 326-3001, (503) 326-6351 (F)

PENNSYLVANIA
1000 Liberty Avenue, 2002 Federal Building, Pittsburgh, PA 15222, (412) 644-2850, (412) 644-4875 (F)

PUERTO RICO
Union Plaza Building, Suite 701, 416 Ponce de leon Avenue, Hato Rey, PR, (787) 763-6811, (787) 763-4629 (F)

RHODE ISLAND
Hartford District Office, 7 Jackson Walkway, Providence, RI 02903, (401) 528-5104, (401) 528-5067 (F)

SOUTH CAROLINA
Charleston Trident Chamber of Commerce, P.O. Box 975, 81 Mary Street, Charleston, SC 29402, (803) 727-4051, (803) 727-4052 (F)

SOUTH DAKOTA
Des Moines District Office, Commerce Center, 200 N Phillips Avenue, Suite 302, Sioux Falls, SD 57102, (605) 330-4264, (605) 330-4266 (F)

TENNESSEE
22 North Front Street, Suite 200, Memphis, TN 38103, (901) 544-4137, (901) 575-3510 (F)

TEXAS
P.O. Box 58130, 2050 N Stemmons Fwy., Suite 170, Dallas, TX 75258, (214) 767-0542, (214) 767-8240 (F)

UTAH
324 S State Street, Suite 105, Salt Lake City, UT 84111, (801) 524-5116, (801) 524-5886 (F)

VERMONT
Vermont Dept. of Economic Development, 109 State Street, Montpelier, VT 05609, (802) 828-4508, (802) 828-3258 (F)

VIRGINIA
700 Centre, 704 East Franklin Street, Suite 550, Richmond, VA 23219, (804) 771-2246, (804) 771-2390 (F)

WASHINGTON
3131 Elliott Avenue, Suite 290, Seattle, WA 98121, (206) 553-5615, (206) 553-7253 (F)

WEST VIRGINIA
405 Capitol Street, Suite 807, Charleston, WV 25301, (304) 347-5123, (304) 347-5408 (F)

WISCONSIN
517 E Wisconsin Avenue, Room 596, Milwaukee, WI 53202, (414) 297-3473, (414) 297-3470 (F)

WYOMING
Served by the Denver District Office

U.S. DEPARTMENT OF COMMERCE COUNTRY DESK OFFICERS (202) 482-2000
U.S. DEPARTMENT OF STATE COUNTRY DESK OFFICERS (202) 647-4000

All office are located in Washington, DC and have the same respective prefix:

Country	Commerce (202) 482-	State (202) 647-
Afghanistan	2954	9552
Albania	4915	3187
Algeria	1870	4680
Andorra	4508	1412
Angola	4228	8252
Anguilla	2527	
Antigua and Barbuda	2527	2621
Argentina	1548	2401
Armenia	4655	8671
Aruba	2527	
Australia	3646	9691
Austria	2920	1484
Azerbaijan	4655	8671
Bahamas, The	2527	2621
Bahrain	5545	6572
Baltic States	3952	3187
Bangladesh	2954	9552
Barbados	2527	2621
Belarus	4655	6764
Belgium	5041	6071
Belize	2527	4980
Benin	4228	2865
Bermuda	2527	8027
Bhutan	2954	2141
Bolivia	2521	3076
Bosnia-Hercegovina	2645	4138
Botswana	4228	8252
Brazil	3871	9407
Brunei	3875	3276
Bulgaria	4915	3188
Burkina Faso	4388	3066
Burma (Myanmar)	3875	7108
Burundi	4388	3139
Cambodia	3875	3133
Cameroon	5149	1707
Canada	3101	2170
Cape Verde	4388	3391
Caribbean	1648	4195
Caymans	2527	
Central African Republic	4388	3139
Chad	4388	1707
Chile	1495	2407
Colombia	1659	3023
Commonwealth of Independent States	4655	9559
Comoros	4564	5684
Congo	5149	3139
Costa Rica	2527	3381
Croatia	2645	4138
Cuba	2527	9272
Cyprus	3945	6113
Czech Republic	2645	3298
Denmark	3254	5669
Djibouti	4564	8852
Dominican Republic	2527	2620
Ecuador	1659	3338
Egypt	4441	1228
El Salvador	2527	4961
Equatorial Guinea	4228	3139
Estonia	2645	3187
Ethiopia	4564	8852
Fiji	4958	3546
Finland	3254	6071
France	8008	2633
French Antilles	2527	2620
French Polynesia	4958	3546
Gabon	5149	1707
Gambia	4388	3395
Georgia, Republic of	4655	8671
Germany	2434	2005
Ghana	5149	4567
Gibraltar	3748	8027
Greece	3945	6113
Greenland	3254	5669
Grenada	2527	2130
Guadeloupe	2527	2620
Guatemala	2527	4980
Guinea	4388	2865
Guinea-Bissau	4388	4567
Guyana	2527	4195
Haiti	2527	4195
Honduras	2527	3381
Hong Kong	3932	6300
Hungary, Republic of	2645	3298
Iceland	3254	5669
India	2954	2351
Indonesia	3875	3276
Iran	1810	6111
Iraq	4441	5692
Ireland	2177	5669
Israel	1870	3672
Italy	2177	2453
Ivory Coast	4388	3391
Jamaica	2527	2620
Japan	2425	3152
Jordan	1857	1022
Kazakhstan	4655	6859
Kenya	4564	5684
Kiribati	4958	3546
Korea, North and South	4957	7717
Kuwait	1860	6562
Kyrgystan	4655	6859
Laos	3875	3133
Latvia	2645	3187
Lebanon	4441	1030
Lesotho	4228	8252
Liberia	4388	3391
Libya	5545	4674
Liechtenstein	2920	1484

Lithuania	2645	3187
Luxembourg	5401	6664
Macau	2482	6300
Macedonia	2645	4138
Madagascar	4584	5684
Malawi	4228	8433
Malaysia	3875	3276
Maldives	2954	2351
Mali	4388	3066
Malta	3748	2453
Marshall Islands	4958	0108
Martinique	2527	2620
Mauritania	4388	2865
Mauritius	4564	5684
Mexico	0300	9894
Micronesia	4958	0108
Moldova	4655	8671
Monaco	2633	
Mongolia	2462	6300
Montenegro	2645	4138
Montserrat	2527	4195
Morocco	5545	4675
Mozambique	5148	8252
Namibia	4228	8252
Nauru	4958	3546
Nepal	2954	1450
Netherlands	5401	6664
Netherlands Antilles	2527	2620
New Caledonia	4958	3546
New Zealand	3647	9691
Nicaragua	2527	4975
Niger	4388	3066
Nigeria	4228	3395
Norway	4414	5669
Oman	1870	6558
Pacific Islands	3647	3546
Pakistan	2954	9823
Palau	4958	0108
Panama	2527	4986
Papua-New Guinea	4958	3546
Paraguay	1548	2296
Peru	2521	3360
Philippines	3875	1221
Poland	2645	1070
Portugal	4508	1412
Puerto Rico	2527	
Qatar	1870	6572
Reunion Island	4958	2453
Romania	2645	3187
Russia	0364	9806
Rwanda	4388	3139
San Marino	2177	2453
Sao Tome & Principe	4388	1707
Saudi Arabia	4652	7550
Senegal	4388	2865
Serbia	2645	4138
Seychelles	4564	5684
Sierra Leone	4388	3395
Singapore	3875	3278
Slovak Republic	2645	3298
Slovenia	2645	4138
Solomon Islands	4958	3546
Somalia	4564	8852
South Africa	5148	8432
Spain	4508	1412
Sri Lanka	2954	2351
ßSudan	4564	9742
Suriname	2527	4195
Swaziland	5148	8252
Sweden	4414	6071
Switzerland	2920	1484
Syria	4441	1131
Taiwan	4957	7711
Tajikistan	4655	8671
Tanzania	4228	5684
Thailand	3875	7108
Togo	5149	2865
Trinidad & Tobago	2527	2621
Tunisia	1860	3614
Turkey	5373	6114
Turkmenistan	4655	8671
Turks and Caicoa Islands	2527	
Tuvalu	3647	3546
Uganda	4564	5684
Ukraine	4655	6795
United Arab Emirates	5545	6558
United Kingdom	3748	8027
Upper Volta	4338	3066
Uruguay	1495	2296
Uzbekistan	4655	6731
Vanuatu	4958	3546
Vatican	2453	
Venezuela	4303	3338
Vietnam	3875	3132
Virgin Islands (U.S.)	2527	2620
Virgin Islands (U.K.)	2527	0827
Western Sahara	5545	4675
Western Samoa	4958	3546
Yemen Arab Republic	1870	6571
Yemen, Dem. Rep. of	1870	6571
Yugoslavia	2645	4138
Zaire	5149	2080
Zambia	4228	8433
Zimbabwe	4228	9429

INTERNATIONAL BUSINESS PUBLICATIONS AND PERIODICALS

AgExporter ($51/year) ISSN SUB 9737 5285 Port Royal Road, Springfield, VA 22161 (703) 487-4630 (p) *Provides current information on exporting agricultural products.*

ATFI News Rijnhaave, 65 Willowbrook Boulevard, Wayne, NJ 07470-9756 (201) 890-3731 (p) *Freight rates and charges in the ATFI tariff environment.*

AID Importer List Agency for International Development, Office of Small and Disadvantaged Business Utilization, 1100 Wilson Blvd., Suite 1220A, Roslyn, VA 22209; (703) 875-1551 (p); (703) 875-1862 (f). *Lists importers in select AID recipient countries who are interested in importing specific U.S. products.*

American Export Register Thomas Publishing Company International Division (212) 629-1131 (p); (f) (212) 629-1140. *The U.S.'s oldest marketing catalog designed to promote U.S. products in foreign markets. The Register is distributed overseas to 20,000 importers in over 170 countries. U.S. exporters and export management companies can be listed in the register free of charge. Advertising is also available.*

Atlas of Eastern Europe ($16.00) S/N 041-015-00170-1 U.S. Superintendent of Documents, P.O. Box 371954, Pittsburgh, PA 15250-7954 (202) 512-1800 (p); (202) 512-2250 (f); gpoaccess@gpo.gov (e) *Provides statistical and demographic information about Eastern Europe.*

Background Notes ($68) S/N 044-000-91214-7 U.S. Superintendent of Documents, P.O. Box 371954, Pittsburgh, PA 15250-7954 (202) 512-1800 (p); (202) 512-2250 (f); gpoaccess@gpo.gov (e) *Brief primers country by country.*

Bankable Deals: A Question & Answer Guide to Trade Finance (free) U.S. Small Business Administration Office of International Trade (202) 205-6720 (p); (202) 205-7272 (f). *A booklet produced by the U.S. Small Business Administration and AT&T with the assistance of Union Bank of Texas. This guide provides valuable information on export finance and answers some of the questions most frequently asked by export businesses.*

Basic Facts About Patents, Basic Facts About Trademarks, Q&A About Trademarks (free), **Patent and Trademark Office** Office of Legislation and International Affairs, U.S. Department of Commerce, 2011 Crystal Drive, Room 208B, Arlington, VA 22202 (703) 305-9300 (p) or (703) 305-8341 (p) *This office assists in filing patent applications for other countries.*

Basic Guide to Exporting, A ($16.50) S/N 003-009-00604-0 ISBN 0-16-0003296 NTIS, Springfield, VA 22161 (703) 487-4650 (p) *A great "beginning to export" resource that provides comprehensive information on all aspects of exporting; last published in 1992.*

Basic Guide to Exporting, A ($16.50) World Trade Press, 1505 Fifth Avenue, San Rafael, CA 94901 (800) 833-8586 (p); (415) 453-7980 (f) *This is the U.S. Department of Commerce's respected introduction to exporting just improved and up-to-date. Includes an expanded and, according to the publisher, correct phone numbers and other contact information.*

BizPlan*Builder*, ($129), JIAN, Inc., 1975 West El Camino Real, Suite 301, Mountain View, CA 94040-2218 (p); (415) 254-5640 (f) *BizPlanBuilder is an outstanding strategic business and marketing plan book/software program. Instead of spending weeks to create an international business plan, this template will guide you through the process in just days. JIAN, Inc. also has other business book/software programs including Employee Manual Maker and Publicity Builder.*

Breaking Into The Trade Game (free) U.S. Small Business Administration, Office of International Trade, 409 Third Street, S.W. Washington, DC 20416 (202) 205-6720 (p) *Excellent primer of how to break into potentially lucrative international markets. Contains an international business template.*

BNA Export Reference Manual ($675) Bureau of National Affairs, Inc., Distribution Center, 9435 Keywest Avenue, Rockville, MD 20850 (800) 372-1033 (p) or (301) 961-6750 (p); www.newstand.lotus.com *Published annually and updated weekly, a three-volume reference service providing up-to-date country-by-country shipping and marketing research information. Social, political, economic, and commercial conditions of each country are profiled including policies, regulations, issues, development, and laws.*

Boycott Law Bulletin ($495/year) Nu-Tec Publishing, 4715 Strack Road, suite 211, Houston, TX 77069-1617 (713) 444-6562 (p); (713) 444-6564 (f); jkamalic@infohwy.com (e) *A fax service that reports on federal and state anti-boycott laws, regulations, enforcement actions, and policies relating to more than 40 countries which are involved in boycotting the State of Israel.*

Business America ($53/year) ISSN 0190-6275 U.S. Superintendent of Documents, P.O. Box 371954, Pittsburgh, PA 15250-7954 (202) 512-1800 (p); (202) 512-2250 (f); gpoaccess@gpo.gov (e) *The principal Commerce Department publication for presenting domestic and international business news. Each monthly issue includes a "how-to" article for new exporters, trade policy discussion, and a list of upcoming trade shows.*

Business Information Service for the Newly Independent States (BISNIS) (free) Business Information Service, U.S. Department of Commerce, Room 7413, Washington, DC 20230 (202) 482-4655 (p); (202) 482-2293 (f) *Excellent newsletter on doing business in the former Soviet Union.*

Building an Import/Export Business ($15) ISBN 0-471-53627-X John Wiley & Sons, Inc., 605 Third Avenue, New York, NY 10158 (800) 225-5945 (p) *How to set up the business, choosing an appropriate product and planning, freight forwarding etc., payment methods, regulations, and how to capitalize on the formation of the EEA.*

Business Transactions In Germany Matthew Bender and Company, 11 Penn Plaza, New York, NY 10001 (800) 223-1940 (p) or (212) 967-7707 (p) *A comprehensive 4-volume guide to doing business in Germany. This treatise provides a basic understanding of the German legal system, private and commercial law, and business regulations.*

Buyer Alert Advertising for Exporters ($15 per announcement) AgExport Services Connections Division, AgBox 1052, USDA/FAS/AGX, Washington, D.C. 20250-1052 (202) 690-3416 (p); (202) 690-4374 (f) *Distributed by USDA's overseas offices, this biweekly newsletter will introduce your food, farm, and forest products to foreign buyers around the world. Buyer alerts help U.S. exporters reach more than 15,000 importers in nearly 60 countries.*

Carnet: Move Goods Duty Free Through Customs (free) U.S. Council for International Business, 1212 Avenue of the Americas, New York, NY 10036 (212) 354-4480 (p) or (800) 5-DUTY FREE (p); (212) 944-0012 (f); atacarnet@uscib.org (e); http://uscib.org *Brochure describing advantages of a carnet and how to obtain one.*

Central Eastern European Business Bulletin (free) Eastern European Business Information Center, Room 7412, U.S. Department of Commerce, 14th and Constitution Avenue, Washington, DC 20230 (202) 482-2645 (p) *Monthly newsletter which provides trade leads and updates on this newly emerging market.*

Commerce Business Daily ($324) U.S. Superintendent of Documents, P.O. Box 371954, Pittsburgh, PA 15250-7954 (202) 512-1800 (p); (202) 512-2250 (f); gpoaccess@gpo.gov (e); free online at http:cbdnet.access.gpo.gov *A daily publication that provides government procurement notices and awards.*

Commercial News USA (free) Associated Business Publications International, 317 Madison Avenue, New York, NY 10017 (212) 490-3999 (p) or (212) 482-4918 (p); (212) 822-2028 (f) *Distributed to 130,000 buyers worldwide, the ten times-yearly publication of the U.S. and Foreign Commercial Service is solely devoted to promoting U.S. products to overseas buyers. This is an excellent service.*

Companies International CD-ROM ($2,495) Gale Research Inc., PO Box 33477, Detroit, MI 48232-5477 (800) 877-4253 (p); (313) 961-6083 (f). *Included on this CD-Rom product is more than 300,000 businesses worldwide (including the U.S.) listing company name and address, phone, fax, financial information, employees, SIC/HS codes, import/export information, contact people, etc.*

Complete Guide to Doing Business in Mexico, The ($29.95) ISBN 0-8144-0211-9 American Demographics, P.O. Box 68, Ithaca, NY 14851 (800) 828-1133 (p); (607) 273-3196 (f) *Offers timely information on Mexican business customs and profiles the tax system, labor force, financial system, import-export regulations, intellectual property protection, NAFTA, etc.*

Comprehensive Guide To Trade Terms ($36.50) U.S. Department of Commerce, Washington, DC 20230, (800) STAT-USA (p); (202) 482-2164 (f); stat-usa@doc.gov (e); http://www.stat_usa.gov (w) *A listing of almost 2,000 terms used in international trade. The lexicon is also available on the NTDB or on floppy disk. In addition, the guide can be ordered from the National Technical Information Service at (703) 487-4650. PB95-50043.*

Consumer International ($900) EP262 1995, Find/SVP, 625 Avenue of the Americas, New York, NY 10011-2002 (800) 346-3737 (p); (212) 807-2676 (f). *Reveals consumer trends for 26 countries from Argentina and Australia to the U.S. and Venezuela.*

Corporate Taxes Worldwide Summary (free) Price Waterhouse, 1251 Avenue of the Americas, New York, NY 10020 (212) 819-5000 (p); (212) 790-6620 (f) *Provides a complete summary of basic information about corporate taxes in 115 countries. Outlines the corporate tax rates and certain features of the tax law that could affect corporate operations.*

Correct Way to Fill Out the Shipper's Export Declaration, The (free) U.S. Bureau of the Census, Washington, DC 20233 (301) 457-1086 (p); (301) 457-1159 (f); http://census.gov.foreign_trade (w) *Illustrates the proper way to fill out the SED and support documents.*

Countertrade Handbook ($55) ISBN 0-89930-320-X Greenwood Publishing, 88 Post Road West, Box 5007, Westport, CT 06881 (203) 226-3571 (p) *Explains countertrade and how it best works for your business.*

Country Business Guides: The Portable Encyclopedia for Doing Business In A Particular Country - Argentina, Australia, Canada, China, Hong Kong, Japan, Korea, Mexico, Philippines, Singapore, Taiwan, USA ($24.95 each, 6 for $134, or 10 for $210) World Trade Press, 1505 Fifth Avenue, San Rafael, CA 94901 (800) 833-8586 (p); (415) 453-7980 (f) *Includes 26 chapters including the economy, current issues, opportunities, import and export procedures, trade fairs, demographics, labor, business law, etc.*

Country Commercial Guides U.S. Department of State *First available in 1994, these annual reports contain chapters on country marketing plans, economic trends and best markets as submitted by embassy commercial and economic attaches.* Available on the National Trade Data Bank, at the State Department web site at www.state.gov, or by visiting a local federal depository library.

Country Reports ($350 each) The Economist Intelligence Unit, 111 West 57th Street, New York, NY 10019 (212) 554-0600 (p); (212) 586-1181 (f). *EIU offers 105 business oriented reports on 180 countries worldwide including quarterly updates. Every Country Report provides 30 pages of the latest political, economic, financial, industrial and commercial trends. Country Reports databases are also available by world region on disc.*

Country Studies: Bulgaria, China, Ethiopia, Guyana, Japan, Nepal, North Korea, South Korea, Spain (prices range from $19 to $27) U.S. Superintendent of Documents, P.O. Box 371954, Pittsburgh, PA 15250-7954 (202) 512-1800 (p); (202) 512-2250 (f); gpoaccess@gpo.gov (e) *Describes the economic, military, political, and social systems and institutions as well as the influence of cultural factors. These cloth bound volumes are part of the highly-regarded Department of the Army Foreign Area Handbook series.*

CulturGrams ($80/nonprofit; $120 without a tax-exempt id number). Kennedy Publications, Brigham Young University Publications, P.O. Box 24538, Provo, UT 84602 (800) 528-6279 (p); (801) 378-5882 (f) http://www.byu.edu/culturgram *Updated yearly, these are invaluable 4-page cultural orientations on 164 countries which are country-specific "newsletters" that outline a nation's customs, people, life style, history, government, and economy.*

Customs Bonded Warehouses (free) U.S. Custom's Service, P.O. 7407, Washington, DC 20044, (202) 927-6724, http://www.customs.ustreas.gov *Explains how to establish a customs bonded warehouse.*

Customs Bulletin and Decisions ($128/52 issues) U.S. Superintendent of Documents, P.O. Box 371954, Pittsburgh, PA 15250-7954 (202) 512-1800 (p); (202) 512-2250 (f); gpoaccess@gpo.gov (e) *Keeps you informed about U.S. customs laws. Each bulletin features regulations, rulings, decisions, and notices concerning the U.S. Customs Service as well as matters and decisions of the U.S. Court of Customs and Patent Appeals.*

Customs Duties & Taxes Worldwide ($500) World tariff, Suite 448, 220 Montgomery Street, San Francisco, CA 94104-9490 (800) 556-9334 (p); (419) 391-7537 (f) *Also on PC-disk with keyword search.*

Datafiles From the Former Soviet Union ($150 3 vol set) **Data files: Poland** ($60) International Division Publications, U.S. Chamber of Commerce, 1615 H Street, NW, Washington, DC 20062-2000 (202) 463-5460 (p); (202) 463-3114 (f) *Contains directories of commercial- and industry-specific contacts on how and with whom to conduct business.*

Destination Japan ($4.00) S/N 003-009099602-3 U.S. Superintendent of Documents, P.O. Box 371954, Pittsburgh, PA 15250-7954 (202) 512-1800 (p); (202) 512-2250 (f); gpoaccess@gpo.gov (e) *Comprehensive information on cultivating business in Japan. Also available on the NTDB.*

Dictionary of International Trade ($16.50) World Trade Press, 1505 Fifth Avenue, San Rafael, CA 94901 (800) 833-8586 (p); (415) 453-7980 (f) *Definitions for more than 4,000 trade, banking, economic finance, and shipping terms. Includes acronyms, an international dialing guide, currencies of the world, weights and measures, maps, and resources international trade.*

Direct Marketing Guide to Canada (free) U.S. Postal Service, International Products Management, Room 1140, 475 L'enfant Plaza, SW, Washington, DC 20260-6520 (202) 268-6095 (p) or contact your local US Postal Service Business Office *Contains an excellent resource guide with accurate phone numbers.*

Directory of American Firms Operating in Foreign Countries ($220) Uniworld Business Publications, Inc., 257 Central Parkwest, New York, NY 10024 (212) 697-4999 (p); http://www.uniworldbp.com (w) *An alphabetical listing of 2,600-plus American companies operating in foreign countries.*

Directory of Freight Forwarders and Custom House Brokers ($30) International Wealth Success, Inc., 24 Canterbury Road, Rockville Centre, NY 11570 (800) 323-0548 (p) *Lists the names and addresses of about 2,000 U.S. firms which will handle the shipping of products for U.S. imports and exporters.*

Directory of U.S. Exporters and **Directory of U.S. Importers** ($399 each) Journal of Commerce, 445 Marshall Street, Philipsberg, NJ 08865 (800) 222-0356 (p) or (908) 454-6879 (p) *Contains verified business profiles of more that 18,000 active exporting companies. Information includes company name, address, line of business, ports of entry, international freight forwarder, etc.*

Directory of U.S. Government Resources (free) Trade Information Center, U.S. Department of Commerce, HCHB 7424, 14th and Constitution, NW Washington, DC 20230 (800) 872-8723 *Lists names and addresses of all government assistance programs and information sources.*

Distribution ($65/year) Distribution Department, P.O. Box 2106, Radnor, PA 19089-9206 (610) 964-4386 (p); (610) 964-5029 (f) *A transportation and business logistics magazine.*

Doing Business In . . . Canada ($645), France ($580), Ireland ($170), Japan ($925), Spain ($205), United Kingdom ($645), United States ($1,105) Matthew Bender and Company, 11 Penn Plaza, New York, NY 10001 (800) 833-9844 (p); (518) 487-3502 (f) *Each series contains comprehensive, technical information regarding the laws, rules, regulations, taxation etc. of engaging business with the stated country.*

Doing Business Under The Foreign Corrupt Practices Act ($135) Practicing Law Institute, 810 Seventy Avenue, New York, NY 10019 (800) 260-4754 (p); (800) 321-0093 (f) *Offers legal guidance on all the FCPA's accounting and payments provisions in a single resource.*

Do's and Taboos Around the World ($14.95) and **Do's and Taboos of International Trade** 3rd ed. ($14.95) ISBN 0-471-59528-4 John Wiley & Sons, 605 Third Avenue, New York, NY 10518-0012 (800) 225-5945 (p) *Provides an entertaining and informative narrative of circumstances to expect and avoid while doing business in foreign countries.*

Drawback: A Duty Refund on Certain Imports (free) U.S. Custom's Service, P.O. 7407, Washington, DC 20044, (202) 927-6724, http://www.customs.ustreas.gov *Lists products eligible for import duty refunds and whether importers qualify for a refund.*

Dun and Bradstreet International Business Resources Series: Asia/Pacific Key Business Enterprise ($575) *lists over 22,000 companies;* **Europe** ($425) *lists over 35,000 companies;* **Latin America** ($250) *lists over 25,000 companies;* **Principal International Businesses** *lists over 55,000 companies in 140 countries* ($595); **Canadian Manufacturers** ($495) lists over 20,000 companies. Dun and Bradstreet, 3 Sylvan Way, Parisppany, NJ 07504 (800) 526-0651, ext. 6714 (p).

Dynamics of Successful International Business Negotiations ($27.50) ISBN: 0-87201-196-8 Gulf Publishing Company, P.O. Box 2608, Houston, TX 77252-2608 (713) 520-4444 (p) or (800) 231-6275 (p) *This guide provides specific solutions to the challenges facing businesses involved in world trade. It covers all aspects of developing strategy and a corporate culture and negotiating in a cross-cultural global marketplace.*

EC 1992: A Practical Guide for American Business update #4 ($21) International Division Publications, U.S. Chamber of Commerce, 1615 H Street, NW, Washington, DC 20062-2000 (202) 463-5460 (p); (202) 463-3114 (f) *Offers a business perspective on changes in the EC and updates standards, the environment, financial services etc.*

EC 1992: The Effects of Greater Economic Integration Within the European Community on the United States U.S. International Trade Commission, Washington, DC 20436 (202) 205-1809 (p); (202) 205-2186 (f) *Describing the effects of the European economic union on U.S. businesses.*

EIU Guide to the New GATT ($225) ISBN: 0 85058 800 6 The Economist Intelligence Unit, 111 West 57th Street, New York, NY 10019 (212) 554-0600 (p); (212) 586-1181 (f) *This report provides a comprehensive and practical analysis of the Uruguay Round. A detailed guide to the final agreement is followed by a comprehensive assessment of its impact by sector and region.*

East Asian Executive Report (*monthly* legal and business guide for executives) 717 D Street, NW, Suite 300, Washington, DC 20004 (202) 628-6900 (p); (202) 628-6619 (f) *Monthly legal and business guide for executives.*

Electric Current Abroad ($3.50) U.S. Superintendent of Documents, P.O. Box 371954, Pittsburgh, PA 15250-7954 (202) 512-1800 (p); (202) 512-2250 (f); gpoaccess@gpo.gov (e) *Describes characteristics of electric current available overseas and types of electric plugs in domestic and commercial use.*

Employment Abroad: Facts and Fallacies ($7.50) U.S. Chamber of Commerce, 1615 H Street, N.W., Washington, D.C. 20062 (202) 463-5460 (p); (202) 463-3114 (f); http://www.uschamber.org *International jobs, where they are, where they're not.*

Encyclopedia of Associations ($460) Gale Research, Inc., 835 Penobscot Building, Detroit, MI 48226-4094 (313) 961-2242 (p) *Provides a comprehensive listing of trade associations for hundreds of industries and fields. Consulting with a trade association will provide valuable insight on what foreign customers are looking for your product.*

Environmental Management Kit ($215) and **Guide to ISO 14001** (free) and **ICC Business Charter for Sustainable Development** (free), ICC Publishing, 156 Fifth Avenue, Suite 305, New York, NY 10010 (212) 206-1150, iccpub@interport.net *ICC produces a number of outstanding publications related to international trade.*

Ernst & Young International Business Series (free) Contact your local Ernst & Young office for the series. Also available from John Wiley and Sons, Inc. (800) 225-5945 *These 100+ country-specific guides provide an overview of the investment climate, taxation, the business environment, and business activities and practices.*

Europa World Year Book Eastern Europe and the CIS ($425); South America, Central America, and the Carribbean ($325); The USA and Canada ($375); Western Europe ($335); Africa South of the Sahara ($350); Middle East and North Africa ($345); and Far East and Australia ($395) International Press Publications, 90 Nolan Court #21, Markham, Ontario, L3R 4L9 (905) 946-9588 (p); (800) 679-2514 (p); (908) 946-9590 (f) *Profiles of more than 250 countries with current political, economic, and cultural affairs.*

European Markets; **Latin American Markets**; and **Asian Markets: Guides to Company and Industry Information Sources** ($335 each) ISBN 1-56365-036-3 Washington Researchers, Ltd., P.O. Box 19005, 20th Street Station, Washington, D.C. 20036-9005 (p); (202) 333-3499 (p); (202) 625-0656 (f) *The format is concise, allowing anyone to quickly pick up ideas on how to approach even the toughest competitive research project.*

EUROpportunities U.S. Department of Commerce, Office of Western Europe, Washington, DC 20230, (202) 482-5341 *This program offers individualized marketing assistance, marketing research information, and recommendations on other forms of export promotion assistance for a particular product.*

Export ABCs, ($25), The Journal of Commerce, 445 Marshall Street, Phillipsburg, NJ, 08865-9984, (800) 221-3777 (p) *This collection of Journal of Commerce columns comes in a convenient binder. Topics range from negotiation tactics to catering to cultural differences, from payment risk to the use of export management companies.*

Export Administration Regulations ($88/year) SN #903-013-00000-7 U.S. Superintendent of Documents, P.O. Box 371954, Pittsburgh, PA 15250-7954 (202) 512-1800 (p); (202) 512-2250 (f); gpoaccess@gpo.gov (e) *This guide provides in-depth information on export licenses, restrictive trade practices or boycotts, import regulations, documentation requirements, etc.*

Export Compliance Guide ($577 plus monthly updates) Thompson Publishing Group, Subscription Service Center, P.O. Box 26185, Tampa, FL 33623-6185, (800) 925-1878 (p); (800) 759-7179 (f) *Covers export trading including licensing agencies, reviewing agencies, applicable laws and regulations, compliance procedures, and export enforcement.*

Export Controls and Nonproliferation Policy ($5.50) S/N 052-003-01371 U.S. Superintendent of Documents, P.O. Box 371954, Pittsburgh, PA 15250-7954 (202) 512-1800 (p); (202) 512-2250 (f); gpoaccess@gpo.gov (e) *Analyzes the benefits and costs of export controls on dual-use goods in U.S. efforts to stem the proliferation of weapons of mass destruction.*

Export Credit Insurance: The Competitive Edge (free) Export-Import Bank of the United States, 811 Vermont Avenue, NW, Washington, DC 20571-0999 (202) 566-4490 (p) *Describes the export insurance programs of FCIA.*

Export Documentation ($69.50) International Trade Institute, 5055 North Main Street, Dayton, OH 45415 (800) 543-2453 (p); (987) 276-5920 (f) *Examines the steps you must go through to process any international order, with examples of each type of document you will experience in an international trade transaction.*

The Exporter ($180 for 12 issues), Trade Data Reports, Inc., 90 John Street, New York, NY, 10038 (212) 587-1340 (p); exporter@exporter.com (e); http://exporter.com (w)

Exporter's Encyclopedia ($545/year) ISBN 0732-0159-3896 Dun and Bradstreet, 3 Sylvan Way, Parisppan, NJ 07504 (800) 234-3867 (p); (201) 605-6911 (f) *Considered the premier source of country-specific information. Provides exhaustive country information for 220 world markets including country profiles, trade regulations, documentation, marketing data, transportation, and business travel information.*

Exporter's Guide to Foreign Sources for Credit Information Trade Data Reports, 6 West 37th Street, New York, NY 10018 (212) 563-2772 (p) *A private-sector credit reporting service that provides evaluations on foreign firms.*

Export/Import Basics: The Legal, Financial, and Transport Aspects of International Trade, $39.95, ICC Publishing, 156 Fifth Avenue, Suite 305, New York, NY 10010 (212) 206-1150 (p), iccpub@interport.net (e) *Focuses on the legal framework underlying export and import transactions and illustrates how international payment, transport, and insurance obligations should follow logically from a well-drafted export contract of sale.*

Export/Import Procedures and Documentation ($75), ISBN 0-8144-0035-0, American Management Association, P.O. Box 169, Saranack Lake, NY 12983, (518) 891-5510 (p); cust_ser@amanet.org (e); http://www.amanet.org (w) *Explains import and export procedures and shows examples of documentation.*

Exporting From Start to Finance ($42.95) ISBN 0-0706-9300-5 McGraw Hill, 13311 Monterey Avenue, Blue Ridge Summit, PA 17214-9988 (800) 262-4729 (p) *Discusses basics of financing through completion of sale.*

Export Letters of Credit and Drafts ($69.50) International Trade Institute, 5055 North Main St., Dayton, Ohio 45415 (800) 543-2453; (937) 276-5920 (f) *Instructs on how to read a letter of credit and what it really means. Provides sample letters showing how to instruct customers in opening and L/C and what to do when collection or compliance issues arise.*

The Export License: How to Fill Out the Application: A step-by-step guide using Form BXA-622P (free) Export Seminar Staff, Office of Export Licensing, Bureau of Export Administration, U.S. Department of Commerce, Room 1608, Washington, DC 20230 (202) 482-8731 (p) *Explains how to complete an application for export licensing.*

Export Marketing and Sales ($69.50) International Trade Institute, 5055 North Main St., Dayton, Ohio 45415 (800) 543-2453; (937) 276-5920 (f) *This comprehensive publication provides methods of finding and analyzing foreign market information to minimize the risks associated with exporting.*

Export Packing List: A Guide ($6) National Council on International Trade and Documentation, 350 Broadway Suite 205, New York, NY 10013 (212) 925-1400 (p) *A guide to creating the export packing list and the accompanying labels.*

Export and Project Financing ($449) Thompson Publishing Group, Subscription Service Center, P.O. Box 26185, Tampa, FL 33623-6185 (800) 925-1878 (p); (800) 759-7179 (f) *A complete reference of major export credit agencies and development banks. Includes chapters on working capital loans, short- and medium-term trade financing, international leasing, major projects financing, and finance agencies from throughout the world.*

Export Reference Glossary ($99.95) International Trade Institute, 5055 North Main Street, Dayton, OH 45415 (800) 543-2453 (p); (937) 276-5920 (f) *A guide to understanding all the export terms in use and how and when to use them. Over 49,000 reference in over 350 pages.*

Export Sales Agents ($49.95) ICC Publishing, 156 Fifth Avenue, Suite 305, New York, NY 10010 (212) 206-1150 (p), iccpub@interport.net (e) *Learn how to hire and keep one.*

Export Sales & Marketing Manual ($295) Export-Link; 9302 Lee Highway, Suite 800, Fairfax, VA 22031 (800) 876-0624 (p); (703) 293-7829 (f); http://www.export-link.com *A step-by-step guide specifically designed for small businesses to help identify foreign markets, price products, locate representatives, budget for exporting, etc.*

Export Shipping ($69.50) International Trade Institute, 5055 North Main St., Dayton, Ohio 45415 (800) 543-2453 (p); (937) 276-5920 (f) *Provides the exporter with an understanding of ocean/air containers, how to obtain international freight quotations, information on shipping documents, packing shipments and basic trade terms.*

Export Today ($49/year) ISSN 0882-4711 Trade Communications, 733 15th St, N.W., Suite 1100, Washington, DC 20005 (202) 737-1060 (p) *Monthly magazine that provides current analysis and information on the world of international business.*

Export Trading Company Guidebook ($11.00) S/N 003-009-00523-0, ISBN 0-16-000-336-9 U.S. Superintendent of Documents, P.O. Box 371954, Pittsburgh, PA 15250-7954 (202) 512-1800 (p); (202) 512-2250 (f); gpoaccess@gpo.gov (e) *A complete guide to all facets of an export company.*

Export Yellow Pages (free from the SBA, USEACs, and U.S. West) ISBN 0-9628513-2-9; Venture Publishing or Delphos Publishing, 1101 30th Street, N.W., Suite 200, Washington, DC 20007; (202) 337-6300 (p) or (800) 288-2582 (p) *A listing of freight forwarders, agents, and various representatives engaged in international trade. Also lists transportation services.*

Far Eastern Economic Review (weekly) Review Publishing Company, Ltd., P.O. box 160, General Post Office, Hong Kong (582) 5-8911533 (p); (582) 5-722436 (f) *An excellent source of information on this trading area.*

Financing and Insuring Exports: A User's Guide to Eximbank and FCIA Programs ($50) Export Import Bank of United States, 811 Vermont Avenue, N.W., Washington, DC 20571 (202) 565-3900; http://www.exim.gov (w). *Outlines Eximbank and FCIA programs and policies. It contains a case study and contact lists.*

FINDEX: The Directory of Market Research Reports, Studies, and Surveys ($390) ISBN 0-942189-08-6 Cambridge Information Group, 7200 Wisconsin Avenue, Bethesda, MD 20814 (800) 843-7751 (p) or (301) 961-6750 (p) *Contains descriptions of consumer and industrial studies and surveys, audits and research services, and reports on general business topics.*

Foreign Agricultural Circular U.S. Department of Agriculture, 12th Street and Jefferson Drive, SW, Washington, DC 20250 (202) 447-7937 (p) *Contains periodic reports covering developments on agricultural production and trade for the U.S. and the world for many different commodities.*

Foreign Agricultural Service Country Reports (free) U.S. Department of Agriculture-Information Division, Reports Office, 14th and Independence Avenue, S.W., Room 6072-S, Washington, DC 20250-1000 (202) 720-6343 (p); (202) 690-0193 (f) *Country Reports are country-specific 2-4 page descriptions of various commodities, 40 overseas markets overview, market trends, and information on U.S. market position, and the competition.*

Foreign Assembly of U.S. Components (free) U.S. Custom's Service, P.O. 7407, Washington, DC 20044, (202) 927-6724 (p), http://www.customs.ustreas.gov (w) *List the products which are exempted from products assembled abroad.*

Foreign Buyer List ($15 for each) AgExport Services Connections Division, AgBox 1052, USDA/FAS/AGX, Washington, D.C. 20250-1052 (202) 690-3416 (p); (202) 690-4374 (f) *Database containing information on more than 15,000 foreign buyers of food, farm, and forest products in 70 countries. Foreign Buyer Lists provide important information on each firm such as contact person, address, telephone, fax, and type of product(s) imported.*

Foreign Labor Trends ($36/60 issues) U.S. Superintendent of Documents, P.O. Box 371954, Pittsburgh, PA 15250-7954 (202) 512-1800 (p); (202) 512-2250 (f); gpoaccess@gpo.gov (e) *Facts on labor-management relations; trade unions; employment and unemployment; wages and working conditions; labor and government; labor administration and legislation; training; labor migration, etc.*

Foreign Tax Credits Internal Revenue Service, U.S. Department of Treasury, 950 L'Enfant Plaza South, SW, Washington, DC 20024 (202) 622-7000 (p) *Publication 514 describes tax credits, who is eligible, and how to calculate the credit.*

Foreign Trade Zones (free) U.S. Custom's Service, P.O. 7407, Washington, DC 20044 (202) 927-6724 (p) http://www.customs.ustreas.gov (w) *Explains how firms can benefit from use of an FTZ.*

The Global Road Warrior ($24.95) World Trade Press, 1505 Fifth Avenue, San Rafael, CA 94901 (800) 833-8586 (p); (415) 453-7980 (f) *A 100-country handbook for the international business traveler. Each country listing includes key facts on the work week, holidays, money, climate, visas, passports, dealing with emergencies, maps, and extensive information on airports, hotels, restaurants, and World Trade Centers.*

Global Trade ($45/year) North American Publishing, 401 North Broad Street, Philadelphia, PA 19108 (215) 238-5300 (p); (215) 238-5457 (f) *Covers transportation, finance, and services.*

Global Trade Talk ($11) U.S. Superintendent of Documents, P.O. Box 371954, Pittsburgh, PA 15250-7954 (202) 512-1800 (p); (202) 512-2250 (f); gpoaccess@gpo.gov (e) *Bi-monthly U.S. Customs Service magazine provides pertinent and timely information about international trade issues and serves as an information exchange forum for the brokerage community.*

Going International ($28.00) ISBN 0-394-54450-1 Random House, 201 East 50th Street, New York, NY 10022 (800) 733-3000 (p) *Provides country-specific, demographic, and cultural information.*

Guide to the Caribbean Basin Initiative ($5.50) U.S. Superintendent of Documents, P.O. Box 371954, Pittsburgh, PA 15250-7954 (202) 512-1800 (p); (202) 512-2250 (f); gpoaccess@gpo.gov (e) *Covers financing, duty-free entry of products from the 24 CBI countries, trade opportunities, country profiles and contacts, etc.*

Guide To Doing Business with the Agency for International Development (free) U.S. AID, Room 1200A, SA-14, Washington, D.C. 20523-1414 (703) 8775-1551 (p); (703) 875-1862 (f) *Includes information on the Section 8(a) Program, Project Development, and mailing list application.*

Guide to Doing Business in Mexico ($35) McGraw-Hill, Inc. Blue Ridge Summit, PA 17214-9984; (800) 262-4729 (p) *Practical, how-to guide on doing business in Mexico.*

Guide to Drafting Distributorship Agreements ($29.95) ICC Publishing, 156 Fifth Avenue, Suite 305, New York, NY 10010 (212) 206-1150 (p); iccpub@interport.net (e) *Provides guidance on protecting the exporter's interests.*

Guide to Europe ($130) ISBN 0-8103-2139-4; Gale Research Company, Book Tower, Dept. 77748, Detroit, MI 48226 (800) 223-GALE (p) *A directory listing major buyers, central purchasing agencies and selected importers of top European markets.*

Guide To INCOTERMS ($19.95) ISBN 92-842-1088-7 The Chamber of Commerce of the United States, 1615 H Street, NW, Washington, DC 20062 (202) 659-6000 (p) *Provides detailed diagrams and descriptions of the INCOTERMS.*

Guide to Uniform Rules for Collections ($39.95) ICC Publishing, 156 Fifth Avenue, Suite 305, New York, NY 10010 (212) 206-1150 (p), iccpub@interport.net (e) *Provides a consistent approach to global collection procedures.*

Handbook of Export Controls ($95) International Division Publications, U.S. Chamber of Commerce, 1615 H Street, NW, Washington, DC 20062-2000 (202) 463-5460 (p); member@uschamber.com (e) *Provides definitions of when and where export controls are in effect for U.S. exporters.*

Health Information for International Travelers ($7.00) U.S. Superintendent of Documents, P.O. Box 371954, Pittsburgh, PA 15250-7954 (202) 512-1800 (p); (202) 512-2250 (f); gpoaccess@gpo.gov (e) *Designed for health departments, physicians, travel agencies, airlines, and shipping companies, includes information on vaccination and foreign countries' entry requirements.*

How to Do Business with the Russians ($45) ISBN 0-89930-211-4; Greenwood Press, 88 Post Road West, Westport, CT 06881 (203) 226-3571 (p) *This handbook was written by a Russian native to provide U.S. businesses with guidance of Soviet foreign trade. In addition to the text, there are examples and outlines that emphasize how to conduct business affairs at home and abroad. Regulations, procedures, strategies, cultural nuances, and more are highlighted.*

How to Find Information About Foreign Firms ($145) ISBN: 1-56365-044-4 Washington Researchers Publishing, Box 19005, 20th Street Station, NW, Washington, DC 20036-9005 (202) 333-3499 (p); (202) 625-0656 (f) *Shows how to research foreign companies using hundreds of domestic and international resources.*

How to Find Manufacturing Agents and Agency Salesmen ($3.50) Manufacturers' Agents National Association, P.O. Box 3467, Laguna Hills, CA 92654 (714) 859-4040 (p) *Learn some of the best and easiest hiring techniques.*

How to Get More of Your Agent's Time ($3.25) Manufacturers' Agents National Association, P.O. Box 3467, Laguna Hills, CA 92654 (714) 859-4040 (p) *Relates the results of a survey question asked of agents: "Assuming that greater commissions are not a factor, how would you respond to a manufacturer who asked what it would take to give his line more time?"*

How to Get the Most Out of Trade Shows ($29.95) ISBN: 0-8442-3193-2 NTC Publishing Group, 4255 W. Touhy Avenue, Lincolnwood, IL 60646-1975 (800) 323-4900 (p) or (708) 679-5500 (p); ntcpubz@aol.com (e) *Provides procedures and guidelines for exhibiting products overseas.*

How To Obtain Copyright, Trademark & Patent Protection (free) Department of Treasury U.S. Customs Service, Public Information Office, 1500 Pennsylvania Avenue, Washington, DC 20044 (202) 927-5580 (p); (202) 622-2599 (f) *This informative brochure explains the intellectual property protection process.*

IDIC Newsletter (free) U.S. Chamber of Commerce, 1615 H Street, N.W., Washington, D.C. 20062 (202) 463-5460 (p); (202) 463-3114 (f); http://www.uschamber.org *International trade updates.*

Implementing the European Community Single Market (free) USITC Publication 2723 Secretary to the Commission, United States International Trade Commission, Washington, DC 20436 *This report provides timely information regarding the state of the EEA and country specific reports.*

Importer's Manual USA ($87) World Trade Press; 1505 Fifth Avenue; San Rafael, CA 04901 (415) 454-9934 (p); (415) 453-7980 (f); worldpress@aol.com (e) *Includes information on how to import on a product-by-product basis for 135 product groups. Also includes sections on letters of credit, U.S. Customs entry and clearance, international law, shipping, insurance, and a 100-country reference section.*

Importing Into United States (4.50) U.S. Government Printing Office, Superintendent of Documents, Washington, DC 20402 (202) 512-1530 (p); gpoaccess@gpo.gov (e); http://www.customs.ustreas.gov (w) *Learn how to import goods, prepare invoices and country of origin procedures.*

Import Procedures ($69.50) International Trade Institute, 5055 North Main St., Dayton, Ohio 45415 (800) 543-2453; (937) 276-5920 (f) *A guide to importing into the United States. Include dutiable status of good entered value, invoicing and marketing, entry procedures and documentation, liquidation and protests, drawback and quotas.*

Import Quotas (free) U.S. Custom's Service, P.O. 7407, Washington, DC 20044 (202) 927-6724 (p); http://www.customs.ustreas.gov (w) *Lists commodities subject to import quotas.*

Income Taxation of Foreign-Related Transactions Pub. No. 337; Matthew Bender and Company, 2 park Avenue, New York, NY 10016 (800) 223-1940 (p) or (212) 967-7707 (p); (212) 532-5737 (f) *The recognized basic text on all aspects of U.S. taxation of Americans doing business abroad. Covers foreign tax credits, section 482, foreign corporations doing business abroad, FSC's and more.*

INCOTERMS - 1990 ($29.95) ISBN 92-842-0087-3; International Chamber of Commerce, 38 Cours Albert, 75008, Paris, France (212) 206-1150 (p); (212) 633-6025 (f) *The official guide to INCOTERMS.*

Index of World Bank Publications (free) World Bank Publications, P.O. Box 7247-8619, Philadelphia, PA 19170-8619 *This index lists all the financial programs the World Bank offers.*

India: Economic Reform in ($25) International Division Publications, U.S. Chamber of Commerce, 1615 H Street, NW, Washington, DC 20062-2000 (202) 463-5460 (p); (202) 463-3114 (f) *A special report by the U.S.-India Business Council on improvements in trade relations.*

Industrial Reps of Overseas Countries and Overseas Buying Reps ($25) International Wealth Success, Inc., 24 Canterbury Road, Rockville Centre, NY 11570 (800) 323-0548 (p) *Lists 400 agencies, trade missions, consulate generals and firms in the U.S. representing 100 foreign countries. Also includes a summary of export control regulations and sample export applications.*

Inside Washington: Government Resources for International Business ($49.95) ISBN 0-96-285 1353; Delphos Publishing, 1101 30th Street, N.W., Suite 200, Washington, DC 20007 (202) 337-6300 (p); ssgatchev@delphos.bocc.com (e) *A complete source for available government programs plus case studies of businesses that have profited from government resources.*

Inside the World Bank Group: The Practical Guide for International Business Executives ($49.95) ISBN 1-883917-10-7 Delphos Publishing, 1101 30th Street, N.W., Suite 200, Washington, DC 20007; (202) 337-6300 (p) or (800) 288-2582 (p) *Includes all the private sector resources for multi-lateral investment guarantee agencies, International Finance Corporation, International Bank for Reconstruction and Development.*

Intermodal Freight Transportation ($35) Eno Foundation for Transportation, P.O. Box 2055, Westport, CT 06880 (703) 729-7200 (p); (703) 729-7219 (f) *A comprehensive overview of intermodality highlighting the current market, statistical, and technical innovations.*

International Business Export Catalogue American International Publishing Corporation, 10711 Burnet Road, Suite 305, Austin, TX 78758 (512) 873-7761 (p) *International circulation to 55,000 qualified subscribers includes only U.S. small manufacturers. Advertising rates start at 1/8 page for $940.*

International Business Quick Reference Guide ($35) International Division Publications, U.S. Chamber of Commerce, 1615 H Street, NW, Washington, DC 20062-2000 (202) 463-5460 (p); (202) 463-3114 (f) *Includes references on foreign chambers abroad and in the U.S., embassies, overseas assistance, state and local assistance, Department of Commerce numbers, etc.*

International Business Videos (prices listed below) Insight Media, 2162 Broadway, New York, NY 10024 (212) 721-6316 (p); (212) 799-5309 (f); insight@echonyc.com (e) *Call for an on-approval preview policy.*

Building Competitive Advantage ($189)
The Challenges of NAFTA ($450)
A Cultural Passport to International Business ($139)
Cross-Cultural Challenges ($450)
Developing Cultural Sensitivity ($189)
Distribution Channels: International Markets ($139)
Global Business: An Overview ($189)
Global Business: The Future ($189)
A Hunger for Pesos: A Yen For Dollars ($139)
International Assignment ($189)
International Financial Management ($179)
International Marketing Management ($189)
Int'l Marketing: Breaking Down the Great Wall ($139)
International Strategy ($189)
International Trade ($189)
International Trade and Exchange Rates ($109)
The International Monetary Fund At Work ($129)
Introduction to ISO 9000 ($159)
Managing in a Global Environment ($139)
Managing Across Cultures ($189)
New Skills for Global management ($450)
One World: Interdependency, Global Market ($139)
Public Debt: International Effects ($129)
Researching World markets ($189)
Understanding Cultural Differences ($189)
Working Together: Managing Cultural Diversity ($495)

International Businesswoman, A Guide to Success in the Global Marketplace ($19.95) ISBN 0-275-9200-1(pb) Greenwood Praeger, 88 Post Road West, P.O. Box 5007, Westport, CT 06881 (203) 226-3571 (p) *Offers sound advice for the international businesswoman.*

International Commodity Trade Series - Wine, Gold, Silver, Grain, Cotton, Cocoa, Lead, Nickel, Rice, Steel, Sugar, Tin, Wool, Zinc ($95.00 each, 3 for $249) World Trade Press, 1505 Fifth Avenue, San Rafael, CA 94901 (800) 833-8586 (p); (415) 453-7980 (f) *Covers history and background of the commodity, world production and consumption, the industry, prices, futures, and international trading environment.*

International Copyright Laws and Practices ($360) Pub. No. 399; Matthew Bender and Company, International Division, 11 Penn Plaza, New York, NY 10001 (212) 967-7707 (p) or (800) 223-1940 (p) *This two-volume set contains copyright laws, regulations, and procedures of over 20 countries. Includes: accession to the Berne Convention, copyright standards, duration of protection, transfer of copyright, and remedies available for infringement.*

International Direct Marketing Guide (free) US Postal Service, International Products Management, Room 1140, 475 L'Enfant Plaza, SW, Washington, DC 20260-6520 (202) 268-6095 (p) or ask your local U.S. Postal Business Office. *Describes all facets of direct marketing techniques.*

International Exporting Agreements ($108) Pub. No. 424; Matthew Bender & Company, International Division, 11 Penn Plaza, New York, NY 10001 (800) 223-1940 (p) or (212) 967-7707 (p); damian@a.burns@bender.com (e); http://www.bender.com (w) *A practical guide to negotiating and drafting international contracts for export sales. Includes material on the international market, commercial contract, relevant international treaties, and strategies in risk management.*

Indochina Project Weekly ($35/year) 2001 S Street, NW, Washington, DC 20009 (202) 483-9222 (p); (202) 483-9314 (f) *Trade and political news.*

International Business ($48/year) ISSN 1060-4073 American International Publishing Corporation, 500 Mamaroneck Avenue, Suite 314, Harrison, NY 10528 (800) 274-8187 (p) or (914) 381-7700 (p) for subscriptions only *Monthly magazine that provides current analysis and factual information on the world of international business.*

International Information Report ($160/year) Washington Researchers, Ltd., P.O. Box 19005, 20th Street Station, Washington, DC 20036-9005 (202) 333-3499 (p); (202) 625-0656 (f) *Keeps you current on the best sources of data and insights on foreign competition, political risks, new export markets, global demographics and more.*

International Mail Manual ($17) U.S. Superintendent of Documents, P.O. Box 371954, Pittsburgh, PA 15250-7954 (202) 512-1800 (p); (202) 512-2250 (f); gpoaccess@gpo.gov (e) *Includes international postal rates, prohibitions, restrictions, and information on insurance availability, special services, etc.*

International Monetary Fund Publications Catalog (free) IMF, Publications Services, 700 19th Street, N.W., Room 10-540, Washington, D.C. 20431 (202) 623-7430 (p); (202) 623-7201 (f) *Listings of publications including world financial surveys, books, economic reviews, occasional papers, videotapes, statistical publications, CD-ROMs, periodicals, pamphlets, etc.*

International Trade Finance Handbook ($15) The Journal of Commerce, 445 Marshall Street, Phillipsburg, NJ 08865-9984 (800) 221-3777 (p); haddock@interport.net (e); http://www.joc.com (w) *The handbook explains the language of international trade, finance methods, and payment mechanisms. Descriptive charts show how to submit required paperwork.*

International Trade Forms: Shipper's Export Declaration; Canada Customs Invoice; and NAFTA Certificate of Origin (each $60 for 500) International Trade Institute, 5055 North Main St., Dayton, Ohio 45415 (800) 543-2453 (p); (937) 276-5920 (f) *Describes common documentation forms.*

International Trade Reporter's "Current Reports" ($1104/year) BNA Editorial Offices, 9435 Key West Avenue, Rockville, MD, 20850 (800) 372-1033 (p); (800) 253-0332 (f). *A weekly publication of the Bureau of National Affairs that identifies and monitors emerging and ongoing issues, provides timely facts and figures, descriptions and just-released official documents, and features focused reports from all regions of the world.*

International Trade Videotape Catalog (Individual Tapes are $89.99 each or an entire series at a discount) Waukesha County Technical College, 800 Main Street, Pewaukee, WI 53072 (414) 691-5550 (p); (414) 691-5089 (f) **Establishing Distribution Channels Overseas Series** (Develop Sales Leads Through U.S. Export Programs; Establishing Distribution Channels; Expand Your Export Potential With State Assistance; Overseas Promotion Through Trade Shows, Missions; Researching International Markets; Strategic Alliances); **Export/Import Documentation and Payment** (Basic Import Document Review; Export Documents and Payment Methods; Incoterms 1990; Payment Terms and the Import Letter of Credit; Simplifying Customs Clearance; U.S. Government Policy Toward Imports); **Export From Start Up To Finance Series** (Blunders and Goofs: Avoiding Company Embarrassment; Calculating An Export Price; Developing A Strategic Plan; Evaluating International Markets; FCIA: Minimizing Your Risk; Financing Your Exports; Product Modification Pricing Factors and Strategies); **International Sales Negotiations** (How Final Is The Contract; The Importance of Good Translation; The Negotiator: Profile of a Successful Negotiator; The Strategy: Guidelines for Successful Negotiations; The Style: International Negotiating Styles); **Legal Aspects of Exporting** (Export License Procedures; JV and License Procedures; Negotiating International Sales Contracts; Negotiating Agent/Distributor Agreements; Protecting International Property Rights; U.S. Law and International Business); **Transporting Products Overseas** (Cargo Insurance, Loss Prevention, and Claims; Choosing the Right Carrier; Packaging Your Exports; The Role of the Freight Forwarder; Transporting Hazardous Materials)

ISO 9000: Explained ($49) ISBN 1-882711-01-7; AQA Company 334 Crane Blvd., Los Angeles, CA 90065 (213) 222-3600 (p) *An excellent background book on this important international quality standard.*

ISO 9000: Handbook and Guide to Registration ($85) McGraw Hill, 10521 Braddock Road, Fairfax, VA 22032-2236 (800) 745-5565 (p); (630) 789-5507 (f) www.mcgrawhill.com (w) *Practical primer for those contemplating or currently involved in the registration process.*

ISO 9000: An Implementation Guide for Small to Mid-sized Businesses ($51.90) ISBN: 1-884015-10-7, St. Lucie Press, 100 E. Linton Blvd., Suite 403B, Delray Beach, FL 33483 (407) 274-9906 (p); (407) 274-9927 (f). *Road map to ISO 9000 certification specifically for small businesses, provides sample procedures, and real-life case studies.*

ISO 9000: Introduction for U.S. Business ($5) International Division Publications, U.S. Chamber of Commerce, 1615 H Street, NW, Washington, DC 20062-2000 (202) 463-5460 (p); (202) 463-3114 (f) *Introduces ISO 9000 standards and offers a list of references.*

ISO 9000: In Your Company ($9) ISBN 1-882711-03-3 AQA Company 334 Crane Blvd., Los Angeles, CA 90065 (213) 222-3600 (p) *Practical, "how-to" guide which explains how to achieve certification.*

ISO 9000: The 90-Day Manual ($184.95) ISBN: 1-884015-11-5 St. Lucie Press, 100 E. Linton Blvd., Suite 403B, Delray Beach, FL 33483 (407) 274-9906 (p); (407) 274-9927 (f). *Explains the concepts of ISO 9000, and includes forms needed to complete certification, a special help telephone number, standard updates, and covers what you need to know if you want to go beyond ISO 9000.*

ISO 9000: Quality Systems ($69) ISBN 1-882711-04-1; AQA Company 334 Crane Blvd., Los Angeles, CA 90065 (213) 222-3600 (p) *Explains how to develop a certifiable quality system.*

ISO 9000: Questions and Answers (free) National Institute of Standards and Technology, Standards Code Information Program, Office of Standards Service, Gaithersburg, MD 20899 (301) 975-4040 (p) *An excellent guide which answers the most commonly asked questions concerning ISO 9000.*

ISO 9000 Registered Company Directory ($195/yr) Irwin Professional Publishing, 11150 Main Street, Fairfax, VA 22030-5066 (800) 353-4809 ()p) or (703) 591-9008 (p); (703) 591-0971 (f) *A newsletter that supplies up-to-date information regarding industry, competition, customer leads, finding suppliers with ISO 9000 systems, choosing a registrar, and how to reduce audit costs.*

ISO 9000: Self-Study Guide ($130) American Management Association, P.O. Box 319, Saranack Lake, NY 12983 (518) 891-5510 (p); (518) 891-0368 (f); cust_serv@amanet.org (e); www.amanet.org (w) *Workbook approach to understanding the ISO 9000 process.*

ISO 9000 Videos ISO 9000: Making Your Company Competitive ($139); Employee Introduction to ISO 9000 ($129); A Practical Guide to Documenting and Implementing ISO 9000 ($379); Internal Auditing for ISO 9000 ($379) The Media Group, Inc., 18 Blair Park Road, Suite 100, Williston, VT 05495 (802) 879-5403 (p) or (800) 678-1003 (p); (802) 879-2702 (f). *This company provides a wide variety of training videos on ISO 9000, ISO 14000 and QS 9000.*

Japan Trade Directory ($265) ISBN 4-8224-0410-2; Gale Research Company, Book Tower, Dept. 77748, Detroit, MI 48226 (800) 223-GALE (p) *Complied by the Japanese External Trading Organization (JETRO), this guide provides information on Japanese companies and associations involved with overseas trade. Also includes a listing of products the Japanese would like to import and an extensive listing of Japanese companies.*

Journal of Commerce ($205/year) The Journal of Commerce, 445 Marshall Street, Phillipsburg, NJ 08865-9984 (800) 221-3777 (p); haddock@interport.net (e); http://www.joc.com (w) *A daily newspaper which provides trade leads, the latest news in the import and export worlds, and focuses upon the transportation field.*

Journal of International Marketing ($75/year) Michigan State University, Center for International Business Education & Research, MSU University Press, 14055 Harrison Road, Suite 25, East Lansing, MI 48823-5202 (517) 353-4336 (p) *A scholarly journal which publishes the latest research findings on export development programs.*

Key Officers of Foreign Service Posts: Guide for Business Representatives. ($5.00) State Department, Document S/N 744-006-00000-7, U.S. Superintendent of Documents, P.O. Box 371954, Pittsburgh, PA 15250-7954 (202) 512-1800 (p); (202) 512-2250 (f); gpoaccess@gpo.gov *This guide lists the key officials at foreign service posts including all embassies, missions, and consulates.*

Key Words In International Trade, ($59.95) ICC Publishing, 156 Fifth Avenue, Suite 305, New York, NY 10010 (212) 206-1150 (p), iccpub@interport.net (e) *Provides common terminology used in import and export transactions.*

Latin America Country Profiles ($55) International Division Publications, U.S. Chamber of Commerce, 1615 H Street, NW, Washington, DC 20062-2000 (202) 463-5460 (p); (202) 463-3114 (f) *Overviews the economic, political, trade and investment climate in 19 nations.*

Letters of Credit ($185) Matthew Bender and Co., International Division, 1275 Broadway, Albany, NY 12204 (800) 424-4200 (p) or (518) 487-3584 (p) *Provides an analysis of the law of commercial standby letters of credit and acceptance financing. Contains credit application forms with step-by-step analysis.*

Managing Cultural Differences ($39.95) Pub. No. 5078; ISBN 0-88415-078-X Gulf Publishing Company P.O. Box 2608 Houston, TX 77252-2608 (713) 520-4444 (p) or (800) 231-6275 (p) *Cultural influences on business management. Provides tips on the art of communicating with foreign nationals, business protocol and cross-cultural courtesy.*

Managing Foreign Exchange Risk ($29.95) ICC Publishing, 156 Fifth Avenue, Suite 305, New York, NY 10010 (212) 206-1150 (p), iccpub@interport.net (e) *Learn to use foreign exchange fluctuations to your advantage.*

Market: Europe ($377/year); ***Market: Asia Pacific*** ($295); ***Market: Latin America*** ($289) W-Two Publications, Ltd., 202 The Commons, Suite 401, Ithaca, NY 14850 (607) 277-0934 (p); (607) 277-0935 (f) *Provides reports on consumer demographic trends and lifestyles in the region each covers.*

Market Research International ($790) S/N: EP245 sub. 1994, Find/SVP, 625 Avenue of the Americas, New York, NY 10011-2002 (800) 346-3787 (p); (212) 807-2676 (f). *A new monthly journal that provides market information on consumer markets across the globe. Each issue features six diverse market reports. A year's subscription includes 72 reports plus quarterly marketing guides providing updates.*

Market Resource Guide to the Pacific Rim (free) U.S. Postal Service, International Product Management Division, Room 1140, 475 L'enfant Plaza, SW, Washington, DC 20260-6520 (202) 268-6095 (p) *Understand the opportunities of this emerging market.*

Market Share Reports ($11) National Technical Information Service, US Department of Commerce, 5285 Port Royal Road, Springfield, VA 22161 (703) 487-4600 (p) *Reports spanning a five-year period for approximately 1,000 commodities. Shows import statistics for eighty-plus countries and the U.S. export share of the import total.*

Marking of Country of Origin Brochure U.S. Customs Service, Public Information Office, Department of Treasury, P.O., Box 7407, Washington, DC 20044 (202) 927-5580 (p) *Explains how to obtain a certificate of origin.*

Mexican Importer ($395/year) The Journal of Commerce, 445 Marshall Street, Phillipsburg, NJ 08865-9984 (800) 221-3777 (p); haddock@interport.net (e); http://www.joc.com (w) *Provides names of importers and overseas suppliers.*

Multilateral Development Banks: Increasing U.S. Exports and Creating U.S. Jobs ($8.50) U.S. Superintendent of Documents, P.O. Box 371954, Pittsburgh, PA 15250-7954 (202) 512-1800 (p); (202) 512-2250 (f); gpoaccess@gpo.gov (e) *Shows how the multilateral development banks cooperate with the Export-Import Bank and other U.S. Government agencies to bolster U.S. exports and create jobs. Lists by state the firms that have won contracts.*

NAFTA: Clinton Administration Statement ($1.25) U.S. Superintendent of Documents, P.O. Box 371954, Pittsburgh, PA 15250-7954 (202) 512-1800 (p); (202) 512-2250 (f); gpoaccess@gpo.gov (e) *Includes questions and answers about the effectiveness of this trade agreement.*

NAFTA: Documentation and Procedures ($88.00) International Trade Institute, 5055 North Main St., Dayton, Ohio 45415 (800) 543-2453 (p); (937) 276-5920 (f) *Understand the documents required of our largest trading partners.*

NAFTA: Full Text (Volumes I and II) ($40) S/N 041-001-00407-6 U.S. Superintendent of Documents, P.O. Box 371954, Pittsburgh, PA 15250-7954 (202) 512-1800 (p); (202) 512-2250 (f); gpoaccess@gpo.gov (e) *U.S. Government-issued actual drafts of the NAFTA document. Treaty text is available at OAS web site at www.sice.oas.org/trade/nafta/nafta.stm.*

NAFTA: Guide to Customs Procedures (free) U.S. Custom's Service, P.O. 7407, Washington, DC 20044 (202) 927-6724 (p), http://www.customs.ustreas.gov (w) *A 55-page book explains how to obtain duty free or reduced duty for goods imported. Gives hypothetical examples of how the new rules affect manufacturers and traders and sources of further information.*

NAFTA: Guide To U.S. Implications for U.S. Business ($15.95) International Division Publications, U.S. Chamber of Commerce, 1615 H Street, N.W. Washington, DC 20062-2000 (202) 463-5460 (p); (202) 463-3114 (f) *This guide offers an analysis of NAFTA.*

NAFTA: Industry Sector Reports ($24) U.S. Superintendent of Documents, P.O. Box 371954, Pittsburgh, PA 15250-7954 (202) 512-1800 (p); (202) 512-2250 (f); gpoaccess@gpo.gov (e) *Articulates opportunities for U.S. industries through industry sector reports.*

NAFTA: An Overview ($40) U.S. Superintendent of Documents, P.O. Box 371954, Pittsburgh, PA 15250-7954 (202) 512-1800 (p); (202) 512-2250 (f); gpoaccess@gpo.gov (e) *Presents the agreement's objectives and guidelines to interpret the provisions.*

NAFTA: Supplemental Agreements ($6.50) S/N 041-001-00411-4 U.S. Superintendent of Documents, P.O. Box 371954, Pittsburgh, PA 15250-7954 (202) 512-1800 (p); (202) 512-2250 (f); gpoaccess@gpo.gov (e)

NAFTA: Tariff Schedule of Canada ($33) S/N 041-001-00409-2 U.S. Superintendent of Documents, P.O. Box 371954, Pittsburgh, PA 15250-7954 (202) 512-1800 (p); (202) 512-2250 (f); gpoaccess@gpo.gov (e)

NAFTA: Tariff Schedule of Mexico ($38) S/N 041-001-00410-6 U.S. Superintendent of Documents, P.O. Box 371954, Pittsburgh, PA 15250-7954 (202) 512-1800 (p); (202) 512-2250 (f); gpoaccess@gpo.gov (e)

NAFTA: Tariff Schedule of the United States ($37) S/N 041-001-00408-4 U.S. Superintendent of Documents, P.O. Box 371954, Pittsburgh, PA 15250-7954 (202) 512-1800 (p); (202) 512-2250 (f); gpoaccess@gpo.gov (e)

NAFTA: Visiting the Accord ($15.95) James Doyle, Inc., International Trade Research Center, 574 McBride Point Drive, St. Louis, MO 63011 (314) 458-0727 (p); (314) 532-5750 (f) *A good analysis of the impacts on the U.S., Canadian, and Mexican economies as a result of this historic trade agreement.*

National Highway and Airway Carriers Directory ($170/2 issues) National Highway Carriers, P.O. Box 6099, Buffalo Grove, IL 60089 (708) 634-0606 (p) *Lists all Less Than Truckload (LTTL) carriers including their routing sections for the U.S. and Canada. Includes a substantial listing of freight forwarders.*

New Standard Export Forms ($29.95) ICC Publishing, 156 Fifth Avenue, Suite 305, New York, NY 10010 (212) 206-1150 (p); iccpub@interport.net (e) *ICC provides a comprehensive collection of common export forms.*

North American Trade Guide ($329) Global Trade Publishing Group, 401 North Broad Street, Philadelphia, PA 19108 (800) 777-8074 (p); (215) 238-5412 (f) *Includes U.S.-Canada-Mexico NAFTA Tariff Schedules, explains how to import, export, and ship in these countries, and includes market profiles, guides to wholesalers and distributors in Canada and Mexico.*

Overseas Phonebooks (prices vary) M. Arman Publishing, Inc., P.O. Box 785, Ormond Beach, FL 32175 (904) 673-5576 (p); (904) 673-6560 (f) *Available 24 hours ($15-$250 per phone book), M. Arman is a distributor of worldwide phone books. Over 1,850 different directories for 120 countries, yellow pages and white pages, all latest editions possible. Complete phonebooks for major cities and countries such as Milan, Italy ($79.50); Al-Munawareh, Saudi Arabia ($93.30); Mainland China $160); Australia ($132); Thailand ($125); Dubai, UAE ($40); Moscow, Russia ($120); Chile ($45); Singapore ($120) .*

Palgrave Dictionary of Money & Finance ($595 = 3 vol.) ISBN 1-56159-041-X Stockton Press, 345 Park Avenue, 10th Floor, New York, NY 10110 (212) 689-9200 (p); (212) 212-689-9711 (f); grove@grovestocktn.com (e) *This encyclopedia of information has over 1,000 entries on money and finance matters.*

Passport Books - - Argentina, Brazil, China, France, Germany, Hong Kong, India, Indonesia, Israel, Italy, Japan, Korea, Mexico, Philippines, Poland, Russia, Singapore, Spain, South Africa, Taiwan, Thailand, United Kingdom, USA, Vietnam ($6.95 each or 10 for $59) World Trade Press, 1505 Fifth Avenue, San Rafael, CA 94901 (800) 833-8586 (p); (415) 453-7980 (f) *Provides country facts, cultural stereotypes, regional differences, overview of the business environment including negotiating tactics, customs and etiquette, and basic language phrases, useful in-country numbers and other useful information.*

PC-Translator ($985) Linguistic Products, Inc., P.O. Box 8263, The Woodlands, TX 77387 (713) 298-2565 (p); (713) 298-1911 (f) *Translates English documents into and from Spanish, French, Italian, Portuguese, Danish, Swedish, Norwegian, German, and Dutch.*

Persian Gulf, Trade and Investment Opportunities in the ($45) International Publications Division, U.S. Chamber of Commerce, 1615 H Street, NW, Washington, DC 20062-2000 (202) 463-5460 (p); (202) 463-3114 (f) *An introduction to U.S. opportunities in this region. Complete with marketing reports, trade contact lists, and regional overviews.*

Personal Safety Guide for International Travelers ($25.00 - quantity discounts available) Lee Security Consultants, 2044 Reynolds Street, Falls Church, VA 22043; (703) 237-3151; (703) 237-0804 (f) *This guide is international travelers. Educates travelers to make them comfortable traveling abroad, prevent incidents, and take appropriate actions.*

Pre-Screening Prospective Agents: Some Guidelines ($3.25) Research Bulletin #534, Manufacturers' Agents National Association, P.O. Box 3467, Laguna Hills, CA 92654 (714) 859-4040 (p) *Illustrates effective screening techniques of a potential agent or distributor to benefit both parties involved.*

Price Waterhouse Doing Business In ... Series (free) Contact your nearest Price Waterhouse office for any country in the 80-volume set. *These are primers on 80 countries throughout the world.*

Profitable Exporting: A Complete Guide To Marketing Your Products Abroad ($90) ISBN 0-471-61334-7 John Wiley & Sons, Inc., 1 Wiley Drive, Sommerset, NJ 08875 (800) 225-5945 (p); http://www/wiley.com (w) *A step-by-step guide on how to enter the export marketplace. This publication gives managers with no export background everything they need to get started in exporting.*

QS 9000 Handbook ($66.90) ISBN 1-57444-011-X, St. Lucie Press, 100 E. Linton Blvd., Suite 403B, Delray Beach, FL 33483 (407) 274-9906 (p); (407) 274-9927 (f). *A survival strategy for suppliers to the automotive industry. This book shows how to document quality systems, train personnel in quality, and improve the effectiveness of any independent quality assurance functions outside your operation.*

Questions & Answers For Export/Import ($44.50) International Trade Institute, 5055 North Main St., Dayton, Ohio 45415 (800) 543-2453 (p); (937) 276-5920 (f) *An excellent guide to the most commonly asked technical exporting questions.*

Registry of Export Intermediaries ($59.95) National Association of Export Companies (NEXCO) (212)725-3311 (p); (212)725-3312 (f). *This directory lists over 4,500 export management and trading companies nationwide who provide export assistance - directly or indirectly to manufacturers wishing to sell their products in foreign markets. The directory provides the names of key contacts, their product specialty, and their country/regional expertise.*

Restricted International Traders ($69) International Division Publications, U.S. Chamber of Commerce, 1615 H Street, NW, Washington, DC 20062-2000 (202) 463-5460 (p); (202) 463-3114 (f); http://www.uschamber.org (w) *A consolidated list of all companies/individuals who have had their trade privileges restricted.*

Schedule B: Statistical Classification of Domestic and Foreign Commodities Exported From The United States ($77) S/N 903-009-00000-4 U.S. Superintendent of Documents, P.O. Box 371954, Pittsburgh, PA 15250-7954 (202) 512-1800 (p); (202) 512-2250 (f); gpoaccess@gpo.gov (e) *This document will help you locate any HS number needed. The CD-ROM version is available from the U.S. Census Bureau for $20 at (301) 457-1086. Schedule B numbers are also available on the Internet at www.census.gov/foreign-trade/www/schedb97.html.*

Services: The Export of the 21st Century ($19.95) World Trade Press, 1505 Fifth Avenue, San Rafael, CA 94901 (800) 833-8586 (p); (415) 453-7980 (f) *Learn how to enter an international markets, which countries are open to different services, and how to break through market barriers. Includes case studies on how firms succeeded in exporting services.*

A Short Course In International Business Culture ($19.95) World Trade Press, 1505 Fifth Avenue, San Rafael, CA 94901 (800) 833-8586 (p); (415) 453-7980 (f) *Identifies cultural differences, explains how to read unspoken cultural signals, and pinpoints conflicts and opportunities facing businessmen and businesswomen.*

A Short Course In International Business Negotiating ($19.95) World Trade Press, 1505 Fifth Avenue, San Rafael, CA 94901 (800) 833-8586 (p); (415) 453-7980 (f) *Topics include the role of the negotiator, choosing your negotiating team, buyer vs. seller strategies, managing the agenda, language and translators, negotiating tactics, etc.*

A Short Course In International Contracts ($19.95) World Trade Press, 1505 Fifth Avenue, San Rafael, CA 94901 (800) 833-8586 (p); (415) 453-7980 (f) *Covers the underlying need for contracts in international business, general terms and provisions of standard contracts, use of attorneys, basics of a one-time sale, dispute resolution, arbitration and litigation. Extensive sample contracts are provided.*

A Short Course In International Economics ($19.95) World Trade Press, 1505 Fifth Avenue, San Rafael, CA 94901 (800) 833-8586 (p); (415) 453-7980 (f) *Provides concepts in balance of trade, trade agreements, foreign exchange, currency devaluation vs. appreciation, free trade vs. protectionism, foreign investment, barriers to trade, etc.*

A Short Course In International Entrepreneurial Trade ($19.95) World Trade Press, 1505 Fifth Avenue, San Rafael, CA 94901 (800) 833-8586 (p); (415) 453-7980 (f) *Covers terminology, sample proposals and contracts, and provides a basic overview of the foreign trade transaction.*

A Short Course in International Marketing (19.95) World Trade Press, 1505 Fifth Avenue, San Rafael, CA 94901 (800) 833-8586 (p); (415) 453-7980 (f) *Divided into 12 chapters and three sections of assessment and planning, market entry and promotion, and cultural issues and customer support.*

A Short Course In International Payments ($19.95) World Trade Press, 1505 Fifth Avenue, San Rafael, CA 94901 (800) 833-8586 (p); (415) 453-7980 (f) *For each party to each transaction, includes lists of what can go wrong and solutions for common problems. The book is a targeted training tool for traders, bankers, and brokers. Also included is coverage of foreign exchange, documents used in trade, letter of credit application and instructions, Incoterms of 1990, cyber transaction, etc.*

Sourcebook of International Trade (free) UNZ & Co., 190 Baldwin Avenue, Jersey City, NJ 07306 (800) 631-3098 (p); (908) 665-7866 (f); unzco@unzexport.com (w); http://www.unzexport.com (w) *This reference manual graphically illustrates how to fill out every type of export documentation.*

Standby/Commercial Letters of Credit ($159.95) ICC Publishing, 156 Fifth Avenue, Suite 305, New York, NY 10010 (212) 206-1150 (p), iccpub@interport.net (e)

Standard Handbook of Industrial Distributors ($95) Bergano Books Co., P.O. Box 190, Fairfield, CT 06430 (203) 254-2054 (p) *Locate distributors in your country of choice for industrial products. Contains a comprehensive analysis of leading distributors, dealers, agents, and representatives in more than 90 countries.*

Tax Havens of the World ($350) Pub No. 722, Matthew Bender and Company, 1275 Broadway, Albany, NY 10224 (800) 223-1940 (p) or (212) 967-7707 (p) *Examines tax havens in 50 areas around the world and rates each on the basis of 30 vital features. Tax reform pitfalls are also analyzed. Gives expert advice on how to gain a foothold in a specific tax haven, qualify for investment and capital incentives, insulate profits, and more.*

Trade Show and Convention Guide ($115) BPI Communications, Amusement Business, Box 24970, Nashville, TN 37202 (615) 321-4250 (p); (615) 327-1575 (f) *Includes dates for five years.*

TradeshoWeek Data Book ($355) Reed Reference Publishing.; 121 Chanton Road, New Providence, NJ (800) 521-8110 (p); info@reedref.com (e) *A weekly source of statistics and new tradeshows.*

Trade Shows Worldwide ($255) ISBN: 0-8103-8079-X; ISSN: 1046-4395; Gale Research, Inc., 835 Penobscot Building, Detroit, MI 48226-4094 (800) 347-GALE (p); (313) 961-6815 (f); galeord@gale.com (e) *Excellent listing of all the major tradeshows held throughout the world.*

Trading Company Sourcebook International Business Affairs Corporation, 4938 Hampden Lane, Suite 346, Bethesda, MD 20814 (301) 907-8647 (p) *A directory of export management/trading company associations.*

Trading With . . . ($25) from The Journal of Commerce ($365 annual subscription price) The Journal of Commerce, 445 Marshall Street, Phillipsburg, NJ 08865-9984 (800) 221-3777 (p); haddock@interport.net (e); http://www.joc.com (w) *Includes current and potential importers and exporters, documentation and entry requirements, tariffs, quotas and currency, restrictions are included, as well as normal business hours and official holidays.*

Translation Services Directory ($75) American Translators Association, 1800 Diagonal Road, Suite 220, Alexandria, VA 22314 (703) 683-6100 (p), 73546.2032@compuserve.com (e). *Lists over 1,500 accredited translators throughout the United States and the world.*

Transportation Telephone Tickler ($94.95) The Journal of Commerce, 445 Marshall Street, Phillipsburg, NJ 08865-9984 (800) 221-3777 (p); haddock@interport.net (e); http://www.joc.com (w) *A complete directory of freight services and facilities in North America. Contains verified information on more than 25,000 companies ranging from airlines to water carriers. Also publishes Eximbank Letter which covers government and private sources of export finance.*

UCP 500/1993 Revision ($10.95); **Uniform Rules: Bank-to-Bank Requirements** ($10.95); **Uniform Rules: Contract Guarantee** ($15.95) ICC Publishing, 156 Fifth Avenue, Suite 305, New York, NY 10010 (212) 206-1150 (p); iccpub@interport.net (e).

U.S. Custom House Guide ($399) North American Publishing Company, 401 North Broad Street, Philadelphia, PA 19108 (800) 777-8074 (p); (215) 238-5412 (f) *Provides the most current U.S. Harmonized Tariff Schedule, complete U.S. Customs Regulations, directories of import service providers, profiles of U.S. and Canadian ports of entry, and import "how-to" advice.*

U.S. Global Trade Outlook, 1995-2000 ($19) S/N 003-009-00650-3 U.S. Superintendent of Documents, P.O. Box 371954, Pittsburgh, PA 15250-7954 (202) 512-1800 (p); (202) 512-2250 (f); gpoaccess@gpo.gov (e) *An annual publication that provides detailed and comprehensive business forecasts for 350 U.S. industries. Forecasts contain information on the condition of the industry domestically and its competitiveness overseas.*

U.S. Trade Shifts in Selected Industries ($15) U.S. Superintendent of Documents, P.O. Box 371954, Pittsburgh, PA 15250-7954 (202) 512-1800 (p); (202) 512-2250 (f); gpoaccess@gpo.gov (e) *A virtual encyclopedia of trade data, complete with performance analysis of more than 300 major U.S. industry groups. Keeps readers abreast of important changes in industrial imports and export in U.S.-bilateral trade balances for key agricultural and manufactured commodities.*

Uruguay Round of Multilateral Trade Negotiations, General Agreement on Tariffs and Trade ($40) U.S. Superintendent of Documents, P.O. Box 371954, Pittsburgh, PA 15250-7954 (202) 512-1800 (p); (202) 512-2250 (f); gpoaccess@gpo.gov (e) *Contains the final act embodying the Uruguay Round, the agreement establishing the World Trade Organization, the agreement of government procurements, etc.*

U.S. Import Requirements (free) U.S. Custom's Service, P.O. 7407, Washington, DC 20044, (202) 927-6724 (p); http://www.customs.ustreas.gov (w) *A concise general guidebook on importing into the United States.*

Washington Researcher's International Information Report ($160) ISSN 0748-206X Washington Researchers, 2612 P Street, N.W. Washington, DC (202) 333-3533 (p) *For company research.*

Washington Tariff & Trade Letter ($437/52 weeks) Washington Tariff & Trade Letter, P.O. Box 467, Washington, D.C. 20044 (800) 270-9989 (p); (301) 570-4545 (f) *Offer insider information on trade bills and current issues in Congress and with agencies including the U.S. Trade Representative, International Trade Commission, International Trade Administration, Bureau of Export Administration, Customs Services, Court of International Trade, Export-Import Bank, U.S. Departments of State and Treasury.*

Weekly Roundup of World Production and Trade (free) U.S. Department of Agriculture, Information Division, Room 5920, S. Building, Foreign Agriculture Service, Washington, DC 20250-1000 (202) 447-7937 (p) *Offers current items and trade statistics on various agricultural commodities and a summary of recent developments in world production and trade.*

West European Country Profiles ($45) International Division Publications, U.S. Chamber of Commerce, 1615 H Street, NW, Washington, DC 20062-2000 (202) 463-5460 (p); (202) 463-3114 (f) *Overviews on the 12 member countries, contact lists, and the investment climate of the EC.*

What's Working for American Companies in International Sales and Marketing ($391/23 issues per year) Progressive Business Publications, P.O. Box 3019, 370 Technology Drive, Malvern, PA 19355-0719 (800) 220-5000 (p); (610) 647-8089 (f) *Provides tips from and experiences of seasoned international traders. Call for a free sample issue.*

Who's Who of American Customs Brokers and International Freight Forwarders ($12) National Customs Brokers and Forwarders Association of America, One World Trade Center, Suite 1153, New York, New York 10048 (212) 432-0050 (p) *This membership directory lists qualified freight forwarders.*

Women's Guide to Overseas Living ($15.95) Intercultural Press, Inc.; P.O. Box 700, Yarmouth, ME 04096; (207) 846-5168 (p); intercultural@internetmci.com (e) *A helpful guide for women executives venturing overseas.*

World Bank Publications, An Index of (free) World Bank Publications, P.O. Box 7247-8619, Philadelphia, PA 19170-8619 (202) 477-1234 (p); (202) 676-0581 (f) *This index lists all the financial programs the World Bank offers.*

Worldcasts 60,000 abstracted product forecasts for 150 countries ($975 per volume or $1,450 for 8 volumes) Predicasts, 11001 Cedar Avenue, Cleveland, OH 44106 (800) 321-6388 (p) or (216) 795-3000 (p) *An 8-volume series with 60,000 abstracted product and market forecasts for 150 countries which provides short- and long-term projections for consumption, employment, production and capacity.*

World Patent Law and Practice Publication No 622, Matthew Bender and Company, 11 Penn Plaza, New York, NY 10016 (800) 223-1940 (p) or (212) 967-7707 (p); (212) 532-5737 (f) *An up-to-date collection of patent statutes, rules and regulations for more than 200 countries.*

World Payment Systems Handbook ($39.95) ICC Publishing, 156 Fifth Avenue, Suite 305, New York, NY 10010 (212) 206-1150 (p), iccpub@interport.net (e)

World Trade ($24/year) World Trade, P.O. Box 3000, Department WT, Denville, NJ 07834-9815 *Monthly magazine that often highlights case studies of successful exporters.*

World Trade Almanac: Economic, Marketing, Trade, Culture, Legal & Travel Surveys for the World's Top 100 Countries ($87.00) World Trade Press, 1505 Fifth Avenue, San Rafael, CA 94901 (800) 833-8586 (p); (415) 453-7980 (f) *The most comprehensive single-volume international trade reference in the world. Includes economic sector profiles, maps, trade statistics, business culture, marketing, legal, monetary, travel, and contact information.*

World Trade and Customs Directory ($399) International Division Publications, U.S. Chamber of Commerce, 1615 H Street, NW, Washington, DC 20062-2000 (202) 463-5460 (p); (202) 463-3114 (f) *Contacts in 100 foreign countries.*

World Trade Mark Law and Practice Pub No. 425, Matthew Bender and Company, 2 Park Avenue, New York, NY 10001 (800) 223-1940 (p) or (212) 967-7707 (p) *The complete guide to world trademark law and practice. Brings together textual analysis of trademark law abroad, practical solutions for day-to-day trademark practices, and essential practice tools.*

World Population ($4.50) S/N 003-024-06706-4 U.S. Superintendent of Documents, P.O. Box 371954, Pittsburgh, PA 15250-7954 (202) 512-1800 (p); (202) 512-2250 (f); gpoaccess@gpo.gov (e)

Worldwide Trading Partner Locating System ($495) Applied Technologies International Corp., 2255 Morello Avenue, Pleasant Hill, CA 94523-1850 (510) 680-0200 (p); (800) 406-1581 (f) *A company profile database of over 250,000 importers, exporters, distributors, wholesalers, manufacturers, direct users and commission agents in 150 countries.*

Year In Trade ($14) U.S. Superintendent of Documents, P.O. Box 371954, Pittsburgh, PA 15250-7954 (202) 512-1800 (p); (202) 512-2250 (f); gpoaccess@gpo.gov (e) *Annual review from the U.S. International Trade Commission covers more than 20 major trade agreements, bilateral trade issues with major U.S. partners, overview of the World Trade Organization, a complete listing of antidumping, countervailing duty, intellectual property right infringement, and section 301 cases, etc.*

Your Trip Abroad and **Tips For Travelers** ($1.00 each) Booklets for Travelers U.S. Superintendent of Documents, P.O. Box 371954, Pittsburgh, PA 15250-7954 (202) 512-1800 (p); (202) 512-2250 (f); gpoaccess@gpo.gov (e) *The booklet, **Your Trip Abroad**, offers information on passports, visas and services overseas. **Tips For Travelers** is available for the Caribbean, China, Eastern Europe, and South Africa.*

INTERNATIONAL BUSINESS RESOURCES ESPECIALLY FOR ECONOMIC DEVELOPERS AND EDUCATORS

This special section was written for international trade professionals seeking to develop or enhance their export assistance program. It includes International Business Publications and Periodicals Especially for Economic Developers and Educators, a Sample International Business Course Outline, an International Business Community Survey Cover Letter And Survey Instrument, and Fostering An Export Development Strategy

American Management & Business Internship Training Program (AMBIT). AMBIT, International Trade Administration, US Department of Commerce, Room 3319, Washington D.C. 20230 (202) 482-2076 (p); (202) 482-2443 (f). *AMBIT is a program of the International Trade Administration whereby U.S. firms provide one- to six-month training programs for managers and technical experts from other countries.*

Clearing House on State International Policies (free) Corporation for Enterprise Development, 1829 East Franklin Street, Suite 800 E, Chapel Hill, NC 27514 (919) 967-5300 (p) *An excellent monthly newsletter which profiles successful state-based export development programs, provides current issue analysis, and highlights the latest trends, tools, and developments in the United States.*

Candidate Evaluator (CEVAL); Company Readiness to Export (CORE IV); Distributor; Freight; and Partner Software Programs (one module $295, each additional is $100, all four is $495) Michigan State University, International Business Center, 6 Kellogg Center, East Lansing, MI 48824-1022 (517) 353-9229 (p) *Software analysis decision support tools to evaluate a firm's capacity and commitment to exporting.*

Directory of Local Chambers Which Maintain International Trade Services ($10.00) U.S. Chamber of Commerce, 1615 H Street, N.W., Washington, D.C. 20062 (202) 463-5460 (p); (202) 463-3114 (f); http://www.uschamber.org (w) *Key contacts throughout the U.S.*

Establishing an International Business Research Program ($8.00) Association of Applied Community Researchers, American Chamber of Commerce, 4232 King Street, Alexandria, VA 22302 (703) 998-0072 (p) or (703) 467-1550 (p) *Offers getting-started advice to economic developers just beginning to focus upon exporting.*

Export Expert Software ($179.95 or $74.95) Columbia Cascade, Inc., 12020 Sunrise Valley Drive, Suite 200, Reston, VA 22091-3429 (703) 860-0866 (p); (703) 860-8449 (f) *DOS and Windows version computer program that walks you through the intricacies of pursuing world markets.*

Export Legal Assistance Network (free) Contact any Small Business Administration District Office or contact the National Coordinator of ELAN, 1667 K Street, N.W., Washington, D.C. 20006 (202) 778-3080 (p); (202) 778-3063 (f); jkelso@porterwright.com (e); http://www.miep.org (w) *ELAN is a nationwide group of attorneys with experience in international trade who provide free initial consults to small business on export matters.*

Gaining the Export Edge: International Business for Small Business ($2000) Michigan Small Business Development Center, 2727 Second Avenue, Detroit, MI 48201 (313) 964-1798 (p), (313) 946-3648 (f); stateoffice@misbdc.wayne.edu (e) *Extensive workbook on the essential elements of an international business plan, developed in a comprehensive training format. State-only licenses granted to statewide organizations. Training offered on an annual basis in Michigan. Call for information on licensing in your state or sending firms to attend the Michigan training program.*

Going Global: How Europe Helps Small Firms Export ($9.95) ISBN 0-8157-6203-8 Brookings Institution, Department 029, Washington, DC 20042-0029 (800) 275-1447 (p) *Profiles successful programs implemented by European countries to help their companies expand into international markets.*

Guide To Doing Business With AID (free) Agency for International Development, Office of Small and Disadvantaged Businesses, 1100 Wilson Blvd. Suite 1220 A, Roslyn, VA 22209 (703) 875-1551 (p); (703) 875-1862 (f) *Lucrative business contracts are awarded to normal, everyday businesses on a regular basis.*

Harmonized Schedule Code Search for Windows 24-697 ($225); **1997 Schedule B 55-837349** ($349); **Layman's Guide To Schedule B** ($29) Unz & Co., 190 Baldwin Avenue, Jersey City, NJ 07306 (800) 631-3098(p) or (201) 795-5400 (p); (908) 665-7866 (f) *The harmonized system is the worldwide standard for classifying products.*

IBEX ($100 per month or $1000 annually) Global Business Alliance, Inc., 1615 H Street, N.W. Washington, D.C., 20062-2000 (800) 537-4239 (p) or (800) 638-6582 (p); http://www.unibex.com (w) *Supported by the U.S. Chamber of Commerce, IBEX is an electronic commerce system containing 13 million firms to identify, qualify, and negotiate confidentially with business partners in the U.S. or abroad. Companies must have a Dun & Bradstreet number to qualify for listing on the service.*

International Business Curriculum Modules ($199 total 5 vol. set) Coastline Community College, 11460 Warner, Fountain Valley, CA 92708 (714) 241-6243 (p) *These are outstanding outlines and primers on over 200 international business issues. Great for class outlines, and research material.*

International Business Teaching ($39.95) ISBN 1-56024-796-7 International Business Press, 10 Alice Street, Bingamton, NY 13904-1580 (800) 429-9678 (p); (800) 895-0582 (f); getinfo@haworth.com (e) *Written to enhance student's understanding of both the structural global dimensions and functional dimensions of international business.*

International Careers ($10.95) ISBN 0-913589 28-4 Williamson Publishing, Church Hills Road, P.O. Box 185 Charlotte, VT 05445 (800) 234-8791 (p) *Where to find jobs abroad.*

The International State ($25) ISBN: 0-89843-186-7 The Aspen Institute, 1333 New Hampshire Avenue, N.W., Washington, D.C. 20036 (202) 736-5804 (p); (202) 467-0790 *This is an outstanding publication which discusses trade assistance programs in the United States and suggests ways to reinvent these programs. Author Carol Conway is a highly regarded expert on the development export development programs.*

International Trade Data Network (ITDN) ($5,000) Rhode Island Export Assistance Center, Bryant College, 1150 Douglas Pike, Smithfield, RI 02917-1284 (401) 232-6239 (p); (401) 232-6416 (f); ptivey@bryant.edu (e) *The ITDN is a non-profit, data multiplier that provides timely, detailed market intelligence needed to be competitive in the global arena. The pc-based, search and retrieval software contains market research, export contacts, travel information, trade leads, and other international business numbers and news.*

Instructional Videos for International Business (prices listed below) Big World Inc., 1350 Pine Street, Suite 5, Boulder, CO 80302 (800) 682-1261 (p) or (303) 444-6179 (p); (303) 444-1261 (f); bigworld@aol.com (e); http://www/bwvideo.com (w) *Call for a free preview.* Ethics In International Business ($450); Building the Transnational Team ($450); Doing Business In Latin America ($450 each or $1,194 series of 4); Doing Business In Southeast Asia ($450 each or $1,195 series of 3); Doing Business Internationally: The Cross-Cultural Challenges ($450); Emerging Markets of Eastern Europe and Russia ($450); Globally Speaking: Asia ($395 each or $1,995 series of 6); Go for the Globe: Game Plans for the New World Market ($450); Going International ($400 each or $2,400 series of 7); The Multicultural Customer ($595) Negotiating in Today's World ($495); New Skills for Global Management ($450); Shedding Light on the Single European Market ($450); Tearing Down The Walls: The CEO Change Forces ($450); Working With China ($395 each or $1,995 series of 6); and Working With Japan ($395 each or $1,995 series of 7)

National Export Strategy ($7.50 each) U.S. Superintendent of Documents, P.O. Box 371954, Pittsburgh, PA 15250-7954 (202) 512-1800 (p); (202) 512-2250 (f); gpoaccess@gpo.gov (e) *Report which highlights progress made by the U.S. government in supporting global commerce, improving trade finance, helping firms export, etc.*

National Trade Data Bank (on CD-ROM) ($575/year or $59/single issue) U.S. Department of Commerce, Room H-4885, Washington, DC 20230 (800) 782-8872 (p) *The NTDB contains statistics and information on fifteen international agencies. Includes Census data by commodity and by country, market reports on specific products, and answers just about any question you might have.*

National Trade Data Bank Manual ($22.50) Bermam Press, 4611-F Assembly Drive, Lanham, MD 20706 (800) 865-3457 (p); (800) 865-3450 (f); order@bernan.com (e); http://www.bernan.com (w) *The manual's easy-to-understand tips and directions allows researchers of all skill levels to quickly access the full scope of the CD-ROM.*

Snowdon International Protocol, Inc.; 235 East 57th Street, Suite 7E; New York, NY 10022 (212) 247-4152; (212) 750-0390 (f) *Trainers of corporate executives, government officials etc., in cross cultural communications. They offer several acclaimed publications and a "Global Protocol Fax Service" for 62 countries.*

Training For Trade: Community College Programs To Promote Exporting ($22.50) ISBN: 87117-222-4 AACC, One DuPont Circle, N.W., Suite 410, Washington, DC, 20036 (202) 728-0200 (p) *Offers case studies of outstanding programs which have successfully helped businesses penetrate export markets.*

Transition: The Newsletter About Reforming Economies ($20/year) The World Bank, Box 7247-7956, Philadelphia, PA 19170-7956 (201) 476-2192 (p); (201) 476-2197 (f) *An excellent guide to changes in developing economies. Sound, reliable, poignant, and interesting.*

The World in 2002: Power, Culture and Prosperity ($24.95) ISBN 0 87584 604 1 Harvard Business School Press, Customer Service Dept., Soldiers Field, Boston, MA 02163 (800) 545-7685 (p); (617) 495-6985 (f). *Offers a vision of a world in which developed nations become increasingly able to imitate one another as innovations cross borders within days. Demonstrates how changes in demography, environment, government, technology, and natural resources will contribute increased competition.*

SAMPLE INTERNATIONAL BUSINESS COURSE SYLLABUS

Business, Economic, and Political Aspects of International Trade

A number of international business instructors have asked how *Trade Secrets* can be used in undergraduate and graduate classes. On the next page you will find a syllabus used in a course cross-listed with business, political science, and economics. *Trade Secrets* should be one of three or four books which covers the business, political, and economic aspects of international trade. Suggested texts are *Annual Editions: Global Issues*, and *Annual Editions: International Business*, Dushkin Publishing Group, (800) 338-5578; *International Economics and International Economic Policy, A Reader*, by Philip King, McGraw Hill, (800) 525-5003; and *Trade Secrets: The Export Answer Book*, second edition, Wayne State University, (313) 964-1798.

Course Description

International relations influence the conducting of business. By the same token, the conducting of business influences international relations. The intent of this course is to provide the student with a variety of concepts, ideas, and theories to create a synergistic understanding of how international trade is conducted in a political environment. It is critically important that students consider the strong forces which have reshaped the world political economy. New social, business, and political conditions include advanced electronic communications, the demise of the authoritarian left as a political ideology, progress toward worldwide economic integration, and a regional redistribution of wealth.

The student will be exposed to the transactional nature of international trade by becoming familiar with the terms, processes, and problems of international trade. Included are marketing, cultural, logistical, regulatory, financial, and regional aspects of conducting international trade. Students will receive a broad overview of international business by considering the multinational corporation and its place in the global economy, emerging and established markets, issues in international production, ethical implications of doing business in a global economy, and regional approaches to conducting international trade. Attention will be given to emerging international political economic concepts in light of the end of the cold war and increasing economic competition. Also covered are the new World Trade Organization, the new world economy, foreign aid and development, and geographic trends. International business, political, economic, and socio-cultural events that occur during the course will be discussed and analyzed in light of the concepts and theories presented.

Course Requirements

Except under exceptional circumstances, no incompletes will be given. Students will write four five-page, double-spaced Position Papers (worth 60%) based on course readings and limited independent research. It is expected that these papers will integrate the various theoretical and practical business concepts presented throughout the course. All papers are to be written in a professional, collegiate manner, including proper sentence structure, grammar usage, and style.

The Class Participation (worth 15%) grade will be awarded at the discretion of the instructor, as an evaluation of the student's participation in class. It is expected that students will give professional attention to assigned readings and arrive prepared to discuss these readings during class. The student is expected to attend class. As part of the overall class participation grade, students will make two presentations to the class by presenting their answers to two of the questions which are presented at the beginning of each class. Students are expected to present a one-page briefing for the class which outlines an answer to the question posed.

The Take Home Final (worth 25%) is a final exercise which will allow students to reflect on and summarize the course material.

International Business Course Outline

Introduction *Do exports really matter to a nation's strategic and competitive advantage?*

Toward A Global Village *What are recent political, technological, and economic changes which have contributed to the development of the "global village?"*

Fair or Free Trade? *Should governments pass legislation and negotiate agreements with other countries to help businesses compete in a global business environment? After presenting both sides of the argument, offer your opinion.*

***Export Development Issues** *What steps should governments take to encourage the development of exports?*

Trade Barriers *Describe types of unfair trade practices. Is it important to open foreign markets? Why or why not?*

Trade Agreements *What are arguments for and against unification of the North American market? Why do you approve or disapprove of NAFTA?*

How Trade Is Conducted *Your boss asks you to write a memorandum to her presenting your opinion on whether or not the company should export its products. Because the company has never exported, tell her how international trade is conducted.*

***Cultural and Ethical Issues** *Why is it important to consider cultural and ethical issues when conducting international trade?*

Environmental Issues *How should business respond to the increasing conflicts between economic freedom and resource conservation?*

North American Economies *What is unique and important about the North America economies?*

***Emerging Economies** *Select an emerging economy. Will your chosen country become a strong market economy in the near future or not? Why is it so difficult for formerly socialist countries to change from a planned economy to a free market economy?*

****Established Economies** *What are the essential elements of being successful in an established economy?*

***The Future Of International Trade** *How will conducting international trade be different in the 21st Century?*

*= position paper due; ** = final exam distributed

International Business Course Final Exam

The final exam of this course will allow you to demonstrate what you have learned. The exam requires that you reflect upon and summarize course material, lectures, and class discussions. It is segmented into five sections, each worth 20 points. Try to limit your answers to not more than two to three pages per question.

1. Identify at least three recent political changes, three recent technological changes, and three recent economic changes which have contributed to the development of the "global village." Include in each of these factors your assessment on why these factors have contributed to the global village.

2. Governments throughout the world develop policies and regulations to encourage the development of exports. Offer a strategic policy which includes 10 to12 ways your particular government can help its companies export. Make sure you consider ways to respond to unfair trade practices in other countries as you design your strategy.

3. Using *Trade Secrets* as your primary reference, what do you see as inherent challenges businesses face as they enter a global market? Include in your discussion marketing, cultural, logistical, financial, and regulatory barriers that are prevalent in the conduct of international trade.

4. List and discuss 10 to 15 factors which contribute to the growth and sustainment of a nation's economy. Make sure you include in your discussion why these factors are important.

5. Select any target market country. Does your chosen country offer strong export opportunities? What are some of the demographic, economic, political, socio-cultural, and market factors which compelled you to select this market? In selecting your target market, it may be helpful to refer to the Market Factor Assessment chart on page 13 of *Trade Secrets* as you evaluate and argue for your target market.

Alternate Question

One of the questions can be substituted if you prefer to conduct an interview with an international trade expert. If you decide to conduct an interview, include the 5 to 10 questions you asked of your expert, a brief synopsis of his or her answer, indicate if you agree or disagree with the response, and, most importantly, tell me why you agree or disagree. Ask anything which interests you, but ensure that your questions are substantive and relate to some of the issues we discussed in class. Suggestion: develop your questions first, then try to find your expert. Also, try to complete this section of the exam first because you may have difficulty tracking someone down and they may provide helpful insights as you complete other sections of the exam.

INTERNATIONAL BUSINESS COMMUNITY SURVEY COVER LETTER

The following survey can be used to ensure that counseling, training, research, advocacy programs, and publications are developed which are responsive to the SME.

Month, date, year

Name
Company Name
Address
City, State Zip

Dear :

Whether or not you export, your perceptions and experiences with trade can become an important factor in delivering quality help to small businesses who would or should export — if they knew how to do it as easily and painlessly as possible.

International trade for small businesses is timely and important. Exporting has never been a more opportune means of expanding sales and profits than it is today. As one business owner has said, "If I hadn't started exporting, I would be out of business today." The growing interdependence in our global economy crystallizes the importance of international trade to business survival and success.

But we know that many small businesses don't even begin exporting and we are interested in determining why. We do know it is imperative that businesses like yours have access to the information, training, and resources you need to be competitive in today's rapidly changing business environment.

To participate in this study, simply take 10 to 15 minutes to complete the enclosed questionnaire. The questions ask about your firm's goals for international market penetration, and the training and services you would need to achieve them. Your participation in this study will be held in the highest regard. Strict confidentiality of all information that you provide is guaranteed.

We realize how valuable your time is and appreciate your willingness to share your thoughts and ideas. A stamped, self-addressed envelope is enclosed for your convenience in returning the questionnaire by [deadline should be within two weeks of receipt of survey].

If you have any questions, please feel free to contact me at ______________________.

Thank you in advance for your participation in this research.

Sincerely,

(Name and title)

INTERNATIONAL BUSINESS COMMUNITY SURVEY INSTRUMENT

This questionnaire is designed to gather information about your attitudes toward developing export markets and to learn about your firm. This survey will be utilized to (give the reason, such as to develop an International Trade Certificate program, develop a publication to help small firms have access to information they need to export their products and services, or to develop an export development program which responds to SME needs, etc.). All information collected here is completely confidential and no firm will ever be identified by name in any report. Please help us make this research a success by answering all the questions as honestly and as completely as you can. Please return the survey in the self-addressed, stamped envelope provided.

Confidential Survey On Company's International Business Practices

MANUFACTURER ______________________________
EXPORT MANAGER/TITLE ______________________________
ADDRESS ____________________ CITY ____________________ ZIP __________
PHONE ____________________ FAX ____________________ EMAIL ____________________

Firm Characteristics ______________________________
Age of firm ______________
Number of employees ______________

1. Describe the nature of your company's products/services. ______________________________
2. Please rate the business experience of the top management team in each of the following areas:
   Little/No Experience = 1; Extensive Experience = 7

International Marketing	❑ 1	❑ 2	❑ 3	❑ 4	❑ 5	❑ 6	❑ 7
International Finance	❑ 1	❑ 2	❑ 3	❑ 4	❑ 5	❑ 6	❑ 7
Transportation/Freight Forwarding	❑ 1	❑ 2	❑ 3	❑ 4	❑ 5	❑ 6	❑ 7
International Business Negotiations	❑ 1	❑ 2	❑ 3	❑ 4	❑ 5	❑ 6	❑ 7
Agent/Distributorship Relationships	❑ 1	❑ 2	❑ 3	❑ 4	❑ 5	❑ 6	❑ 7
Documentation for Export Sales	❑ 1	❑ 2	❑ 3	❑ 4	❑ 5	❑ 6	❑ 7
Protecting Products In Foreign Markets	❑ 1	❑ 2	❑ 3	❑ 4	❑ 5	❑ 6	❑ 7

   Please give the names and title of those employees currently involved in exporting:

   ____________________ ____________________
   ____________________ ____________________

   Question #2 allows the surveyor the opportunity to determine overall company weaknesses and to establish a database by functional category.

3. How does exporting play a role in your long-range corporate goals and objectives?

   ____

   Question #3 allows the surveyor the opportunity to target those firms serious about expanding their market.

4. What percentage of company revenue is attained overseas_____% Our goal is to reach _____% by 2000.

   Typically, the average response is that 5% of company revenues is attained overseas and the goal is 20%. Although each year, the percentages are increasing.

5. What percentage of purchases are from overseas (i.e., imported?) _____%

   Typically, the average response is 1% but some companies import 95% of their components.

6. What forms of marketing are enlisted for company sales?

DOMESTIC	INTERNATIONAL	
___Catalogue	___Catalogue	___Production Overseas
___Direct Sales	___Direct Sales	___Agent/Distributor
___Licensing	___Licensing	___ExportManagement Company
___Trade Show	___Trade Show	
___Sales Representative	___Sales Representative	
___Yellow Pages	___Export Yellow Pages	

   Question #6 is designed to change the mindset of the firm that is reluctant to export (i.e., it gets them thinking that marketing products abroad is not that different than marketing domestically).

7. Have potential international customers contacted you requesting bids for your products?

   ___No ___Yes
   ___order was too small to ship.
   ___did not respond—lack of expertise in quoting the bid.
   ___unfamiliar with country's import rules/regulations.
   ___staff unable to research/develop bid proposal.
   ___company does not manufacture what customer needs.
   ___we filled requested order and are pursuing other leads.

Question #7 allows the surveyor the opportunity to understand how reactive the firm is.

8. Do you feel the opportunity exists for your company to export (more)?
If yes, why? ____
___ Production capabilities under-utilized for the domestic market.
___ Aware of domestic competitors active in global market.
___ Received bid request from potential customers.
___ Stagnate domestic sales or slow growth.

If no, why not?____
___ Capital investment required.
___ Uncertain of market potential.
___ Lack of in-house expertise.

Question #8 allows the surveyor the opportunity to understand why the firm seeks sales and to understand overall barriers to exporting.

9. If you are not exporting or not meeting its export potential, what are the obstacles?
___ Unfamiliarity with export payment terms.
___ Unfamiliarity on how to generate international sales.
___ Unfamiliarity with export distribution channels.
___ Inability to research the appropriate market.
___ Unaware of export marketing.
___ Our sales literature is not developed for foreign markets.
___ Export licensing regulations to cumbersome.
___ Uncomfortable with determining an appropriate price when responding to bids.

Question #9 allows the surveyor the opportunity to find out how to target or focus on problematic areas by developing responsive training programs, etc.

10. In which of the following areas do you feel need strengthening in order to become an efficient exporter?

___ Payment and collection methods	___ Exposure to Cultural Differences	___ Licensing
___ Identifying foreign markets	___ Overseas Procurement	___ Marketing and Sales
___ Documentation	___ Distribution Channels	___ Shipping

Question #10 is used to show where to push for special marketing efforts (used primarily to market an international trade certificate program).

11. On a scale from 1 - 7, with 1 being "irrelevant" to 10 being "useful," please rate how useful the following topics would be to a business owner, international sales manager, or someone looking to learn about international trade.

Case Studies of Successful Small Business Exporters	❑ 1	❑ 2	❑ 3	❑ 4	❑ 5	❑ 6	❑ 7
International Marketing	❑ 1	❑ 2	❑ 3	❑ 4	❑ 5	❑ 6	❑ 7
International Finance	❑ 1	❑ 2	❑ 3	❑ 4	❑ 5	❑ 6	❑ 7
Transportation/Freight Forwarding	❑ 1	❑ 2	❑ 3	❑ 4	❑ 5	❑ 6	❑ 7
International Business Negotiations	❑ 1	❑ 2	❑ 3	❑ 4	❑ 5	❑ 6	❑ 7
Agent/Distributorship Relationships	❑ 1	❑ 2	❑ 3	❑ 4	❑ 5	❑ 6	❑ 7
Documentation for Export Sales	❑ 1	❑ 2	❑ 3	❑ 4	❑ 5	❑ 6	❑ 7
Contract/Legal Agreements	❑ 1	❑ 2	❑ 3	❑ 4	❑ 5	❑ 6	❑ 7
Tax/Accounting Methods	❑ 1	❑ 2	❑ 3	❑ 4	❑ 5	❑ 6	❑ 7
Protecting Products In Foreign Markets	❑ 1	❑ 2	❑ 3	❑ 4	❑ 5	❑ 6	❑ 7
Cultural Comparisons	❑ 1	❑ 2	❑ 3	❑ 4	❑ 5	❑ 6	❑ 7
Resources Available	❑ 1	❑ 2	❑ 3	❑ 4	❑ 5	❑ 6	❑ 7
Sources of Market Information	❑ 1	❑ 2	❑ 3	❑ 4	❑ 5	❑ 6	❑ 7
ISO 9000	❑ 1	❑ 2	❑ 3	❑ 4	❑ 5	❑ 6	❑ 7
Country-Specific Studies	❑ 1	❑ 2	❑ 3	❑ 4	❑ 5	❑ 6	❑ 7

Again, answers to this question will showcase firms' overall concerns.

12. Please indicate to which regions the firm has/seeks to export, by indicating C for current or P for planned.

❑ C ❑ P Africa	❑ C ❑ P Central Europe	❑ C ❑ P North America	❑ C ❑ P Scandinavia
❑ C ❑ P ASEAN	❑ C ❑ P Eastern Europe	❑ C ❑ P Pacific Rim	
❑ C ❑ P CIS	❑ C ❑ P Near/Middle East	❑ C ❑ P South America	

Answers to question #12 will allow the EDO the chance to design programs and publications around the firms' target markets.

13. If you decided to expand/explore your international business potential, what sort of information would you be seeking?

14. Where would you call in search of this international business information?

Question #14 will identify the respected (real or perceived) trade organizations and if the EDO is considered a respected player. It is suggested that an advisory board be formed by these respected organizations.

15. Comments

MOTIVATING FACTORS TO EXPORT

Attract new sources of demand
Promote products in markets where little competition exists
Benefit from economies of scale
Exploit monopolistic advantages
Capitalize on cyclical downturns
Trade where the local currency is strong
Penetrate markets with negligible trade restrictions
Trade in markets where the government does not control the price of products
Respond to cyclical downturns

FIRMS' CONCERNS REGARDING EXPORTING

Fear of not getting paid
Burdensome paperwork
Limited access to export financing
Banks unwilling or unable to facilitate the export transaction
Protectionism or closed foreign market entry
Lack of in-house expertise to conduct market research
Language barriers and cultural differences
Shipping procedures
Perception of little return for a high degree of investment
Competition
Channels of distribution
Payment conditions
Transferability of money

CORE FUNCTIONS OF AN EXPORT DEVELOPMENT PROGRAM

Counseling
Training/Education
Research
Publications
Partnership building
Advocacy

CORE FOCI OF AN EXPORT DEVELOPMENT PROGRAM

Basics of exporting
Cultural comparisons
Documentation
Finance
Insurance
Pricing
Quality standards
Marketing
Packaging
Resources Available
Regulations
Shipping

HOW TO ACHIEVE THE CORE FUNCTIONS OF AN EXPORT DEVELOPMENT PROGRAM

Counseling activities

Offer one-on-one counseling with new-to-export firms and current exporters
Offer exporter roundtable discussions by industry sector
Create mentor/protégé relationships with existing/prospective exporters
Provide trade leads from various public and private sources
Conduct agent and distributor searches
Support overseas offices (leads, promotion, trade intelligence, contacts)
Offer assistance in obtaining financing
Represent companies through catalogue and on-site trade shows
Establish an Office of Trade Show Development

Training activities

Offer a comprehensive, on-going international business certificate training program
Organize and run one-time only seminars, workshops, lectures, and conferences

Research activities

Identify public or private sources of information and assistance
Create a public access library
Customize market research through arrangements with students/firms
Establish student and business intern programs with successful exporters
Send trade delegations overseas and invite trade delegations from other countries
Design and conduct an annual business community survey
Publish trade leads, how-to guides, success stories, databases, newsletters, and software programs
Develop an electronic newsletter to communicate international business opportunities
Organize an automated information retrieval system (e.g., Flash Fax system)
Prepare, maintain, and publish importer directories
Develop directories of businesses seeking joint venture partners
Publish handbooks on the transactional process of trade, including local case studies
Publish trade leads by industry sector
Produce foreign market studies (e.g., market characteristics, distribution channels, import and export data)
Prepare foreign trade statistics based on information found in the NTDB
Collect and publish current prices and price indexes for a selected range of products

Advocacy activities

Create export awareness among firms reluctant to export
Establish an advisory board of public and private organizations including EDOs, freight forwarders, banks, Chambers, legislators, etc. (strategic plan key board function)
Establish working partnerships with trade-focused organizations
Create a comprehensive listing of public and private EDOs within the state of region
Identify distinct service delivery activities of these groups
Offer an annual legislative symposium to promote a better understanding among legislators of international trade and its importance to the state
Establish an annual Export Award (firms, and public, private, and nonprofit organizations)
Foster a community-based export strategy

FOSTERING A COMMUNITY-BASED EXPORT STRATEGY

Coalesce Key Leaders

When developing a community-based export strategy, it is critically important to the synergistic and long-term success of a program that partnerships be developed with all economic development groups that consider international trade a component of their mission or activities. The following core group should decide upon and implement the export strategy, developed according to the region's unique practices and resources.

- Leading exporters
- SMEs currently not exporting
- Private and public sector export intermediaries
- Legislative decisionmakers
- Educators

Articulate a Strategic, Shared Vision

Although difficult and time consuming to achieve, it is imperative that this group agrees to the vision and commits to working through a process that may be fraught with tension. Groups will begin to understand that clearly defined activities lends to greater accountability in the delivery of services, causing some to be hesitant to participate in this process. However, a strategic, widely-shared vision is imperative to more broadly assist SMEs through the export process.

Clearly articulate export development goals

Once the vision has been articulated, broad goals need to be developed (i.e., what are the overall goals or reasons why an export strategy is being developed?). The next phase will involve defining objectives or delivery activities which will achieve the goals.

Create a Deeply Integrated, Public-Private Trade Development System

- Clearly identify the core service delivery areas of all organizations. Because there are many distinct, niche services that can be offered, the success of the strategy will be directly related to how well groups can identify all of the services that can be offered at a national, regional, state, and local level.
- Adopt a clear understanding of which group will provide which service.
- Ensure that services are offered based on client-articulated needs.
- Divide the system into core performance areas (counseling, training, research, publications, partnership building, and advocacy).
- Articulate key services under each core performance area. It is at this point that all of the partners to the strategy define "who will do what."

Operate Based on Memoranda of Understanding

Once the system has been adopted, memoranda of understanding should be developed which commit the partners to providing the distinct services which were defined during the process of structuring of the export development system.

PRIVATE AND PUBLIC SECTOR EXPORT INTERMEDIARIES

- Accountants
- Airlines
- Banks
- Chambers of commerce
- Current and prospective exporters
- District Export Councils
- Educators
- Embassies and Consulates
- Export management/trading companies
- Foreign trade zones
- Foundations
- Freight forwarders/customhouse brokers
- Insurance providers
- International Visitors Councils
- Japanese External Trade Organization
- Lawyers
- Legislators
- Local government officials
- Media
- Multilateral development banks
- National Association of State Development Agencies
- Port authorities
- Postal/shipping services
- Small Business Development Centers
- Service Corps of Retired Executives
- Sister Cities International
- Small Business Administration
- State Departments of Commerce
- State international offices
- Telephone companies
- Trade and industry associations
- Trade consultants
- Department of Commerce—International Trade Administration
- Utilities
- World Trade Centers Association
- United Nations and other multilateral organizations
- Venture capitalists

The establishment of advisory boards, strategic planning committees, and conference development committees are excellent means to develop and maintain communication and solid, working partnerships with public and private export intermediaries. In order to accomplish a synergistic and comprehensive approach, these groups should be brought together to develop a strategic plan, analyze problems, formulate recommendations, contribute to the formulation of policies, help develop the community-based export strategy, and coordinate activities of public and private export development organizations.

EXAMPLES OF PARTNERSHIPS DEVELOPED BY THE MICHIGAN SMALL BUSINESS DEVELOPMENT CENTER TO FOSTER INCREASED EXPORTS

In 1996, the U.S. Small Business Administration named the Michigan Small Business Development Center Export Partner of the Year. Following are some of the collarborative relationships developed to foster an increase in Michigan's exports.

Annual World Trade Week Conference and Exhibition
The World Trade Week conference and exhibition is a partnership involving more than twenty export-oriented organizations, including the Greater Detroit Chamber of Commerce, which coordinates the event. Organized by executive, marketing, finance, and program committees, representatives from these groups meet on a monthly basis throughout the year to plan and share costs of the four-track conference which attracted a record 350 firms and organizations in 1997. Sponsoring partners to the program benefit by being recognized as a key player in the export community and by having the ability to network with private sector export intermediaries throughout the year which often results in additional unrelated partnership opportunities.

Gaining the Export Edge: International Business for Small Business
This international trade certificate program is a 56-hour multi-topical program which is licensed for use throughout the United States. The Michigan SBDC identified a national corporate sponsor to fund the development, marketing, and printing costs of this comprehensive export education program. The sponsoring firm benefits from national marketing efforts undertaken by the SBDC, public relations/goodwill, and the nurturing of exporting firms that can later use services of the sponsoring organization.

International Trade Research Program and Library
The International Trade Research Program offers graduate student research assistants the opportunity to conduct internatioanl trade research on behalf of small firms. Students gain practical experience through nine months spent at the SBDC and three months at the sponsoring firm. Benefits from subsidization of this program are multiple: business counselors don't spend time on market research and analysis, clients can make informed decisions through research provided, and the firm benefits from national/statewide marketing, goodwill, and a opportunity for the firm to have customized research and analysis undertaken by students during summer months.

International Business Resources Listing
In an attempt to reduce costs of maintaining its library, the Michigan SBDC seeks donations of often expensive materials. Because many publishers are reluctant to donate resources without a direct benefit in return, the Michigan SBDC has agreed to list donated products in a comprehensive list. Distributed throughout the U.S., the International Trade Resources guide is considered a definitive listing of international trade resources by educators, consultants, and librarians. Containing more than 600 books, guides, periodicals, software programs, etc., this guide contains complete ordering and pricing information along with a brief description of each product.

Equipment, Publications, Software Donations
In an effort to limit the expense of purchasing equipment, publications, and software programs for 55 SBDCs located throughout Michigan, the Michigan SBDC has developed a number of partnerships whereby a manufacturer or publisher will donate products to the SBDC in exchange for the distribution of up to 10,000 press releases which gives thanks for the donation, describes the product, and advertises the availability of the product for use at the SBDC. Such arrangements have worked very well for JIAN (business planning software), DataMerge (financing sources software), Gale Research (CD-ROM databases), Microsoft (training videos, computers), etc. Donating firms benefit by expanding market opportunities in hard to reach markets, and the SBDC benefits by substantially reducing the cost of buying products and by providing useful business tools to its firms.

SBDC License or Donation of SBDC Publications
The Michigan SBDC is recognized as credible source of international business information and, as such, is contacted by organizations seeking low-cost or no-cost information on a variety of topics. In an attempt to cover costs of research and to more widely distribute this information, the Michigan SBDC will license for a nominal fee to other organizations the rights to reprint publications which gives clear benefits to both parties. For example, *Trade Secrets: The Export Answer Book* has been licensed to Idaho, Illinois, South Carolina, Maryland, and Virginia. The International Trade Centre in Geneva is currently adapting the publication for use in twenty developing countries.

***NAFTA Opportunities* Newsletter**
The NAFTA Opportunities newsletter offer firms practical, actionable information on exporting to Canada. Export intermediaries, marketing experts, and educators supply articles for the newsletter which Michigan SBDC designs, publishes, and distributes. The contributor benefits by getting published and is recognized by firms as a respected expert. The SBDC benefits from reduced time and expense writing and researching for the publication, the content of which is current, cutting edge. Please note: Other SBDC publications are directly subsidized by firms. In return for printing the publications, SBDC places their logos on the publication as a contributing sponsor. Other organizations could produce country-specific newsletters.

Internet Access and Web Server
The Michigan SBDC Internet Marketing Study is an 18-month research study which tracks the successes, failures, and frustrations of 15 firms as they internationally (and domestically) market their product through the Internet. BizServe serves as the Internet Service Provider at no cost to the firm under study. BizServe has benefited from public relations and media exposure which has generated a number of fee-paying clients. The SBDC benefits through a reduction in cost of home-page maintenance and the access to technical expertise at BizServe.

International Business Center Advisory Board
The International Center Advisory Board is a 15-member board comprised of local, small, and successful exporters. Members benefit by serving and influencing their community while the SBDC benefits by receiving advice in the development of practical counseling, training, and research programs that are responsive to the business community's need for assistance. The SBDC's role is to coordinate the program with advice and consent of the community board.

Private Sector Donation of Counseling Hours to SBDC Clients
Attorneys, bankers, finance specialists, marketing consultants, graphic designers, Internet consultants, etc. provide pro bono counseling to SBDC clients throughout the state. This is emphasized in our program for two reasons. First, it gives clients the finest knowledge available in areas which extend beyond SBDC in-house capabilities. Secondly, it reduces concern that SBDCs are providing, free of charge, services which the private sector offers. The SBDC benefits from access to expertise at no charge and the firms benefit by gaining the opportunity to forge longer term, fee-based relationships with client.

ABOUT THE NATIONAL ASSOCIATION OF SMALL BUSINESS INTERNATIONAL TRADE EDUCATORS

The National Association of Small Business International Trade Educators (NASBITE) was formed in 1988 to promote and enhance the involvement and competitiveness of small businesses in international trade through education and training. NASBITE has a board of governors, executive committee, and three working committees. The board of governors is comprised of international trade professionals from community colleges, economic development organizations, private sector businesses, and universities. These international trade experts offer their experience and expertise to this international organization. NASBITE is a 501 (c) (3) nonprofit Oregon Corporation.

MISSION OF NASBITE

To improve global competitiveness through effective education and training.

OBJECTIVES

Facilitate the exchange of information among those involved in international trade education of small business;

Provide professional development for those involved in support of small business international trade education; and

Provide advocacy and leadership for international trade education professionals through establishing linkages and working relationships with public and private sector organizations.

BENEFITS OF JOINING NASBITE

Access To Expertise. NASBITE consists of high caliber international trade experts.

Annual Conference. Experts present workshops and seminars of current interest to international trade educators, trainers, and consultants. Attendees consistently rave about the high "take away" value of the conference.

Communication Linkages. NASBITE offers a listserv for its current members. The electronic network provides immediate access to international trade professionals, educational initiatives, and international trade developments.

International Trade Educator of The Year Award and Program Excellence Awards. As a national organization, NASBITE recognizes excellence in the field of international business training and education.

Membership Directory. Annual listing of member name, address, phone, fax and e-mail numbers.

Professional Development. NASBITE offers an exceptional opportunity to remain on the cutting edge of international trade issues, programs, innovative curricula, and resources.

WHO SHOULD JOIN NASBITE?

In order to keep businesses competitive, partnerships must form between a diverse group of professionals from a variety of points of view. NASBITE is an exceptional organization for interaction with international trade professionals including:

Business Assistance Organizations

Chamber of Commerce International Trade Officers
District Export Council Appointees
Small Business Development Center Directors
State Officers of International Trade

Educators

Community College Business Instructors
Community College Training Directors
University Business Professors
International Business Students
Title VI B Grant Winners

Federal Government

Agency for International Development
Department of Commerce
Department of Education
Department of State Country Desk Officers
Ex-Im Bank
Federal Trade Commission
International Trade Commission
US & FCS International Trade Specialists
U.S. Small Business Administration
World Bank

Private Sector

Corporations
International Trade Consultants
Small- and Medium-sized Businesses
World Trade Center Association staff

Get involved with an international network of trade educators, consultants, and policy makers. **Expand** your professional and career development. **Meet** educators from public and private colleges and universities; representatives from state, regional, national organizations; and private sector businesses and individuals. **Receive** program development updates. **Interact** with small business international trade educators. **Gain access** to program development resources, curricula, course outlines, and data bases. **Learn** about upcoming international trade grants and RFPs. **Gather** trade legislation information. **Receive** special discounts on NASBITE-sponsored events. **Associate** with trade professionals worldwide. **Keep informed** of employment opportunities. **Attend** the annual international conference and specialized "train the trainer" workshops on model programs, curriculum development, and international business trends and developments.

MEMBERSHIP APPLICATION

Membership in NASBITE is open to any person or organization interested in international trade education and small business issues. Annual membership dues are:

Individual:	US $ 75.00
Institutional:	US $ 225.00

The membership year is one year from date of receipt of membership application.

1. Name ______________________________

   Title ______________________________

Please include names of three other members from your organization, if you are joining under an institutional membership:

2. Name ______________________________

   Title ______________________________

3. Name ______________________________

   Title ______________________________

4. Name ______________________________

   Title ______________________________

ORGANIZATION ______________________________

ADDRESS ______________________________

CITY ______________________ STATE ______________________

ZIP ______________________ COUNTRY ______________________

PHONE ______________________ FACSIMILE ______________________

E-MAIL ______________________

A check for ____________ is enclosed.

Please mail application form to:

NASBITE
c/o Michigan Small Business Development Center
2727 Second Avenue
Detroit, MI 48201
(313) 964-1798 (p)
(313) 964-3648 (f)
stateoffice@misbdc.wayne.edu

The International Business Plan

PRODUCTS/SERVICES

STEP 1: Select the most exportable products to be offered internationally.

To identify products with export potential for distribution internationally, you need to consider products that are successfully distributed in the domestic market. The product needs to fill a targeted need for the purchaser in export markets according to price, value to customer/country, and market demand.

What are the major products your business sells?

1. ____________
2. ____________
3. ____________

What products have the best potential for international trade?

1. ____________
2. ____________
3. ____________

STEP 2: Evaluate the products to be offered internationally.

What makes your products unique for an overseas market?

1. ____________
2. ____________
3. ____________

Why will international buyers purchase the products from your country?

1. ____________
2. ____________
3. ____________

How much inventory will be necessary to sell overseas?

1. ____________
2. ____________
3. ____________

EXCERCISE:

IDENTIFYING PRODUCTS WITH EXPORT POTENTIAL

List below the products you believe have export potential. Indicate the reasons you believe each product will be successful in the international marketplace.

PRODUCTS/SERVICES	REASONS FOR EXPORT SUCCESS
1.	1.
2.	2.
3.	3.
4.	4.
5.	5.
6.	6.
7.	7.
8.	8.
9.	9.
10.	10.

PLANNING

What is the purpose of completing this workbook?
You know that you want to see your company grow through exporting.

Five reasons it will be worth your time and effort:

1. Careful completion of this workbook will help evaluate your level of commitment to exporting.
2. The completed workbook can help you evaluate your product's potential for the international trade market.
3. The workbook gives you a tool to help you better manage your international business operations successfully .
4. The completed workbook will help you communicate your business ideas to persons outside your business and can be an excellent starting point for developing an international financing proposal.
5. Businesses managed are more successful when working from a business plan.

Can't I hire someone to do this for me?
This is your business. If the business plan is to be useful, it must reflect your ideas and efforts-not those of an outsider.

Why is planning so important?
The planning process forces you to look at your future business operations and anticipate what will happen. This process better prepares you for the future and makes you more knowledgeable about your business. Planning is vital for marketing your product in an international marketplace.

Any firm considering entering into international business transactions must understand that doing business internationally is not a simple task nor one for the faint of heart. It is stimulating and potentially profitable in the long-term but requires much preparation and research prior to the first transaction.

In considering products for the international market, a business needs to be:

1. Successful in its present domestic operation.
2. Willing to commit its resources of time, people and capital to the program. Entry into the international market may take as long as two years to generate profit with cash outflow during that period.
3. Sensitive and aware of the cultural implications of doing business internationally.

Developing a business plan helps you assess your present market situation, business goals, and commitment which will increase your opportunities for success.

What's the bottom line for me if I do the plan?
Research shows that small business failure rates among new businesses are significantly higher than for new businesses that have developed a business plan.

Isn't planning just for the big companies?
Planning is important for any organization that wants to approach the future with a plan of action. The future comes, whether you are prepared for it or not. A business plan helps you anticipate the future and make well-informed decisions because you have thought about the alternatives you will be facing.

How often do I have to do this?
A plan must be revised as needed, at least once a year. Planning is a continuous process. You will be surprised how much easier it is to develop a business plan after the first time. Plus, after a revision or two you will know more about your international business market opportunities to export products.

GOAL SETTING

Determine your business goals can be a very exciting and often challenging process. It is, however, a very important step in planning your entry into the international marketplace. The following exercise is intended to help you clarify your short and long-term business goals.

STEP 1: Define long-term goals.

A) What are your long-term goals for this business in the next 5 years? Examples: increase export sales by ______% annually; develop country cultural profiles.

B) How will the international trade market help you reach your long-term goals?

STEP 2: Define short-term goals

A) For your international business, what are your first year goals?

Examples: attend export seminars, select a freight forwarder.

B) What are your two-year goals for your international business products/ services?

STEP 3: Develop an action plan to reach your short-term goals by using international trade.

INDUSTRY ANALYSIS

STEP 1: Determine your industry's growth for the next 3 years.

Talk to people in the same business or industry, research industry-specific magazines, attend trade fairs and seminars.

STEP 2: Research how competitive your industry is in the global markets.

Utilize the National Trade Data Bank (NTDB), obtain import/export statistics from the Bureau of the Census, and contact the U.S. Small Business Administration (SBA) or the U.S. Department of Commerce (DOC) district office in your area.

STEP 3: Find out your industry's future growth in the international market.

Contact the SBA or the U.S. Foreign & Commercial Service (US&FCS) district office and contact a DOC country or industry desk in Washington, DC

STEP 4: Research federal or state government market studies that have been conducted on your industry's potential international markets.

Contact SBA, your state international trade office, a DOC country or industry desk in Washington, D.C,

STEP 5: Find export data available on your industry.

Contact your SBA or DOC district office.

YOUR BUSINESS/COMPANY ANALYSIS

STEP 1: Why is your business successful in the domestic market? What's your growth rate?

STEP 2: What products do you feel have export potential?

STEP 3: What are the competitive advantages of your products or business over the domestic and international businesses?

EXERCISE:

PROS AND CONS OF MARKET EXPANSION

Brainstorm a list of pros and cons for expanding your market internationally. Based on your product and market knowledge, determine your probability of success in the international market.

Industry/Product: ____________________

PROs

1. ____________
2. ____________
3. ____________
4. ____________
5. ____________
6. ____________
7. ____________
8. ____________
9. ____________
10. ____________

CONs

1. ____________
2. ____________
3. ____________
4. ____________
5. ____________
6. ____________
7. ____________
8. ____________
9. ____________
10. ____________

PROBABILITY OF SUCCESS

0% — 25% — 50% — 75 — 100%

WORKSHEET

EXPORT PROGRAMS & SERVICES

This worksheet helps you identify organizational resources that can provide programs and services to assist you in developing your international business plan and increase your export sales.

	ORGANIZATIONS					
SERVICES	***SBA Office***	***USDOC Office***	***SBDC***	***Trade Association***	***University/ Community College***	***World Trade Center***
Readiness to Export						
Assessment						
Market Research						
Studies						
Counseling						
Training Seminars						
Education Programs						
Publications						
Export Guides						
Data Banks						
Trade Shows						
Financing						

MARKETING YOUR PRODUCT

Given the market potential for your products in international markets, how is your product unique?

1. What are your product's advantages?
2. What are your product's disadvantages?
3. What are the competitive product's advantages?
4. What are the competitive product's disadvantages?

What are the needs that will be filled by your product in a foreign market?

What competitive products are sold abroad and to whom?

How complex is your product? What skills or special training are required to:

1. Install your product?
2. Use your product?
3. Maintain your product?

MARKETING YOUR PRODUCT *Continued*

4. Service your product?

What options and accessories are available?

1. Has an aftermarket been developed for your product?
2. What other equipment does the buyer need to use your product?
3. What complementary goods does your product require?

If your product is an industrial good:

1. What firms are likely to use it?
2. What is the useful life of your product?

3. Is use or life affected by climate? If so how?

4. Will geography affect product purchase, for example transportation problems?

5. Will the product be restricted abroad, for example tariffs, quotas or non-tariff barriers?

If the product is a consumer good:

1. Who will consume it? How frequently will the product be bought?

2. Is the consumption affected by climate?

3. Is consumption affected by geography, for example transportation problems?

4. Will the product be restricted abroad for example tariffs, quotas or non-tariff barriers?

5. Does your product conflict with traditions, habits or beliefs of customers abroad?

STEP 1: Select the best countries to market your product.

The first step in a sequential screening process for the company is to select the more attractive countries for your product. Preliminary screening involves defining the physical, political, economic and cultural environment.

(1) Select 4 countries you think have the best market potential for your product;
(2) Research data/information for each country;
(3) Rate each factor on a scale of 1-5 with 5 being the best; and
(4) Select a target market country based on your ratings

MARKET FACTOR ASSESSMENT	COUNTRY	COUNTRY	COUNTRY	COUNTRY
Demographic/Physical Environment:				
• Population size, growth, density				
• Urban and rural distribution				
• Climate and weather variations				
• Shipping distance				
• Product-significant demographics				
• Physical distribution and communication network				
• Natural resources				
Political Environment:				
• System of government				
• Political stability and continuity				
• Ideological orientation				
• Government involvement in business				
• Attitudes toward foreign business (trade restrictions, tariffs, non-tariff barriers, bilateral trade agreements)				
• National economic and developmental priorities				
Economic Environment:				
• Overall level of development				
• Economic growth: GNP, industrial sector				
• Role of foreign trade in the economy				
• Currency: inflation rate,availability, controls				
• Balance of payments				
• Per capita income and distribution				
• Disposable income				

MARKET FACTOR ASSESSMENT	COUNTRY	COUNTRY	COUNTRY	COUNTRY
Social/Cultural Environment:				
• Literacy rate, educational level				
• Existence of middle class				
• Similarities and differences in relation to home market				
• Language and other cultural considerations				
Market Access:				
• Limitations on trade: high tariff levels, quotas				
• Documentation and import regulations				
• Local standards, practices				
• Patents and trademark protection				
• Preferential treaties				
• Legal considerations for investment, taxation, repatriation, employment, code of laws				
Product Potential				
• Customer needs and desires				
• Local production, imports, consumption				
• Exposure to and acceptance of product				
• Availability of linking products				
• Industry-specific key indicators of demand				
• Attitudes toward products of foreign origin				
• Competitive offerings				
Local Distribution and Production:				
• Availability of intermediaries				
• Regional and local transportation facilities				
• Availability of manpower				
• Conditions for local manufacture				

Indicators of population, income levels and consumption patterns should be considered. In addition, statistics on local production trends, along with imports and exports of the product category, are helpful for assessing industry market potential. Often, an industry will have a few key indicators or measures that will help them determine the industry strength and demand within an international market. A manufacturer of medical equipment, for example, may use the number of hospital beds, the number of surgeries, and public expenditures for health care as indicators to assess the potential for its products.

What are the projected growth rates for the two countries selected over in the next 3-5 years?

STEP 2: Determine Projected Sales Levels

What is your present U.S. market percentage?

What is the projected growth in these international markets over the next five years?

What sales volume will you project for your products in these international markets for the coming year?

What is the projected growth in these international markets over the next five years?

STEP 3: *Identify Customers Within Your Chosen Markets*

What companies, agents or distributors have purchased similar products?

What companies, agents, or distributors have purchased similar products?

What companies, agents, or distributors would most likely be prospective customers for your export products?

STEP 4: Determining Method Of Export

How do other U.S. firms sell in the markets you have chosen?

Will you sell direct to the customer?

1. Who will represent your firm?

2. Who will service the customers needs?

STEP 5: Building A Distributor or Agent Relationship

Will you appoint an agent or distributor to handle your export market?

1. What facilities does the agent or distributor need to service the market?

2. What type of client should your agent or distributor be familiar with in order to sell your product?

3. What territory should the agent or distributor cover?

4. What financial strength should the agent or distributor have?

5. What other competitive or non-competitive or non-competitive lines are acceptable or not acceptable for the agent or distributor need and how often will they cover the territory?

6. How many sales representatives does the agent or distributor need and how often will they cover the territory?

Will you use an export management company to do your marketing and distribution for you? **YES NO**

If yes, have you developed an acceptable sales and marketing plan with realistic goals you can agree to?

YES NO

Comments:

SUPPORT FUNCTIONS

To achieve efficient sales offerings to buyers in the targeted markets, several concerns regarding products, literature and customer relations should be addressed.

STEP 1: Identify product concerns.

Can the potential buyer see a functioning model or sample of your product that is substantially the same as would be received from production?

YES **NO**

Comments:

What product labeling requirements must be met? (Metric measurements, AC or DC electrical, voltage, etc.) Keep in mind that the European Community now requires 3 languages on all new packaging.

When and how can product conversion requirements be obtained?

Can product be delivered on time as ordered? **YES** **NO**

Comments:

STEP 2: Identify literature concerns.

If required, will you have literature in language other than English?

YES **NO**

Do you need a product literature translator to handle the technical language?

YES **NO**

What special concerns should be addressed in sales literature to ensure quality and informative representation of your product?

STEP 3: Identify customer relations concerns.

What is delivery time and method of shipment?

What are payment terms?

What are the warranty terms?

Who will service the product when needed?

How will you communicate with your customer?...through a local agent, telex or fax?

Are you prepared to give the same order and delivery preference to your international customers that you give to your domestic customers?

YES **NO**

MARKETING STRATEGY

In international sales, the chosen "terms of sale" are most important. Where should you make the product available: at your plant, at the port of exit, landed at the port of importation, or delivered free and clear to the customer's door? The answer to this question involves determining what the market requires, and how much risk you are willing to take.

Pricing strategy depends on "terms of sale" and also considers value-added services of bringing the product to the international market.

STEP 1: Define International Pricing Strategy.

How do you calculate the price for each product?

What factors have you considered in setting prices?

What products' sales are very sensitive to price changes?

How important is pricing in your overall marketing strategy?

What are your discount policies?

What terms of sales are best for your export product?

STEP 2: Define promotional strategy

What advertising materials will you use?

In what trade show or trade missions will you participate, if any?

What time of year and how often will foreign travel be made to customer markets?

STEP 3: Define customer services

What special customer services do you offer?

What types of payment options do you offer?

How do you handle merchandise customers return?

SALES FORECAST

Forecasting sales of your product is the starting point for your financial projections. The sales forecast is extremely important, so it is important you use realistic estimates. Remember that sales forecasts show the expected time the sale is made. Actual cash flow will be impacted by delivery date and payment terms.

STEP 1: Fill in the units-sold line for markets 1, 2, and 3 for each year on the following worksheet.

STEP 2: Fill in the sales price per unit for products sold in markets 1, 2, 3.

STEP 3: Calculate the total sales for each of the different markets (units sold x sales price per unit).

STEP 4: Calculate the sales (all markets) for each year - add down the columns.

STEP 5: Calculate the five year total sales for each market - add across the rows.

SALES FORECASTS - FIRST FIVE YEARS

	1	*2*	*3*	*4*	*5*
Market 1					
Units Sold					
Sale Price/Unit					
Total Sales					
Market 2					
Units Sold					
Sale Price/Unit					
Total Sales					
Market 3					
Units Sold					
Sale Price/Unit					
Total Sales					
Total Sales					
All Markets					

COSTS OF GOODS SOLD

The cost of goods sold internationally is partially determined by pricing strategies and terms of sale. To ascertain the costs associated with the different terms of sale, it will be necessary to consult an international freight forwarder. For example, a typical term of sale offered by a U.S. exporter is cost, insurance and freight (CIF) port of destination. Your price includes all the costs to move product to the port of destination. A typical cost work sheet will include some of the following factors, These costs are in addition to the material and labor used in the manufacture of your product.

export packing
container loading
inland freight
truck/rail unloading
wharfage
handling
terminal charges
ocean freight
bunker surcharge
courier mail

forwarding
documentation
consular legalization
bank documentation
dispatch
bank collection fees
cargo insurance
other misc.
telex

STEP 1: Fill in the units-sold line for market 1, 2, and 3 for each year.

STEP 2: Fill in the sales price per unit for products sold in markets 1, 2, 3.

STEP 3: Calculate the total cost for each of the products (units sold x sales price per unit).

STEP 4: Calculate the costs of goods sold — all products for each year — add down the columns.

STEP 5: Calculate the five-year cost of goods for each market-add across the rows.

COSTS OF GOODS SOLD FIRST FIVE YEARS - FIRST FIVE YEARS

	1	*2*	*3*	*4*	*5*
Market 1					
Units sold					
Sale Price/Unit					
Total Cost					
Market 2					
Units Sold					
Sale Price/Unit					
Total Cost					
Market 3					
Units Sold					
Sale Price/Unit					
Total Cost					
Cost of Goods Sold					
All Markets					

INTERNATIONAL OVERHEAD EXPENSES

To determine overhead costs for your export products, you should be certain to include costs that pertain only to international marketing efforts. For example, costs for domestic advertising of services that do not pertain to the international market should not be included. Examples of most typical expense categories for an export business are listed on the next page. Some of these expenses will be first year start-up expenses, and others will occur every year.

STEP 1: Review the expenses listed on the next page. These are expenses that will be incurred because of your international business. There may be other expense categories not listed-list them under "other expenses".

STEP 2: Estimate your cost for each expense, category.

STEP 3: Estimate any domestic marketing expenses including that is not applicable to international sales.

STEP 4: Calculate the total for your international overhead expenses.

EXPENSE **COST**

EXPENSE	Market 1	Market 2	Market 3	Total Year 1
Legal Fees				
Accounting Fees				
Promotional Material				
Travel				
Communication Equip/Telex				
Advertising Allowances				
Promotional Expenses (e.g., trade shows, etc.)				
Other Expenses				
Total Expenses				
Less Domestic Expenses Included Above, if any				
Total International				
Start-up Expenses				

PREPARING AN EXPORT PRICE QUOTATION

Setting proper export prices is crucial to a successful international sales program; prices must be high enough to generate a reasonable profit, yet low enough to be competitive in overseas markets. Basic pricing criteria - costs, market demand, and competition - are the same for domestic and foreign sales. However, a thorough analysis of all cost factors going into a cost, insurance and freight (CIF) quotation may result in prices that are different from domestic ones.

"Marginal cost" pricing is the most realistic and frequently used pricing method. Based on a calculation of incremental costs, this method considers the direct out-of-pocket expenses of producing and selling products for export as a floor beneath which prices cannot be set without incurring a loss. There are important principles that should be followed when pricing a product for export, summarized below.

There are important principles that should be followed when pricing a product for export, summarized below.

COST FACTORS

In calculating an export price, be sure to take into account all the cost factors for which you, the exporter, are liable.

1. Calculate direct materials and labor costs involved in producing the goods for export.
2. Calculate your factory overhead costs, prorating the amount of overhead chargeable to your proposed export order.
3. Deduct any charges not attributable to the export operation (i.e., domestic marketing costs, domestic legal expenses), especially if export sales represent only a small part of total sales.
4. Add in the other out-of-pocket expenses directly tied to the export sales, such as:

travel expenses	catalogs, slide shows, video presentations
promotional material	export advertising
commissions	transportation expenses
packing materials	legal expenses*
office supplies*	patent and trademark fees*
communication*	taxes*
rent*	insurance*
interest*	provisions for bad debts
market research	credit checks
translation costs	product modification
consultant fees	freight forwarder fees

*These items will typically represent the cost of the total operation, so be sure to pro-rate these to reflect only the cost of producing the goods for export.

5. Allow yourself a realistic price margin for unforeseen costs, unavoidable risks, and simple mistakes that are common in any new undertaking.
6. Also allow yourself a realistic profit or mark-up.

OTHER FACTORS TO CONSIDER

Market Demand - As in the domestic market, product demand is the key to setting prices in a foreign market. What will the market bear for a specific product or service? What will the estimated consumer price for your product be in each foreign market? If your prices seem out of line, try some simple product modifications to reduce the selling price, such as simplification of technology or alteration of product size to conform to local market norms. Also keep in mind that currency valuations alter the affordability of gods. A good pricing strategy should accommodate fluctuations in currency.

Competition - As in the domestic market, few exporters are free to set prices without carefully evaluating their competitor's pricing policies. The situation is further complicated by the need to evaluate the competition's prices in each foreign market an exporter intends to enter. In a foreign market that is serviced by many competitors, an exporter may have little choice but to match the going price or even go below it to establish a market share. If, however, the exporter's product or service is new to a particular foreign market, it may be possible to set a higher price than normally charged domestically.

BREAK-EVEN ANALYSIS

The break-even is the level of sales at which your total sales exactly covers your total costs and operating expenses. This level of sales is called the Break-Even Point Sales Level (BEP).

In other words, at the BEP, you will make a zero profit. If you sell more than the BEP, you will make a net profit. If you sell less than the BEP, you will have a net loss.

The worksheet will calculate your BEP for any year of operation. The steps listed below will assume that you are calculating the BEP for Year 1.

STEP 1: Fill in your Total Sales, Total Cost of Goods Sold, and Total Gross Margin for Year 1 on the following page.

STEP 2: Calculate the Gross Margin percent using the formula which is given on the work sheet. The Gross Margin percent tells you what percentage of each dollar of sales results in Gross Margin.

STEP 3: Fill in the Total Operating Expenses for Year 1.

STEP 4: Calculate the BEP sales level using the formula which is given. Your need to reach this level of sales just to break even.

Note: In addition to a break-even analysis, it is highly recommended that a profit and loss statement be generated for the first few actual international transactions. Since there are a great number of variables relating to costs of goods, real transactions are required to establish actual profitability and minimize the risk of losses.

STEP 1:

Total Sales	$__________
Total Cost of Goods Sold	$__________
Total Gross Margin	$__________

STEP 2

Total Gross Margin	$__________
Gross Margin	$__________
Total Sales	$__________

Gross Margin % = 0
(Leave the Gross Margin $ in a decimal format. The format is 0.347 - not 34.7%).

STEP 3:

Total Operating Expenses	$__________

STEP 4:

Total Operating Expenses	$__________
BEP Sales Level	$__________
Gross Margin %	$__________
BEP Sales Level	$__________

PROJECTED INCOME STATEMENT - YEAR 1 TO 5, ALL MARKETS

You are now ready to assemble the data for your projected income statement. This statement will calculate your net profit or net loss (before income taxes) for each year.

STEP 1: Fill in the sales for each year. You already estimated these figures; just recopy them onto the work sheet.

STEP 2: Fill in the cost of goods sold for each year. You already estimated these figures, just recopy onto the work sheet.

STEP 3: Calculate the Gross Margin for each year (Sales minus Cost of Goods Sold).

STEP 4: Calculate the Total Operating Expenses for each year.

STEP 5: Calculate the Net Profit or Net Loss (Before Income Taxes) for each year (Gross Margin minus Total Operating Expenses).

PROJECTED INCOME STATEMENT - YEAR 1 TO 5, ALL MARKETS

	1	*2*	*3*	*4*	*5*
International Sales					
Cost of Goods Sold					
Gross Margin					
International Operating Expenses					
Legal					
Accounting					
Advertising					
Travel					
Trade Shows					
Promotional Material					
Supplies					
Communication Equipment					
Interest					
Insurance					
Other					
Total International Operating Expenses					

TIMETABLE

This is a worksheet that you will need to work on periodically as you progress in the workbook. The purpose is to ensure that key tasks are identified and completed to increase the success of your international business.

STEP 1: Identify key activities

By reviewing other portions of your business plan, compile a list of tasks that are vital to the successful operations of your business. Be sure to include travel to your chosen market as applicable.

STEP 2: Assign responsibility for each activity

For each identified activity, assign one person primary responsibility for the completion of that activity.

STEP 3: Determine scheduled start date

For each activity, determine the date when work will begin. You should consider how the activity fits into your overall plan as well as the availability of the person responsible.

STEP 4: Determine scheduled finish date

For each activity, determine when the activity must be completed.

SUMMARY

STEP 1: Verify completion of previous pages.

You should have finished all the other sections in the workbook before continuing any further.

STEP 2: Identify your business plan audience.

What type of person are you intending to satisfy with this business plan? The summary should briefly address all major issues that are important to this person. Keep in mind that this page will probably be the first read by this person. It is extremely important the summary be brief yet contain the information most important to the reader. This section should make the reader want to read the rest of your plan.

STEP 3: Write a one-page summary.

You will now need to write no more than a one-page summary of all the previous work sheets you have completed.

Determine which sections are going to be most interesting to your reader. Write one to three sentences that summarize each of the important sections.

These sentences should appear in the order of the sections of your business plan.

The sentences must fit together to form a summary and not appear to be a group of loosely related thoughts.

You may want to have several different summaries, depending on who will read the business plan.

SELECTED PUBLICATIONS OF THE MICHIGAN SMALL BUSINESS DEVELOPMENT CENTER

The Business Planning Series - $25 or $10 each retail - The biggest cause of business failure (which effects large manufacturing firms and home-based businesses) is the inability to plan, control cash flow, and/or improve sales through marketing. *The Business Planning Guide, The Cash Flow Control Guide,* and *The Market Planning Guide* present the essential elements of a winning business plan and financing proposal; offer expert cash flow and control tips; and outline no cost/low cost marketing tips to increase your sales and expand your customer base.

Essential Elements Of Running A Business - $25 retail - This guide contains information on Entrepreneurship, Marketing, Legal Issues, Managing Growth, Financing, and Business Planning. Targeted to small businesses that employ between 5 and 25 people, this guide offers tips and tricks on how to grow your business.

Financing Your Business - hard copy no longer sold - available on web site - Growing a successful business is a challenging endeavor, and managing the financial side of a business is one of the most critical aspects of its success. *Financing Your Business* answers questions on how to manage cash flow, how to choose an investment for excess cash flow, and how to obtain a loan. It discusses finance programs, bookkeeping systems, how to hire a CPA, and banking services.

International Business Resources - $25 retail - It has been said that the arms race has been replaced by the export race. The Michigan SBDC has recognized that small businesses can compete in a global economy and has developed a number of excellent resources for businesses seeking international markets. This guide to international business resources contains over 500 periodicals, books, guides, videotapes, services, software programs, and fax retrieval systems. Designed for the consultant, librarian, or business owner seeking a definitive guide on "what's available," this resource contains titles, addresses, phone and fax numbers, prices, and brief descriptions.

Internet Marketing Study - $25 retail - In this path-breaking study, 15 small businesses in Michigan profile their experiences marketing their products and services on the web. Is marketing on the Internet the wave of the future for small businesses? You be the judge, based on this thought-provoking study.

Michigan County Profiles - $20 each - Michigan Small Business Development Center and Michigan Metropolitan Information Center have created a series of Michigan County Profiles. The initial profiles contain information on Population Patterns; Race; Age; Age of Householders; Living Arrangements; Marital Status; Labor Force Characteristics; Commuting Patterns; Income Levels; Poverty; Housing Age, Value and Type; Economic Structure; and Agricultural Rank. These profiles are excellent for libraries, chambers, business consultants, market researchers, the media, and county agencies.

Retail Business Planning Guide - $25 each - Produced by the Association of SBDCs and Inc. Magazine, this unique publication contains sections on developing a business plan, a resource directory, sample legal forms, bibliography, glossary, and business plans of retail businesses.

Service Business Planning Guide - $25 each - Covers areas similar to the Retail Business Planning Guide.

Small Business Barometer - free - The *Small Business Barometer* is co-sponsored by the Small Business Association of Michigan and the Michigan SBDC. Public Policy Associates of Lansing coordinates a scientific survey of a randomly-selected panel of 200 small businesses three times a year to track changes in attitudes over time. This newsletter, analyzing the results, is especially useful to lawmakers and government officials as well as the business community and the media. Results are shared with the Federal Reserve System which tracks the economy of the nation.

Small Business Guide To Effective Marketing Communications - $5 retail - Used for a number of years by thousands of Small Business Development Center clients, this guide contains useful information on understanding your market, positioning your business, advertising on a small budget, developing newsletters and publications, extending your message through publicity, building community relations, and measuring results.

Small Business Needs Assessment Report, 1998 - $25 retail - Understand what's on the minds of small businesses from the analysis of a statewide needs assessment of small businesses in Michigan. Covers issues on strategic planning, economic expectations, financing, government regulations, human resource, legal, marketing, use of computer, work force development, assistance needs, and performance activity.

Small Business Sources - $25 retail - Imagine having access to hundreds of cross-referenced resources produced solely for small businesses. This guide contains the most current periodicals, books, guides, videotapes, services, software programs, and fax retrieval systems. Designed for the consultant, librarian, or business owner seeking a definitive guide on "what's available," this resource contains titles, addresses, phone and fax numbers, prices, and brief descriptions.

Starting Your Business - hard copy no longer sold - available on web site - Since 1983, the Michigan Small Business Development Center Network has helped create more than 25,000 jobs by helping entrepreneurs start or expand a business. Professional, certified counselors of the Small Business Development Center Network use this guide when consulting with those contemplating starting a business. This resource guide provides practical, how-to information for those needing a basic overview of the key elements of starting a business in Michigan.

Trade Secrets: The Export Answer Book - Second Edition - $25 retail - *Trade Secrets* was written for economic development professionals needing quick references and answers to the most commonly asked questions on international trade. Covers the terms, processes, resources, and possibilities of exporting.

Woman's Business Resource Directory - $5 retail - Developed in partnership with the U.S. Small Business Administration, the Woman's Business Resource Directory contains information on where to locate women business owner programs in Michigan and describes various SBA loan programs, government contracting and certification programs, and small business assistance programs.

Business Building Software - $83.40 - The Michigan SBDC has created a win-win-win deal with JIAN, Inc., the creators of award winning business software designed. The following software is available to clients for $83.40: Agreement*Builder*, BizPlan*Builder*, EmployeeManual*Maker*, LivingTrust*Builder*, Publicity*Builder*, SafetyPlan*Builder*, and Marketing*Builder*. All JIAN software is available for use at Michigan Small Business Development Centers. Call JIAN at (800) 896-5426 to order.

Financing Sources Databank Software - No Charge Access - Each year, SBDC counselors report that capital formation is in a list of top ten critical issues for businesses. In response to this problem, counselors now have the ability to identify 10,000 potential financiers, lenders, and investors located throughout the U.S. through the *Financing Sources Databank*. Financing sources include venture capital firms, asset-based lenders, factoring firms, microlenders, small business investment companies, leasing companies, private placement underwriters, investment bankers and SBA LOWDOC lenders, as well as commercial real estate lenders, buyers, JV partners, and REITs. To access this database, firms should contact a local Michigan Small Business Development Center or call DataMerge at (800) 580-1188.

Phone orders will be taken. Please have your name, address, phone, and fax number available when you place your order. Orders will be shipped and invoiced the same day the order is placed. Payment is due within thirty days of receipt of order. Quantity discounts available.

Michigan Small Business Development Center (313) 964-1798

KEY WORD INDEX

KEY INTERNATIONAL BUSINESS CONTACTS

Advocacy Center, to help firms land foreign contracts - (202) 482-3896
Agents/Distributors, to find - (202) 482-4204
Anti-Dumping Administrative Investigations - (202) 482-1768
Bankers Association for Foreign Trade - (202) 452-0942
Bilateral Investment Treaty - (202) 482-3229
Business America Magazine - (202) 482-3251
Catalog Exhibitions and Trade Shows - (202) 482-3973
Certified Trade Fairs - (202) 482-1609
Commerce Business Daily - (202) 482-0632
Commercial News USA - (202) 482-4918
Compliance with Import Laws - (202) 482-2104
Countervailing Duty Investigations - (202) 482-1768
Customs Valuation Codes - (202) 482-3583
District Export Councils - (202) 482-2975
E and E Star Awards - (202) 482-1289
Employment Opportunities - (202) 482-1533
Exchange Rates - (202) 482-5333
Eximbank Liaison - (202) 482-3277
Export Assistance Centers - (202) 482-3277
Export Legal Assistance Network - (202) 778-3080
Export Yellow Pages - (202) 482-5131
Foreign company background - (202) 482-4204
Freedom of Information - (202) 482-3756
General Agreements on Tariffs and Trade /
World Trade Organization - (202) 482-0603
Generalized System of Preferences - (202) 482-3493
Gold Key Service - (800) 872-7723
Government Printing Office - (202) 512-1800
Industrial reports and Studies - (202) 482-4356
Intellectual Property - (202) 482-2915
International Buyer Program - (202) 482-0481
International Contacts/Trade Leads -(202) 482-2505
Investigations of Unfair Trade Practices - (202) 482-5497
Market Development Cooperator Program - (202) 482-3197
Matchmaker Program, foreign and US business - (202) 482-3119
National Technical Information Service - (703) 487-4605
National Trade Data Bank - (800) 782-8872
North American Free Trade Agreement - (202) 482-0305
Organization Charts for ITA - (202) 482-5436
Patent and Copyright Office - (202) 707-6800
Personnel Locator - (202) 482-2000
President's Export Council - (202) 482-1124
Procurement Contracts - (202) 482-5436
Public Affairs - (202) 482-3808
Publications Officer - (202) 482-5467
Small Business Development Center - (703) 271-8700
Trade Advisory Center Reading Room - (202) 482-3268
Trade Information Center - (800) 872-7723
Trade Opportunities Program - (202) 482-2505
Trade Reference Room - (202) 482-5241
World Bank Liaison - (202) 482-3277
Bureau of Export Administration - (202) 482-4811
U.S. Customs Service - (202) 927-2077
U.S. Department of Agriculture - (202) 720-0924
U.S. Department of State - (202) 512-1530

USEFUL EXPORT PUBLICATIONS

Background Notes - (202) 512-1800
Bankable Deals: Q&A Guide to Trade Finance - (202) 205-6720
Basic Guide to Exporting, A - (703) 487-4650
Breaking Into the Trade Game - (202) 205-6720
Bureau of National Affairs Export Reference Manual - (800) 372-1033
Business America - (202) 512-1800
Carnet: Move Goods Duty Free Through Customs - (212) 354-4480
Commercial News USA - (212) 490-3999
Correct Way to Fill Out the Shipper's Export Declaration - (301) 457-1086
Country Reports - (212) 554-0600
CulturGrams - (800) 528-6279
Directory of Freight Forwarders and Custom House Brokers - (800) 323-0548
Export Documentation - (800) 543-2453
Exporter's Encyclopaedia - (800) 234-3867
Exporter's Guide to Foreign Sources for Credit Information - (212) 563-2772
Export/Import Procedures and Documentation - (518) 891-5510
Export Legal Assistance Network- (202) 778-3080
Export Letters of Credit and Drafts - (800) 543-2453
Export Sales & Marketing Manual - (800) 876-0624
Export Shipping - (800) 543-2453
FINDEX: The Directory of Market Research Reports - (800) 843-7751
The Global Road Warrior - (800) 833-8586
Guide to Drafting Distributorship Agreements - (212) 206-1150
Guide to INCOTERMS - (202) 659-6000
How to Obtain Copyright, Trademark & Patent Protection - (202) 927-5580
IBEX: Finding Foreign Buyers - (800) 537-4239
Importer's Manual USA - (415) 454-9934
Importing Into United States - (202) 512-1530
Import Procedures - (800) 543-2453
INCOTERMS - 1990 - (212) 206-1150
Industrial Overseas Buying Representatives - (800) 323-0548
Inside Washington: Government Resources - (202) 337-6300
ISO 9000: Introduction for U.S. Business - (202) 463-5460
ISO 9000: Questions and Answers - (301) 975-4040
International Trade Data Network (ITDN) - (401) 232-6239
Journal of Commerce - (800) 221-3777
Key Officers of Foreign Service Posts - (202) 512-1800
Key Words in International Trade - (212) 206-1150
Managing Foreign Exchange Risk - (212) 206-1150
Market Share Reports - (703) 487-4600
Marking of Country of Origin - (202) 927-5580
National Trade Data Bank - (800) 782-8872
National Trade Data Bank Manual - (800) 865-3450
Questions & Answers for Export/Import - (800) 543-2453
Services: The Export of the 21st Century - (800) 833-8586
Sourcebook of International Trade - (800) 631-3098
Trade Shows Worldwide - (800) 347-4253
Translation Services Directory - (703) 683-6100
U.S. Global Trade Outlook - (202) 512-1800
Washington Researcher's International Information Report - (202) 333-3533

Notes

Notes